THE MODERN
STUDENT'S LIBRARY

EACH VOLUME EDITED BY A LEADING
AMERICAN AUTHORITY

This series is composed of such works as
are conspicuous in the province of literature
for their enduring influence. Every volume
is recognized as essential to a liberal education and will tend to infuse a love for true
literature and an appreciation of the qualities which cause it to endure.

*A descriptive list of the volumes published in
this series appears in the last pages
of this volume*

CHARLES SCRIBNER'S SONS

THE MODERN STUDENT'S LIBRARY

CONTEMPORARY ESSAYS

CONTEMPORARY ESSAYS

EDITED BY
ODELL SHEPARD

CHARLES SCRIBNER'S SONS

NEW YORK   CHICAGO   BOSTON

For permission to include selections in this book we are indebted to the following:

Dodd, Mead and Company for "Impatient 'Culture' and the Literal Mind" by Frank Moore Colby from *Constrained Attitudes*

Doubleday, Doran & Co. for "Red-Bloods and Mollycoddles" by G. Lowes Dickinson from *Appearances*, and for "Holidays" by C. E. Montague from *The Right Place*

Gerald Duckworth & Co. for "An Autumn House" by Edward Thomas from *Rose Acre Papers*

E. P. Dutton & Company and Methuen & Co. for "On Coming to an End" by Hilaire Belloc from *On Nothing*

Harcourt, Brace and Company for "Back to Nature" by Henry S. Canby from *Definitions*

Harper & Brothers and Gerald Duckworth & Co. for "The Dictatorship of the Dull" by Alexander Black from *The Latest Thing*

Henry Holt and Company for "The Tyranny of Mere Things" by L. P. Jacks from *The Human End*

Houghton, Mifflin Company for "On Being Original" by Irving Babbitt from *Literature and the American College*

Alfred A. Knopf for "The Art of Writing" by H. M. Tomlinson from *Old Junk*

Longmans, Green & Co. for "The Place of Science in a Liberal Education" by Bertrand Russell from *Mysticism and Logic*

E. V. Mitchell for "Bibliomania" from *Book Notes*

The North American Review for "Laughter" by Max Beerbohm, for "The Aristocratic Spirit" by Hanford Henderson with the kind consent of the author, and for "Our Fear of Excellence" by Margaret Sherwood with the kind consent of the author

Oxford University Press for "Beginnings" by Maurice Hewlett from *Extempory Essays*

G. P. Putnam's Sons for "The Art of the Essayist" by Arthur Christopher Benson

The Yale Review and the author for "Plato as a Novelist" by Vida D. Scudder

Charles Scribner's Sons for "The Practical Value of Poetry" by Max Eastman from *Enjoyment of Poetry*, for "Quality" by John Galsworthy from *The Inn of Tranquillity*, for "The Extirpation of Culture" by Katharine Fullerton Gerould from *Modes and Morals*, for "On Knowing the Difference" by Robert Lynd from *The Pleasures of Ignorance*, for "Writing" by Edward Sandford Martin from *In a New Century*, for "A Plea for the Platitude" by Brander Matthews from *The Tocsin of Revolt*, for "The Horizon" by Alice Meynell from *The Colour of Life* and "Shadows" and "Clouds" by Alice Meynell from *Essays*, for "Skylarks" and "At Heaven's Gate" by George Santayana from *Soliloquies in England*, for "Tradition" by Stuart P. Sherman from *Americans*, for "The Way of Imperfection" by Francis Thompson from *The Renegade Poet*, and for "The Book of Books" by Henry van Dyke from *Companionable Books*.

CONTENTS

vii

INTRODUCTION

THERE are some ways in which the essay seems fitted to provide an exact and adequate expression of contemporary thought and feeling. Almost always it has been a vehicle of that individualism which is nowadays, at least in theory, dear to us all. Usually capricious in technic, following closely the dartings of whim and the curves of fancy, it has demanded for itself precisely that freedom from the restraints imposed by external models which is now claimed by many other forms of art. From the beginning it has avoided dogmatism, over-emphasis, and heat of controversy, running true to the spirit of the great sceptic Montaigne, commonly regarded as its inventor, who kept ever before his eyes the chastening motto "What do I know?" All of this, it would seem, should help to endear the essay to a time which is in many respects, though not in all, less certain of itself and of its own beliefs than the past has been and which is at any rate pretty well convinced of the folly of preaching.

As a matter of fact, however, although what may be called the mood of the essay pervades much of our fiction, poetry, and drama, the form itself cannot be called either popular or highly influential. But then perhaps it has never been either the one or the other. Most readers, it seems likely, have always wished either to be informed or to be excited, and the essay is not adapted, at least in an obvious and elementary way, to the service and satisfaction of these fundamental literary desires. Perhaps it has always been written "for a little clan," so that one need be only mildly surprised, in thinking of the several ways in which the twentieth century is suited to the writing and enjoyment of essays, to find how little we have made of our opportunities.

One reason, however, why this literary form is less cultivated at present than we might expect lies on the surface. Although it answers exactly to the tentative and exploratory habit of our thought, to our scepticism, to our distrust of violent emotion and of heavy-handed moralizing, as also to our curiosity about persons and the inner life of the mind, it has one major quality to which we are incapable just now of doing justice—a quality, indeed, which many readers of our time are likely to resent somewhat as they would a "class distinction." The essay at its best and purest is a product of a leisurely mood, and it is addressed to minds at leisure. Perhaps we cannot define it more compactly than by calling it the literary expression of a cultivated play of mind, the word "play" being understood to signify an activity engaged in with no ulterior motive but solely for its own sake. Now this mood of leisure is one of those in which contemporary life is most obviously deficient, and for play of the sort defined we have, in spite of our violent emphasis upon "sport," little talent or sympathy. Whether because of some Puritanical virus still lingering in our veins or because we have not yet rolled down our mental sleeves after the long labor of pioneering, leisure and the play of mind, once considered by wise men almost the chief goals of human effort, seem to many of us a mere waste of time. Worse still, they suggest to many an aristocratic attitude toward life which is vaguely resented as untimely anti-social, and not without invidious implications.

Lovers of the essay will do well to admit that it is indeed quite incorrigibly aristocratic, using that word with any shreds of true meaning that may yet be clinging to it, but they will not see that this amounts to a condemnation. On the contrary, they find it actually a cheering fact, of which the essayists assure them, that not quite everyone conforms to type, votes with the mob, adds his voice to the greatest shouting. The essayist, in whatever age we find him, is sure to be a man of his own kind, going his own way, speaking out of his own thoughts and moods. Because his modesty is innate and intrinsic he is undaunted by the possible imputation of egotism, and he uses the first personal pronoun without a qualm. Even when he develops his whims and opinions with what looks like serious conviction, we see that there is nothing argumentative, certainly nothing hortatory in his manner or purpose. Always he seems to be saying: "Thus it is with me; of course I know that you will not see the matter quite as I do, but perhaps my experience will suggest something to you, and even from complete opposition at least a spark of illumination may be struck out." This is evidently a civilized attitude, and whatever tinge or taint of the aristocratic it may have will do us no harm. A good essayist is likely to be good company, being one of the few who are actually delighted by the varieties of human nature and of human experience that they see about them. Those varieties he tends to increase.

A good essayist, however, is not "too soon made glad." For whole-hearted and unquestioning approval of the present scheme of things we must look to those who are of that scheme rather than to these who stand somewhat aside and wonder, not unhopefully, what it is all coming to. Having maintained the mood of leisure, he is undeafened and undazzled by contemporary noise and glitter; he retains the peace and the poise of mind requisite for sober thought; as an aristocrat he is likely to find much of his best company in the past and to care a good deal about tradition. For all these reasons, his work is a steady though usually implicit criticism of the life about him. And while we read this criticism we should remember that it is no concern of his to soothe, to flatter, or to cajole us, for he is not a demagogue and he can do very well without our approval; his business as critic is simply to "see the thing as in itself it really is."

The effect of a democratic environment upon this form of writing which has hardly any but aristocratic traditions seems to be working out in two different ways. On the one hand we have a complete abandonment of every mark of distinction—the learning of Lowell, for example, the serene elevation of Emerson, the frosty individualism of Thoreau—and a frank catering to the multitude. On the other hand we have the innumerable writers of "articles," who struggle month by month and even day by day to satisfy America's enormous appetite for information upon things in general. In neither of these camps is anything done for the true essay. There is another kind of writing, however, which, although it does not stem from Montaigne but rather from Cicero and Seneca, is certainly a variety of the essay and which has won during recent years, both in England and America, a large public. Less whimsical and idiosyncratic than the Montaigne essay, this is a serious and extended presentation of an idea or belief or point of view which has a social rather than a merely personal significance. Considering the elasticity of the term "essay," I have felt justified in including a considerable number of papers of this kind in the present book.

It is customary, I believe, for compilers of books such as this, to gather their materials, such as they happen to like for a variety of reasons, from here and there, and then to toss them together in almost any order or disorder that suits the whim of the moment. By this lack of method they often convey an effect of wealthy profusion which is not unpleasing, and frequently they make us wonder at the catholicity of their reading and taste. My own effort in compiling this volume of selections has been, whether for better or worse, somewhat different, for I have tried to produce here, out of the writings of other people, a book with as definite a shape and trend as it would have had if produced by a single mind. The collection has taken form about Mr. Hanford Henderson's essay on "The Aristocratic Spirit," as a nucleus, and my effort has been to provide that essay with an ample setting, suitable illustration, and some deduction of results. There are at least a dozen other essays in the book that might have been used as pivots or nuclei in a similar way, but each of these would have called for a book with a somewhat different tendency, and it happened that just this kind of book was the kind I wished to make. To Mr. Henderson and to all the others who have made the book possible my thanks, and whatever credit there may be in the performance, are due.

ODELL SHEPARD

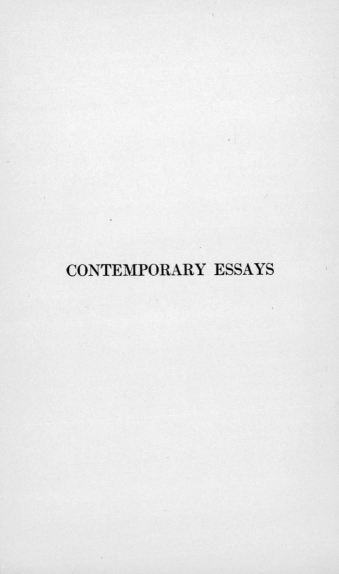

CONTEMPORARY ESSAYS

BEGINNINGS

BY MAURICE HEWLETT

POETRY, which is so much older than the printing-press as to be older than writing, still preserves as habit what it once employed as machinery. Rime was a machine, the stanza a machine, rhythm itself, and certainly the exordium. It was found necessary to begin with the bill of fare. When prose, from being oratory, became literature, another necessity was felt—that you must begin at the beginning, that is to say, with the soup. The two were used alternatively, or, as we shall see, compounded, presented together; but it was reserved to days comparatively recent to introduce the *aperitif*.

To serve our own times I must vary the figure. As you look upon your novel—for what is left to literature now besides the novel?—as a chronicle or a symphony, so you will invite the reader on your first page—to listen to an overture, or to begin at the beginning. 'There was a man—dwelt in a churchyard': nothing could be better than that in the way of opening. It was the old way:

'Hit befel in the days of Uther Pendragon when he was Kynge of all England, and so regned, that there was a myghty duke in Cornewaill that helde warre ageynst hym long tyme.'

That is how the greatest of all romances begins—at the beginning; and yet it has in it the germ of the overture; for it gives you the things upon which the romance depends, colour and theme. It is not the epic manner, remark; there the convention is clear. In epic you begin with the theme. It is not for nothing that the *Iliad* begins with a wrath, and the *Odyssey* with a man. But

3

romance, which breathes by colour, adds it to the theme, and so it is with the ballad:

> It fell about the Martinmas time,
> When the Wind blew snell and cauld:

there, and in things like it, is the theme presented as colour. Some such thing, no doubt, was in Stevenson's mind when he held forth to a correspondent upon the necessity for a novel to 'begin to end badly,' or 'well,' as may be. He quarrelled with the happy opening of *Richard Feverel,* if I remember rightly.

Well then, with the opening of the *Morte d'Arthur* in our heads, here is its lineal descendant of the nineteenth century, in a brisk exordium:

'About thirty years ago, Miss Maria Ward, of Huntingdon, with only seven thousand pounds, had the good luck to captivate Sir Thomas Bertram, of Mansfield Park, in the county of Northampton, and to be thereby raised to the rank of a baronet's lady, with all the comforts and consequences of a handsome home and large income.'

As I say, brisk, business-like, crisp, epigrammatic. Colour is watered down to a question of the almanacs; theme is there, without being forced upon us. Yet it is entirely adequate to the matter in hand. In its way it is an overture, if only to a toy-symphony. It tunes us up. We stand upon the shore of an unknown sea, ready for the baronet's lady and all her *sequelae.* Miss Austen is, I consider, one of our best beginners. How admirable is that of *Emma!*

Much had happened in the interval between Sir Thomas Malory and her. Among other things Defoe had invented the novel, and therefore, in a way, Miss Austen herself. He saw, however, no better way of doing it than to make a chronicle of it, which had been Sir Thomas's way too; but there was one vast difference

between them. Both began at the beginning; but Sir
Thomas used colour to enhance his tale, and Defoe to
lower it. Sir Thomas would enchant you, lift you into
'realms of old'; Defoe would sober you down. Both used
persuasion—literature is for ever linked with cookery
—but Sir Thomas would have you see reality as a dream,
Defoe a dream as a reality. Here is Defoe at his best:

'I was born in the year 1632, in the city of York, of a good
family though not of that county, my Father being a For-
eigner of Bremen, who settled first at Hull. . .'

He runs on with his particulars: his mother's name
Robinson, his father's Kreutznaer, and so on. That was
Defoe's manner, which I suspect to have been derived
from Cervantes. He had the same love of verisimilitude,
and the same need of it, though more daintiness in its
employ.

'In a village of La Mancha, the name of which I have no
desire to call to mind, there lived not long since one of those
gentlemen that keep a lance in the lance-rack, an old buckler,
a lean hack, and a greyhound for coursing.'

That is a much more literary, but not more artful,
manner than Defoe's, though essentially the same. It
is carefully compressed; Defoe's, with equal care, is
diffuse. Both have had their followers. Defoe's has
outlasted the greater man's. Meantime another style of
narration had been discovered which I hope I shall be
forgiven for calling the Cheap-Jack manner. The
Cheap-Jack persuades by dazzle, by hypnosis. He has
unlimited words at his tongue's end, and bemuses you
with the flood of them. Rabelais is answerable for
that:

'Most noble and illustrious drinkers, and you thrice-precious
profligates (for to you and none else do I dedicate my
writings), Alcibiades, in that dialogue of Plato's . . .'

and so on, and so on—for ever. And that also is Sterne's
way of doing it. True, *Tristram Shandy* begins at the
beginning, and indeed at the very beginning—but with
what chirping, with what prattle!

'I wish either my father or mother, or indeed both of them,
as they were in duty both equally bound to it, had minded
what they were about when they begot me . . .'

Tristram does not get himself born at that rate until
the beginning of Chapter V, there being so much more
of Opinions than of Life in his immortal memoir. With
a book like that you have neither theme nor colour to
dispose you to its perusal. You have curiosity, that only.
I know people who have tried to read *Tristram Shandy*
for the story, to see what happened. And I know what
did happen. 'Fratello, tu non voi esser inteso: io non ti
voglio intendere—vai con cento diavoli.' That is how
an Italian, according to Dean Church, treated an 'enigmatic prophet,' before throwing him into the fire. 'My
dear man, you have no desire to be understood, and I
have no desire to understand you. Go to the deuce.' A
good many novel-readers have bidden Sterne to the
deuce; and I don't at all shrink from owning that I have
never reached the end of *Shandy*—or of *Gargantua*
either, for that matter. The Cheap-Jack, in fact, must
stand or fall upon his own gifts. If his kind of nonsense suits yours, well and good.

Fielding had not the patter for that way of opening.
You may call his the arm-chair port-and-walnuts way,
and not be wrong. He had the passion for dissertation;
he loved it for its own sake as well as his own; he must
buttonhole the reader. That made him a bad starter,
though not nearly so bad as Sir Walter Scott; both
Amelia and *Tom Jones* begin at Chapter II, *Tom Jones*
hardly there. I think the appetite grew upon him with

his growing facility. In *Tom Jones* you have an overture to pretty well every chapter, asides and prosceniumappearances which really hold up the action. Thackeray, deriving very much from him, was nevertheless better at getting away with the thing. Nothing could be better than the openings of *Vanity Fair* and *Pendennis,* nothing more sententious and ambagical than the first chapter of *The Newcomes,* which, however, is put into the pen of Pendennis himself, a first-class prig. In *Esmond* you are, or ought to be, prepared for the easy circumlocutions of Sir Richard Steele—but except you are uncommonly quick on the uptake, you are *not* so prepared. As a consequence, *Esmond* succeeds generally on a second perusal, and better and better as you re-read. But comparatively few there be of the ordinary run of readers who find it again after the first rebuff. Dickens was an excellent starter, using many manners, mostly well. 'The kettle began it' is not a happy instance. That is a bang on the drum, like a showman's at a fair. But what could be better than the beginning of *Dombey?*

'Dombey sat in the corner of the darkened room in the great arm-chair by the bedside, and Son lay tucked up warm in a little basket bedstead, carefully disposed on a low settee immediately in front of the fire, and close to it, as if his constitution were analogous to that of a muffin, and it was essential to toast him to brown while he was very new.'

Allowing for Dickens' weakness for far-fetched images, that is as good a formula as you could want for the beginning of a novel. Theme and colour are both there. The next paragraph is quite as good, and the whole chapter keeps it up. What is especially artful about it is that, while it is beginning at the beginning in the good old way, it is also an overture, according to new doctrine. Others followed him hard—Charles

Reade, Wilkie Collins, Walter Besant, and the smaller fry.

'She went into the garden to cut a cabbage to make an apple pie. And while she was there . . .'

From the genius to whom that opening was revealed come Henry James and all the modern novelists, 'so many and so many and such glee,' who begin their books in the middle—Mr. Conrad and a countless host. Mr. James did not hit upon the device until the *mezzo del cammin* of his mortal career, and, as some would have it, at the end of his immortal. *The Portrait of a Lady* begins with a dissertation about tea, very much as *Tom Jones* with one about things in general. But later on we come to 'She went into the garden,' or even to '*So* she went into the garden,' which is to take a very high line with the reader. I neither accuse nor defend. All that I am concerned to say about it is that, beginning in the middle, he was generally skilful enough to avoid the explicit harking-back which others have not been able to do—to their detriment, I think. For see what happens. If the middle of the story is the beginning of the novel, the beginning of the novel will be the middle of the story; and what then becomes of Form, which all discuss and none understand? I don't pretend to admire the formula, anyhow, and have never been tempted to adopt it. You gain very little by it, and inevitably lose much. Mr. James became its bond-slave at the last, and wound himself in webs of explication which involved him ever the deeplier. I daresay he did it as well as it could be done—but was it worth doing? I doubt it.

Lastly, you can begin at the end. Mr. de Morgan did that once. His hero, the teller of the tale, is on his death-bed when the scene opens. This dismal fact haunted me. The tale was long. 'He'll never last out, poor wretch,' was always at the back of my mind as I read on.

But here is enough of novels. *Per correr miglior acque,* for a moment.

I began with prose, and shall end with it, but wish to say a word about epics while it is in my head. It is quite true that the practice of Homer, to begin strictly with the theme, has been observed in Europe from Apollonius Rhodius, through Virgil, and the Italian sugar-baker epopoeists—of whose openings Tasso's full-sounding line,

Canto l'armi pietose, e 'l capitano,

is much the best—; through the mock-epics down to the parlour-epics of Cowper—

I sing the Sofa.

It has been followed, I take it, for the plain reason that there is no better way of beginning a really great piece of work than by telling yourself and the rest of the world just what you are going to do. But the absence of colour, the avoidance of all pretence to an overture, must have some other reason—which I suppose to be this, that the Epic has been and has remained a classical composition, making no attempt at spheral music, having neither space, time, nor inclination for it, depending wholly on character and plot. Even in modern, romantic times, even when built upon romance, as most of the confectionery epics were—Boiardo's, Pulci's, Ariosto's— the rule has held. I am not ready to admit that the *Chanson de Roland* is the exception which it seems to be. That, as we have it, is an epic fragment. Nobody can be sure how it began, except that it was not as it begins now. The invocation of the muse, another convention of the Epic, is a piece of piety, archaistic or not, with which I don't at all mind confessing my sympathy.

The Task is not a mock-epic. Part of its humour consists in the employment of heavy machinery for a light purpose—as if you should use a Nasmyth hammer for pounding sugar, or a steam-roller for a cider-press; and it is just possible that his word of extenuation is noticeable. If it is noticeable it is wrong—that's certain. I must now give the exordium:

> I sing the Sofa. I, who lately sang
> Truth, Hope, and Charity, and touch'd with awe
> The solemn chords, and with a trembling hand,
> Escap'd with pain from that advent'rous flight,
> Now seek repose upon an humbler theme;
> The theme though humble, yet august and proud
> Th' occasion—for the Fair commands the song.

What a gentleman Cowper was! There is no other way of appraising the mastery and courtliness of that beginning. The next paragraph is exactly right:

> Time was, when clothing sumptuous or for use,
> Save their own painted skins, our sires had none,
> As yet black breeches were not; satin smooth,
> Or velvet soft, or plush with shaggy pile:
> The hardy chief upon the rugged rock
> Wash'd by the sea, or on the grav'lly bank,
> *Fearless of wrong*, repos'd his weary strength.

Surely, a masterpiece of serio-comic writing. The more one reads of Cowper the more one loves him.

'Nothing shows up a bad sonnet so well as to imagine a church built on such lines.' I am reminded of that saying of Renan's by coming naturally to Wordsworth and his way of opening a great poem, and recollecting the figure which he used to describe it, borrowed from architecture, not from music. *The Recluse* he said was to have been conceived of as a 'Gothic Cathedral,' of which *The Prelude* might be considered as the 'ante-chapel.' It is calling one a symphony and t'other an overture, in other words, and distinguishing the work from Epic. *The Recluse* was certainly not an epic. The subject of it was much too subtle for epic treatment. But it was of epic proportions. One book of it, the only one we now have, is of 9,000 lines; *The Prelude* is of 7,000. Whether you pound upon the theme or not by way of opening, whether you stand in an ante-chapel and look before you into the soaring immensities of a nave; whether your mind is prepared by solemn organ-tones, or the shrilling of a trumpet—whatever or whichever you do, I cannot allow that Wordsworth did fairly by a poem which was designed to be the longest, if not the weight-iest in our tongue when he began *The Prelude* by a re-mark about the weather—

Oh there is blessing in this gentle breeze!

But to return to prose, and sum up this curious matter, one would say that, for a great book, a significant prel-ude, some 'music of preparation and awakening sus-pense,' was required. But, to judge by examples, it would seem that it is not so. There is Gibbon. If ever a man felt the solemnity of dedication to a life's work, took up the yoke, knew the touch of the live coal, heard the voice saying, Write, it was Gibbon. He has told us himself how and when he learned what his task was to be. But how placidly he sets out the counters on the board—like an old woman going to play draughts!

'In the second century of the Christian Era, the Empire of Rome comprehended the fairest part of the earth, and the most civilized portion of mankind. The frontiers of that exten-sive monarchy were guarded by ancient renown and disciplined valour. The gentle, but powerful, influence of laws and manners had gradually cemented the union of the provinces. Their peaceful inhabitants enjoyed and abused the advantages of wealth and luxury. . . .'

It is a mild, though an adequate beginning to a work which was (and he knew it) to assure him immortality. Yes, it is 'adequate'—but for one word, the word 'abused.' He should have left that out. No doubt the Roman citizens did abuse their advantages—Gibbon is there to say so—but do you, should you, beg the question of your whole twelve volumes in the first paragraph of the first of them? I cannot think it.

Try another. Here is the beginning of *Travels in Arabia Deserta,* a great book, done with a great gesture:

'A new voice hailed me of an old friend when, first returned from the Peninsula, I paced again in that long street of Damascus which is called Straight; and suddenly taking me wondering by the hand, "Tell me (said he) since thou art here again in the peace and assurance of Ullah, and whilst we walk, as in the former years, toward the new blossoming orchards, full of the sweet spring as the garden of God, what moved thee, or how couldst thou take such journeys into the fanatic Arabia?"'

Mr. Doughty is employing a machine, somewhat worn down in these days, the machine of the inquiring friend and the long recital; the machine indeed of the *Arabian Nights.* Yet it is a beautiful prelude: and it is all the prelude. The next paragraph plunges into the middle of the beginning, and we are off into the dangerous wild. I repeat, a beautiful prelude; but to end I will cap it with a better—Kinglake's to *Eöthen.*

'At Semlin I still was encompassed by the scenes and sounds of familiar life; the din of a busy world still vexed and cheered me; the unveiled faces of women still shone in the light of day. Yet, whenever I chose to look southward, I saw the Ottoman's fortress—austere, and darkly impending high over the vale of the Danube—historic Belgrade. I had come, as it were, to the end of this wheel-going Europe, and now my eyes would see the splendour and havoc of the East.'

'The splendour and havoc of the East.' I cannot charge my memory or find in my library a more fitting prelude to adventure or a more infallible bar of music upon which to open the pages of a good book.

THE ART OF THE ESSAYIST

BY ARTHUR CHRISTOPHER BENSON

THERE is a pleasant story of an itinerant sign-painter who in going his rounds came to a village inn upon whose sign-board he had had his eye for some months and had watched with increasing hope and delight its rapid progress to blurred and faded dimness. To his horror he found a brand-new varnished sign. He surveyed it with disgust, and said to the inn-keeper, who stood nervously by hoping for a professional compliment, "This looks as if someone had been doing it himself."

That sentence holds within it the key to the whole mystery of essay-writing. An essay is a thing which someone does himself; and the point of the essay is not the subject, for any subject will suffice, but the charm of personality. It must concern itself with something "jolly," as the schoolboy says, something smelt, heard, seen, perceived, invented, thought; but the essential thing is that the writer shall have formed his own impression, and that it shall have taken shape in his own mind; and the charm of the essay depends upon the charm of the mind that has conceived and recorded the impression. It will be seen, then, that the essay need not concern itself with anything definite; it need not have an intellectual or a philosophical or a religious or a humorous motif; but equally none of these subjects are ruled out. The only thing necessary is that the thing or the thought should be vividly apprehended, enjoyed, felt to be beautiful, and expressed with a certain gusto. It need conform to no particular rules. All literature answers to

14

something in life, some habitual form of human expression. The stage imitates life, calling in the services of the eye and the ear; there is the narrative of the teller of tales or the minstrel; the song, the letter, the talk—all forms of human expression and communication have their anti-types in literature. The essay is the reverie, the frame of mind in which a man says, in the words of the old song, "Says I to myself, says I."

It is generally supposed that Montaigne is the first writer who wrote what may technically be called essays. His pieces are partly autobiographical, partly speculative, and to a great extent ethical. But the roots of his writing lie far back in literary history. He owed a great part of his inspiration to Cicero, who treated of abstract topics in a conversational way with a romantic background; and this he owed to Plato, whose dialogues undoubtedly contain the germ of both the novel and the essay. Plato is in truth far more the forerunner of the novelist than of the philosopher. He made a background of life, he peopled his scenes with bright boys and amiable elders—oh that all scenes were so peopled!—and he discussed ethical and speculative problems of life and character with vital rather than with a philosophical interest. Plato's dialogues would be essays but for the fact that they have a dramatic colouring, while the essence of the essay is soliloquy. But in the writings of Cicero, such as the *De Senectute,* the dramatic interest is but slight, and the whole thing approaches far more nearly to the essay than to the novel. Probably Cicero supplied to his readers the function both of the essayist and the preacher, and fed the needs of so-called thoughtful readers by dallying, in a fashion which it is hardly unjust to call twaddling, with familiar ethical problems of conduct and character. The charm of Montaigne is the charm of personality—frankness, gusto, acute observation, lively acquaintance with men and manners. He is ashamed of recording nothing that interested him; and a certain discreet shamelessness must always be the characteristic of the essayist, for the essence of his art is to say what has pleased him without too prudently considering whether it is worthy of the attention of the well-informed mind.

I doubt if the English temperament is wholly favourable to the development of the essayist. In the first place, an Anglo-Saxon likes doing things better than thinking about them; and in his memories, he is apt to recall how a thing was done rather than why it was done. In the next place, we are naturally rather prudent and secretive; we say that a man must not wear his heart upon his sleeve, and that is just what the essayist must do. We have a horror of giving ourselves away, and we like to keep ourselves to ourselves. "The Englishman's home is his castle," says another proverb. But the essayist must not have a castle, or if he does, both the grounds and the living-rooms must be open to the inspection of the public.

Lord Brougham, who revelled in advertisement, used to allow his house to be seen by visitors, and the butler had orders that if a party of people came to see the house, Lord Brougham was to be informed of the fact. He used to hurry to the library and take up a book, in order that the tourists might nudge each other and say in whispers, "There is the Lord Chancellor." That is the right frame of mind for the essayist. He may enjoy privacy, but he is no less delighted that people should see him enjoying it.

The essay has taken very various forms in England. Sir Thomas Browne, in such books as *Religio Medici* and *Urn-Burial*, wrote essays of an elaborate rhetorical style, the long fine sentences winding themselves out in delicate weft-like trails of smoke on a still air, hanging in translucent veils. Addison, in the *Spectator*, treated with delicate humour of life and its problems, and created what was practically a new form in the essay of emotional sentiment evoked by solemn scenes and fine associations. Charles Lamb treated romantically the homeliest stuff of life, and showed how the simplest and commonest experiences were rich in emotion and humour. The beauty and dignity of common life were his theme. De Quincey wrote what may be called impassioned autobiography, and brought to his task a magical control of long-drawn and musical cadences. And then we come to such a writer as Pater, who used the essay for the expression of exquisite artistic sensation. These are only a few instances of the way in which the essay has been used in English literature. But the essence is throughout the same; it is personal sensation, personal impression, evoked by something strange or beautiful or curious or interesting or amusing. It has thus a good deal in common with the art of the lyrical poet and the writer of sonnets, but it has all the freedom of prose, its more extended range, its use of less strictly poetical effects, such as humour in particular. Humour is alien to poetical effect, because poetry demands a certain sacredness and solemnity of mood. The poet is emotional in a reverential way; he is thrilled, he loves, he worships, he sorrows; but it is all essentially grave, because he wishes to recognise the sublime and uplifted elements of life; he wishes to free himself from all discordant, absurd, fantastic, undignified contrasts, as he would extrude laughter and chatter and comfortable ease from some stately act of ceremonial worship. It is quite true that the essayist has a full right to such a mood if he chooses; and such essays as Pater's are all conceived in a sort of rapture of holiness, in a region from which all that is

common and homely is carefully fenced out. But the
essayist may have a larger range, and the strength of a
writer like Charles Lamb is that he condescends to use
the very commonest materials, and transfigures the
simplest experiences with a fairy-like delicacy and a
romantic glow. A poet who has far more in common
with the range of the essayist is Robert Browning, and
there are many of his poems, though perhaps not his
best, where his frank amassing of grotesque detail, his
desire to include rather than exclude the homelier sorts
of emotion, his robust and not very humorous humour,
make him an impressionist rather than a lyrist. As
literature develops, the distinction between poetry and
prose will no doubt become harder to maintain. Coleridge said in a very fruitful maxim: "The opposite of
poetry is not prose but science; the opposite of prose
is not poetry but verse." That is to say, poetry has as
its object the kindling of emotion, and science is its opposite, because science is the dispassionate statement of
fact; but prose can equally be used as a vehicle for the
kindling of emotion, and therefore may be in its essence
poetical: but when it is a technical description of a certain kind of structure its opposite is verse—that is to
say, language arranged in metrical and rhythmical form.
We shall probably come to think that the essayist is more
of a poet than the writer of epics, and that the divisions
of literature will tend to be on the one hand the art of
clear and logical statement, and on the other the art of
emotional and imaginative expression.

We must remember in all this that the nomenclature
of literature, the attempt to classify the forms of literary
expression, is a confusing and a bewildering thing unless
it is used merely for convenience. It is the merest
pedantry to say that literature must conform to established usages and types. The essence of it is that it is a

large force flowing in any channel that it can, and the classification of art is a mere classification of channels. What lies behind all art is the principle of wonder and of arrested attention. It need not be only the sense of beauty; it may be the sense of fitness, of strangeness, of completeness, of effective effort. The amazement of the savage at the sight of a civilised town is not the sense of beauty, it is the sense of force, of mysterious resources, of incredible products, of things unintelligibly and even magically made; and then too there is the instinct for perceiving all that is grotesque, absurd, amusing, and jocose, which one sees exhibited in children at the sight of the parrot's crafty and solemn eye and his exaggerated imitation of human speech, at the unusual dress and demeanour of the clown, at the grotesque simulation by the gnarled and contorted tree of something human or reptile. And then, too, there is the strange property in human beings which makes disaster amusing, if its effects are not prejudicial to oneself; that sense which makes the waiter on the pantomime stage, who falls headlong with a tray of crockery, an object to provoke the loudest and most spontaneous mirth of which the ordinary human being is capable. The moralist who would be sympathetically shocked at the rueful abrasions of the waiter, or mournful over the waste of human skill and endeavour involved in the breakage, would be felt by all human beings to have something priggish in his composition and to be too good, as they say, to live.

It is with these rudimentary and inexplicable emotions that the essayist may concern himself, even though the poet may be forbidden to do so; and the appeal of the essayist to the world at large will depend upon the extent to which he experiences some common emotion, sees it in all its bearings, catches the salient features of the scene, and records it in vivid and impressive speech.

The essayist is therefore to a certain extent bound to be a spectator of life; he must be like the man in Browning's fine poem "How it strikes a Contemporary," who walked about, took note of everything, looked at the new house building, poked his stick into the mortar.

> He stood and watched the cobbler at his trade,
> The man who slices lemons into drink,
> The coffee-roaster's brazier, and the boys
> That volunteer to help him turn its winch;
> He glanced o'er books on stalls with half an eye,
> And fly-leaf ballads on the vendor's string,
> And broad-edge bold-print posters by the wall;
> He took such cognizance of men and things!
> If any beat a horse, you felt he saw—
> If any cursed a woman, he took note,
> Yet stared at nobody—they stared at him,
> And found less to their pleasure than surprise,
> He seemed to know them, and expect as much.

That is the essayist's material; he may choose the scene, he may select the sort of life he is interested in, whether it is the street or the countryside or the sea-beach or the picture-gallery; but once there, wherever he may be, he must devote himself to seeing and realizing and getting it all by heart. The writer must not be too much interested in the action and conduct of life. If he is a politician, or a soldier, or an emperor, or a plough-boy, or a thief, and is absorbed in what he is doing, with a vital anxiety to make profit or position or influence out of it; if he hates his opponents and rewards his friends; if he condemns, despises, disapproves, he at once forfeits sympathy and largeness of view. He must believe with all his might in the interest of what he enjoys, to the extent at all events of believing it worth recording and representing, but he must not believe too solemnly or urgently in the importance and necessity of any one sort of business or occupation. The eminent banker, the social reformer, the forensic pleader, the fanatic, the crank, the puritan—these are not the stuff out of which the essayist is made; he may have ethical preferences, but he must not indulge in moral indignation; he must be essentially tolerant, and he must discern quality rather than solidity. He must be concerned with the pageant of life, as it weaves itself with a moving tapestry of scenes and figures rather than with the aims and purposes of life. He must, in fact, be preoccupied with things as they appear, rather than with their significance or their ethical example.

I have little doubt in my own mind that the charm of the familiar essayist depends upon his power of giving the sense of a good-humoured, gracious and reasonable personality and establishing a sort of pleasant friendship with his reader. One does not go to an essayist with a desire for information, or with an expectation of finding a clear statement of a complicated subject; that is not the mood in which one takes up a volume of essays. What one rather expects to find is a companionable treatment of that vast mass of little problems and floating ideas which are aroused and evoked by our passage through the world, our daily employment, our leisure hours, our amusements and diversions, and above all by our relations with other people—all the unexpected, inconsistent, various, simple stuff of life; the essayist ought to be able to import a certain beauty and order into it, to delineate, let us say, the vague emotions aroused in solitude or in company by the sight of scenery, the aspect of towns, the impressions of art and books, the interplay of human qualities and characteristics, the half-formed hopes and desires and fears and joys that form so large a part of our daily thoughts. The essayist ought to be able to indicate a case or a problem that is apt to occur in ordinary life and suggest the theory of it, to guess what it is that makes our moods resolute or fitful, why we act consistently or inconsistently, what it is that repels or attracts us in our dealings with other people, what our private fancies are. The good essayist is the man who makes a reader say: "Well, I have often thought all those things, but I never discerned before any connection between them, nor got so far as to put them into words." And thus the essayist must have a great and far-reaching curiosity; he must be interested rather than displeased by the differences of human beings and by their varied theories. He must recognise the fact that most people's convictions are not the result of reason, but a mass of associations, traditions, things half-understood, phrases, examples, loyalties, whims. He must care more about the inconsistency of humanity than about its dignity; and he must study more what people actually do think about than what they ought to think about. He must not be ashamed of human weaknesses or shocked by them, and still less disgusted by them; but at the same time he must keep in mind the flashes of fine idealism, the passionate visions, the irresponsible humours, the salient peculiarities, that shoot like sunrays through the dull cloudiness of so many human minds, and make one realize that humanity is at once above itself and in itself, and that we are greater than we know; for the interest of the world to the ardent student of it is that we most of us seem to have got hold of something that is bigger than we quite know how to deal with; something remote and far off, which we have seen in a distant vision, which we cannot always remember or keep clear in our minds. The supreme fact of human nature is its duality, its tendency to pull different ways, the tug-of-war between Devil and Baker which lies inside our restless brains. And the confessed aim

of the essayist is to make people interested in life and
in themselves and in the part they can take in life; and
he does that best if he convinces men and women that
life is a fine sort of game, in which they can take a hand;
and that every existence, however confined or restricted,
is full of outlets and pulsing channels, and that the
interest and joy of it is not confined to the politician or
the millionaire, but is pretty fairly distributed, so long
as one has time to attend to it, and is not preoccupied
in some concrete aim or vulgar ambition.

Because the great secret which the true essayist whispers in our ears is that the worth of experience is not
measured by what is called success, but rather resides
in a fulness of life: that success tends rather to obscure
and to diminish experience, and that we may miss the
point of life by being too important, and that the end
of it all is the degree in which we give rather than
receive.

The poet perhaps is the man who sees the greatness
of life best, because he lives most in its beauty and fineness.   But my point is that the essayist is really a lesser
kind of poet, working in simpler and humbler materials,
more in the glow of life perhaps than in the glory of it,
and not finding anything common or unclean.

The essayist is the opposite of the romancer, because
his one and continuous aim is to keep the homely materials in view; to face actual conditions, not to fly from
them.   We think meanly of life if we believe that it has
no sublime moments; but we think sentimentally of it if
we believe that it has nothing but sublime moments.   The
essayist wants to hold the balance; and if he is apt to
neglect the sublimities of life, it is because he is apt to
think that they can take care of themselves; and that
if there is the joy of adventure, the thrill of the start
in the fresh air of the morning, the rapture of ardent

companionship, the gladness of the arrival, yet there must be long spaces in between, when the pilgrim jogs steadily along, and seems to come no nearer to the spire on the horison or to the shining embanked cloudland of the West. He has nothing then but his own thoughts to help him, unless he is alert to see what is happening in hedgerow and copse, and the work of the essayist is to make something rich and strange of those seemingly monotonous spaces, those lengths of level road.

Is, then, the Essay in literature a thing which simply stands outside classification, like Argon among the elements, of which the only thing which can be predicated is that it is there? Or like Justice in Plato's Republic, a thing which the talkers set out to define, and which ends by being the one thing left in a state when the definable qualities are taken away? No, it is not that. It is rather like what is called an organ prelude, a little piece with a theme, not very strict perhaps in form, but which can be fancifully treated, modulated from, and coloured at will. It is a little criticism of life at some one point clearly enough defined.

We may follow any mood, we may look at life in fifty different ways—the only thing we must not do is to despise or deride, out of ignorance or prejudice, the influences which affect others; because the essence of all experience is that we should perceive something which we do not begin by knowing, and learn that life has a fulness and a richness in all sorts of diverse ways which we do not at first even dream of suspecting.

The essayist, then, is in his particular fashion an interpreter of life, a critic of life. He does not see life as the historian, or as the philosopher, or as the poet, or as the novelist, and yet he has a touch of all these. He is not concerned with discovering a theory of it all, or fitting the various parts of it into each other. He works rather on what is called the analytic method, observing, recording, interpreting, just as things strike him, and letting his fancy play over their beauty and significance; the end of it all being this: that he is deeply concerned with the charm and quality of things, and desires to put it all in the clearest and gentlest light, so that at least he may make others love life a little better, and prepare them for its infinite variety and alike for its joyful and mournful surprises.

WRITING

BY EDWARD SANDFORD MARTIN

PERHAPS the practised reader who has learned how, can read so that you forget that he is reading, and take his words as though they were popping at you fresh from the mind that thought them; but with most of us it happens that the instant we proceed from talk into reading there comes a change in the quality of our intonations. It is not our talk any longer, but some one else's, of which we are the mouthpiece.

A subtle distinction very like this difference between talk that is talk and talk that is read is apt to obtain between talk and writing. Most of us, when we undertake to write anything, instinctively assume, as our pen comes out of the ink-pot, a tone a little different from our natural tone of voice. Practice of the right kind tends to obliterate this difference, and to make the writer's writing more like good talk, and, incidentally, to make his talk more like good writing. It is not a bad thing for a man to talk like a book, provided it is exactly the right sort of book, and he doesn't talk like too much of it at once. It is high praise for some kinds of writing to say that it reads like oral speech, but it won't be good writing unless the talk it sounds like is very good talk. In good writing there is the sound of the writer's voice. Surely Milton's living voice is in his prose, and Ruskin's voice in Ruskin's prose, and another voice in Hawthorne's, and another in Newman's, and another in Thackeray's. Style is not an arbitrary thing. It is personal. It has a different tone in every writer, just as the living voice and enunciation is different in each person, and no two painters paint alike. Style regards words as sounds, and puts them together so that they sound well. To reconcile them to grammar is not difficult. To observe how alliterations and assonances enter into style is analytically interesting, but of no practical value in writing. The ear attends to those details.

It is wonderful what subtleties of tone, of feeling, of sentiment, of emotion, can be put into written words, and into very common little words at that. Provided you know something—not so very much—about how to use them, words seem to hold just what you entrust to them, both the sense and the spirit, and keep it to show to any pair of eyes that comes looking for it, and have a discerning and sympathetic mind behind them. You put tears into your words, and the sympathetic reader will snuffle when he comes to them, but you must have snuffled first yourself; put in a smile, and he will smile; catch your spirit at a moment of exaltation or of strong emotion and capture its message with a pencil—there it will be alive and inspiring for whoever reads it with competent eyes.

A great charm about writing is the possibility of writing better than you know; of getting hold of better thoughts than you are fairly entitled to think, or do think, as a rule, and putting them into words of unsuspected felicity. But you must think the thoughts for the moment. You can't put down what you never had, but you can put down what you had and lost.

Most of us are uneven in our mental processes. We don't think big thoughts all the time. We think them under pressure of strong emotions or of fortunate physical conditions. Even when there is no special occasion to inspire a thought that is better than common, it will often come as the result of concentration of the mind, conscious or unconscious, on some particular subject. The mind's automatic action is a very important phase of its activities. It keeps going all the time, and strikes a good many sparks on its own hook. Once a good mind has been headed on a certain course, it is apt to hold that course more or less closely, or at least to revert to it, until it arrives somewhere; and this it will often do whether its owner keeps his watch at the wheel or not. I think that most writers, when they have got some particularly good idea into some particularly lucid and effective form of words, often feel that the job is only part of their doing, and that a good deal of it, and probably the very best of it, came to them by processes more or less independent of their volition. Nobody writes without putting his will into the work and making the indispensable effort, but what comes is partly what is in him and partly what is given him to say, and which is which he may not know, nor whence came what was given. What we call literary talent, or, in its rarer and more remarkable form, genius, seems to be the gift of having extra good ideas come into the mind, and clothe themselves with extra good language. Very young writers have sometimes powers of expression which persons less lucky never get. There is an ear for language like the ear for music, and akin to it. Girls of the most limited experience and youths of inadequate education seem now and then to possess by instinct the faculty of expression; of putting their words where they ought to go, and doing the trick that makes literature.

It is a great advantage to a writer to have sense, but he can get along with a moderate supply of it if only he is a good enough writer. It is an advantage to him to have learning, provided he has it under good control and doesn't let it run away with him or dam him up. But the thing he *must* have is ideas. It is hard sledding for a writer to get along without ideas. Somehow, if he is going to be a writer, he must have bubbles in his mind. He can borrow a great many thoughts if he knows where to find them. What is learning but the assimilation of other men's ideas! But while some persons are writers because they are possessed with ideas that demand to be expounded, a good many others attain more or less painfully to the possession of ideas because they are called to be writers and are peremptorily constrained to have something to impart. It isn't quite enough to have language, though if you know enough words and attain to a truly skilful use of them, you can make them go a good ways. You must have some kind of an idea to string them on if you are going to make a tolerable literary job. Sit down with pen, ink, paper, and a dictionary—if you need one. Then we all know what happens. You have got to think. There is no way out of it. Thinking is to the natural man a severe and repugnant exercise, but the natural man is not a writer. Before anybody becomes a writer he must subjugate nature to the extent of partially overcoming his distaste for consecutive thought. I dare say it is a healthy distaste. I think the repugnance can be overcome, especially if the writer aspires to have many readers. If a writer thinks too fluently and exhaustively, even though he thinks well, he is liable to tire his reader out before he lets go himself. And when a reader is thoroughly tired he quits. That is his privilege, and that is one of the writer's risks that he must consider. If you sit under a speaker, you must often sit him out whether he thinks too exhaustively for you or not, but a writer can hardly put any one to so much inconvenience as that. If his thought is too protracted or doesn't strike you as edifying, you can shut him off in the middle of a sentence, without any lapse of manners or offense to any one. A man who has been a fairly successful writer for a good many years has been heard to attribute his success to the exceptionally feeble quality of his mind, which brought it about that he always got tired of any line of thought he was expounding before the reader did. There is something in that idea, though presumably that was not the whole story, but the same instinct that saves a talker from being a bore must save a writer from being the same. The proper aim of writers, however, is not so much to relieve the reader from the trouble of assimilating thoughts as to put the thought to him so skilfully, so concisely, in such an orderly way, and with such felicities of illustration and diction, that he will take it in gladly, and without too much consciousness of effort.

I don't mean to say that it should be the chief end of every writer to make easy reading. A proper handling of his subject may not admit that. But he should make as easy reading as the proper handling of his subject will allow. He ought to marshall his ideas, or his facts, in their proper order, and to use the right words, and to put them in the right places, so that the reader will have no unnecessary trouble in taking in what he gives out, but may find profit in what he says and a pleasure in the way he says it.

*   *   *

And besides all that, writing is interesting work. A man's *work* is the thing that is going to take most of his time and energy, that he is going to put his best into, and that is going to be his chief reliance for entertainment. Work in the long run is a vastly more durable form of entertainment than play, though play has its uses and is good for a change. Any work a man devotes himself to is apt to interest him, but some kinds of work are pleasanter and more intrinsically interesting than other kinds. Writing is exceedingly pleasant if you can make it go well enough. It is the practice of an art, and to practice an art with skill is delightful. It is a pleasure to be able to kick a football so that it will go between the goal-posts, or where you want it to. That is a mighty skilful job, and it gives pleasure in the doing because it is pretty and because it is difficult. To catch an idea, and send it where you want it to go, and have it go as it should and land where it is needed, is also an exploit that makes you happy. To do a good piece of work satisfies a certain hunger of the mind. Not that a writer always knows when a piece of his work is particularly good or not. Very often he doesn't. Once he gets started on his subject, all he can do is to keep his mind at work on it and put down, the best he knows how, the best his mind will yield. What he gets depends on what is in him and whether he manages to get it out.

Writing verses is an entertaining branch of the literary calling, provided you can do it to your taste. Somehow, our faculties being such as they are, there are wonderful possibilities in poetry for stirring them. Verse-writing is good practice in getting the run of words and determining their order. You not only have to have a good many words at your command in order to choose such as make rhyme and rhythm come right, but you are apt to have to put them together in ever so many different combinations before you get the one you want. And there are such astounding possibilities in those combinations. The words are the same, or as good, as have served the English-writing poets since Chaucer. Is there not always the possibility that you may string a few dozen or a few hundred of them together in such a fashion that mankind will neither suffer them nor you to be forgotten? It has been done. Why may it not be done again? It can. There are all the pieces if one can only invent a surpassing pattern. It always seems *possible* to put the familiar little words together so as to make a surpassing poem, but very, very few writers have done it, and those few have not done it by accident, but commonly as the fruit, more or less immediate, of long-continued effort coupled with genius.

Of making many books and myriads of magazines and newspapers there is no end, and armies of writers and would-be writers are always at it. And yet the supply of good writers is, nowadays, never equal to the demand. That is a great advantage. It keeps up rates, and makes it unnecessary for writers to form unions and have strikes. There is a natural monopoly of high talent. Money can stimulate the production of good writing somewhat by offering inducement to good minds to take literary exercise, but it cannot buy good writing unless it is written, and it very often pays for qualities that are not delivered. Inducement and inspiration are not identical. Money may offer inducement, but inspiration comes from other sources. The love of approbation is one source of inspiration, and in particular the hunger for the special approbation of careless young women of no particular discrimination about literature has been the inspiration of more good verse than all the gold pieces that any one ever saw. And the love of truth, and the love of beauty, and the love of nature and of mankind are all inspirations of endless effectiveness.

THE ART OF WRITING

BY H. M. TOMLINSON

WHETHER I placed the writing-pad on my knees in a great chair, or on the table, or on the floor, nothing happened to it. I can only say that that morning the paper was full of vile hairs, which the pen kept getting into its mouth—enough to ruin the goodwill of any pen. Yet all the circumstances of the room seemed luckily placed for work to flow with ease: but there was some mysterious and inimical obstruction. The fire was bright and lively, the familiar objects about the table appeared to be in their right places. Again I examined the gods of the table to be sure one had not by mischance broken the magic circle and interrupted the current of favour for me. They were rightly orientated—that comic pebble paper-weight Miss Muffet found on the beach of a distant holiday, the chrysanthemums which were fresh from that very autumn morning, stuck in the blue vase which must have got its colour in the Gulf Stream; and the rusty machete blade from Peru, and the earthenware monkey squatting meekly in his shadowy niche, holding the time in his hands. The time was going on, too.

I tried all the tricks I knew for getting under way, but the pen continued to do nothing but draw idle faces and pick up hairs, which it held firmly in its teeth. Then the second telegram was brought to me. "What about Balkan article?" it asked, and finished with a studied insult, after the manner of the editor-kind, whose assurance that the function of the universe is only fulfilled when they have published the fact makes them behave as would Jove with a thick-headed immortal. "These Balkan atrocities will never cease," I said, dropping the telegram into the fire.

Had I possessed but one of those intelligent manuals which instruct the innocent in the art, not only of writing, but of writing so well that a very disappointed and world-weary editor rejoices when he sees the manuscript, puts his thumbs up and calls for wine, I would have consulted it. (I should be glad to hear if there is such a book, with a potent remedy for just common dulness—the usual opaque, gummous, slow, thick, or fat head.) As for me, I have nothing but a cheap dictionary, and that I could not find. I raised my voice, calling down the hollow, dusty, and unfurnished spaces of my mind, summoning my servants, my carefully chosen but lazy and wilful staff of words, to my immediate aid. But there was no answer: only the cobwebs moved there, though I thought I heard a faint buzzing, which might have been a blow-fly. No doubt my staff—small blame to them—were dreaming somewhere in the sun, dispersed over several seas and continents.

Well, a suburb of a big town, and such jobs as I find for them to do, are grey enough for them in winter. I have no doubt some were nooning it in Algiers, and others were prospecting the South Seas, flattering themselves, with gross vanity, how well they could serve me there, if only I would give them a chance with those coloured and lonely islands: and others were in the cabins of ships far from any land, gossiping about old times: and these last idle words, it is my experience, are the most stubborn of the lot, usually ignoring all my efforts to get them home again and to business. I could call and rage as I chose, or entreat them, showing them the urgency of my need. But only a useless and indefinite article came along, as he usually does, hours and hours before the arrival of a lusty word which could throw about the suggestions quicker than they might be picked up and examined.

Very well. There was nothing for it but to fill another pipe, and dwell with some dismay upon such things as, for instance, the way one's light grows smoky with age. Is there a manual which will help a man to keep his light shining brightly—supposing he has a light to keep? But if he has but the cheapest of transient glims, good and bright enough for its narrow purpose, is it any wonder it burns foul, seeing what business it gets to illuminate in these exciting and hurried times. What work! I think it would make rebels of the most quiet, unadventurous, and simple-featured troop of words that ever a man gathered about him for the plain domestic duties to employ them regularly, for example, in sweeping into neat columns such litter as the House of Commons makes. It would numb the original heart of the bonniest set of words that rightly used would have made people happy —sterilize them, make them anaemic and pasty-faced, so that they would disturb the peace of mind of all compassionate men who looked upon them. That my own staff of words refused my summons . . .

But what was it I said I wanted them for just now? I gazed round the walls upon the portraits of the great writers of the past, hoping for inspiration. Useless! Upon Emerson's face there was a faint smile of most infuriating benevolence. Lamb—but I am getting tired of his smirk, which might be of irony or kindness. He would look savage enough to-day, hearing his constantly returning Dissertation on Roast Pig thump the door-mat four times a week; for that, he can be assured, is the way editors would treat it now, and without even preliminary consultations with lady typist-secretaries. Of the whole gallery of the great I felt there was not one worth his

wall room. They were pious frauds. This inspiration
business is played out. I have never had the worth of
the frames out of those portraits. . . . Ah, the Balkans.
That was it. And of all the flat, interminable Arctic
waves of bleak wickedness and frozen error that ever a
shivering writer had to traverse. . . .

My head was in my hands, and I was trying to get
daylight and direction into the affair with my eyes shut,
when I felt a slight touch on my arm. "I'm sorry we're
in your way. Are you praying? Look who's here."

I looked. It was Miss Muffet who spoke. She shook
the gold out of her eyes and regarded me steadily. Well
she knew she had no right there, for all her look of
confident and tender solicitude. The Boy, who is a
little older (and already knows enough to place the
responsibility for intrusion on his sister with her innocent eyes and imperturbable calm and golden hair), stood
a little in the background, pretending to be engrossed
with a magnet, as though he were unaware that he was
really present. Curls hopped about on one leg frankly,
knowing that the others would be blamed for any naught-
iness of hers. Her radiant impudence never needs any
apology. What a plague of inconsequential violators of
any necessary peace! When would my lucky words come
now?

The Boy probably saw a red light somewhere.
"Haven't you finished uncle we thought you had has a
topsail schooner got two or three masts I saw a fine little
engine up in the town and an aeroplane it was only
seventeen shillings do you think that is too much?"

"I am learning the sailor's hornpipe at school," said
Miss Muffet, slowly and calmly; "you watch my feet.
Do I dance it nicely?"

I watched her feet. Now it is but fair to say that
when Miss Muffet dances across a room there is no

international crisis in all this world which would distract any man's frank admiration. When Miss Muffet steps it on a sunny day, her hair being what it is, and her little feet in her strap shoes being such as they are, then your mood dances in accord, and your thoughts swing in light and rhythmic harmony. I got up. And Curls, who is one of those who must mount stairs laboriously secure to the rails—she has black eyes only the bright light of which is seen through her mane—she reached up for my hand, for she cannot imitate her sister's hornpipe without holding on.

Miss Muffet reached a corner of the room, and swung round, light as a fairy, her hands on her hips, and said, "What do you think of that?" Some of my lucky words instantly returned. I suppose it was more to their mind. But I had nothing to give them to do. They could just stand around and look on now, for when Curls seriously imitates her sister, and then laughs heartily at her own absurd failure, because her feet are irresponsible, that is the time when you have nothing to do, and would not do anything if it had to be done. . . .

What time it was the next interruption came—it was another telegram—I don't know. Time had been obliterated. But then it began to flow again; though not with a viscid and heavy measure. And when I took up my light and ready pen, there, standing at eager attention, was all my staff, waiting the call. What had happened to bring them all back? If the writers of literary manuals will explain that secret to me, I should acquire true wealth.

ON BEING ORIGINAL

BY IRVING BABBITT

THERE has been a radical change during the last hundred years in the world's attitude toward originality. An age of conformity has given way to an age of self-assertion; so that nowadays a man makes a bid for fame by launching a paradox, much as he might have done in the time of Pope by polishing a commonplace. Then, even a person of genuine originality was in danger of being accounted freakish. Now, many a man passes for original who is in reality only freakish. Boileau, speaking for the old criticism, says that Perrault was "bizarre;" Sainte-Beuve, speaking for the new, says that Perrault had genius. From the outset, the neo-classic critics stifled free initiative in the name of the "rules," and opposed to every attempt at innovation the authority of Aristotle and the ancients. The relation of the literary aspirant to the "models" during this period is not unfairly summed up in the words of the comic opera—

> "Of course you can never be like us,
> But be as like us as you're able to be."

Later, under French influence, the tyranny of etiquette was added to the tyranny of classical imitation. Aristotle was reinforced by the dancing master. Social convention so entwined itself about the whole nature of a Frenchman of the Old Regime that it finally became almost as hard for him as we may suppose it is for a Chinaman to disengage his originality from the coils of custom. The very word original was often used as a

term of ridicule and disparagement. Brossette writes
of the Oriental traveler Tavernier that he is "brutal and
even a bit original." "When it is desired to turn any
one to ridicule," writes Boursault about the same time,
"he is said to be an *original sans copie*." Anything in
literature or art that departed from the conventional type
was pronounced "monstrous." La Harpe applies this
epithet to the "Divine Comedy," and points out how inferior the occasional felicities of this "absurd and shapeless rhapsody" are to the correct beauties of a true epic
like Voltaire's "Henriade."

And so we might go on, as Mr. Saintsbury, for example, does for scores of pages in his "History of Criticism," exposing the neo-classic narrowness, and setting
forth in contrast the glories of our modern emancipation.
But this is to give one's self the pleasure, as the French
would say, of smashing in open doors. Instead of en-
gaging in this exhilarating pastime, we might, perhaps,
find more profit in inquiring, first, into the definite historical reasons that led to the triumph of the so-called
school of good sense over the school of genius and originality; and second, in seeking for the element of truth
that lurked beneath even the most arid and unpromising
of the neo-classic conventions. For if, like Mr. Saintsbury and many other romanticists, we reject the truth
along with the convention, we shall simply fall from
one extreme into another.

The whole subject of originality is closely bound up
with what is rather vaguely known as individualism.
We must recollect that before the disciplinary classicism of the later Renaissance there was an earlier Renaissance which was in a high degree favorable to originality. At the very beginning of this earlier period,
Petrarch made his famous plea for originality, in a letter to Boccaccio, and established his claim, in this as

in other respects, to be considered the first modern man. "Every one," says Petrarch, "has not only in his countenance and gestures, but also in his voice and language, something peculiarly his own (*quiddam suum ac proprium*), which it is both easier and wiser to cultivate and correct than it is to alter." And so many of the Italians who followed Petrarch set out to cultivate the *quiddam suum ac proprium*, often showing real ardor for self-expression, and still oftener, perhaps, using the new liberty merely as a cloak for license. Society finally took alarm, not only at the license, but at the clash of rival originalities, each man indulging in his own individual sense without much reference to the general or common sense of mankind. This reaction, especially in France and Italy, soon ran into excesses of its own. Yet we must not forget that, at the moment when the neoclassic disciplinarian appeared on the scene, the great creative impulse of the early Renaissance was already dying out or degenerating into affectation. The various forms of bad taste that spread like an epidemic over Europe at the end of the sixteenth century and beginning of the seventeenth (cultism, Marinism, euphuism, préciosité, etc.), have their common source in a straining to be original in defiance of sound reason. We may say of the writers of these different schools as a class that, in spite of occasional lyrical felicities, they have "all the nodosities of the oak without its strength and all the contortions of the Sibyl without the inspiration."

The school of good sense was the natural and legitimate protest against this pseudo-originality. But this school can be justified on higher grounds than simply as a reaction from a previous excess. It tried to apply, however imperfectly, the profound doctrine of Aristotle that the final test of art is not its originality, but its truth to the universal. The question is one of special interest because we are living in an age that comes at the end of a great era of expansion, comparable in some ways to that of the Renaissance. Now, as then, there is a riot of so-called originality. In the name of this originality art is becoming more and more centrifugal and eccentric. As the result of our loss of standards, the classicist would complain, we are inbreeding personal and national peculiarities and getting farther and farther away from what is universally human.

In other words, the chief ambition of our modern art, which resembles in this respect some of the art of the later Renaissance, is to be original. The first aim of both classic and neo-classic art, on the other hand, was to be representative. Aristotle had said that it is not enough to render a thing as it is in this or that particular case, but as it is in general; and he goes on to say that the superiority of poetry over history lies in the fact that it has more of this universality, that it is more concerned with the essentials and less with the accidents of human nature. The weakness of neo-classic art was that it substituted the rule of thumb and servile imitation for direct observation in deciding what were accidents and what were essentials. It was ready to proscribe a thing as "monstrous,"—that is, as outside of nature,—when in reality it was simply outside the bounds set by certain commentators on Aristotle. The artist had to conform to the conventional types established in this way, even if he sacrificed to them poignancy and directness of emotion. He was limited by the type not only in dealing with any particular literary form,— tragedy, epic, and so forth,—but even in his creating of individual characters. For example, he must be careful not to paint a particular soldier, but the typical soldier, and of course he was not to depart too far from the classical models in deciding what the traits of the

typical soldier are. Thus Rymer condemns Iago because
he is not true to the "character constantly worn by soldiers for some thousands of years in the world." According to Rymer, again, the queen in one of Beaumont
and Fletcher's plays oversteps the bounds of decorum.
Some particular queen, Rymer admits, may have acted
in this way; but she must be rid of all her "accidental
historical impudence" before she can become an orthodox, typical queen, entitled to "stalk in tragedy on her
high shoes."

The attempt of the neo-classicists to tyrannize over
originality and restrict the creative impulse in the name
of the type was bound in the long run to provoke a reaction. To carry through the difficult and delicate task
of breaking with convention some man of more than
Socratic wisdom was needed; instead, this task was un-
dertaken by the "self-torturing sophist, wild Rousseau."
In almost the opening sentence of his "Confessions"·
Rousseau strikes the note that is heard throughout the
nineteenth century, from the early romanticists to Ibsen
and Sudermann: "If I am not better than other men, at
least I am different." By this gloating sense of his
own departure from the type Rousseau became the father
of eccentric individualists. By his insistence on the
rights and legitimacy of unrestrained emotion he in-
augurated the age of storm and stress, not only in
Germany, but throughout Europe. Our modern impressionists, who would make of their own sensibility the
measure of all things, are only his late-born disciples.

Emotion, insists the classicist, must be disciplined
and subdued to what is typical; else it will be eccentric
and not true to the human heart. "The human heart of
whom?" cries Alfred de Musset, like a true disciple of
Jean-Jacques. "The human heart of what? Even
though the devil be in it, I have my human heart of my

own—*j'ai mon cœur humain, moi.*" The whole of French romanticism is in that *moi*. Away with stale authority, usage, and tradition, that would come between a man and his own spontaneity, and keep him from immediate contact with "nature." Let him once more see the world bathed in the fresh wonder of the dawn. To this end let him discard books ("a dull and endless strife") and live as if "none had lived before him."

Every man, in short, is to be an original genius. It was the assumption of this attitude by Rousseau's followers in Germany that gave its name to a whole literary period (*Geniezeit*). Germany sought its emancipation from convention, not, as Lessing would have wished, through the discipline of reason, but through "genius" and "originality," which meant in practice the opening of the floodgates of sentiment. We can imagine the disgust with which Lessing looked on the Rousseauism of the youthful Goethe. In "Werther," critics are accused of being in a conspiracy against originality. Their rules are compared to a system of dams and trenches with which the critics protect their own little cabbage-patches against genius, whose impetuous waves would otherwise burst forth and overwhelm them, and at the same time astound the world. One thinks of Lessing's admirable defense of criticism, of the passage in which he confesses that he owes all he has, not to genius and originality, but to a patient assimilation of the wisdom of the past. "Without criticism I should be poor, cold, short-sighted. I am, therefore, always ashamed or annoyed when I hear or read anything in disparagement of criticism. It is said to suppress genius, and I flattered myself that I had gained from it something very nearly approaching genius. I am a lame man who cannot possibly be edified by abuse of his crutch."

We are still inclined to side with original genius

against what Lessing calls criticism. Criticism itself
has come to mean nowadays mere appreciativeness, instead of meaning, as it did for Lessing, the application
of standards of judgment. It may, however, appear
some day how much the great romantic leaders, Shelley
for example, suffered from the absence of just what
Lessing called criticism. Men may then grow weary
of a genius and originality that are at bottom only an
outpouring of undisciplined emotion. One whole side
of our American transcendental school is only a belated
echo of German romanticism, which itself continues the
age of original genius. There is special danger even
in Emerson's conception of originality, and the un-
bounded deference with which it fills him for the un-
trained individual. Every man, to become great, merely
needs, it would appear, to plant himself indomitably
on his instincts; but it is not safe for the average person
to trust so blindly to what Rymer would have called his
own "maggot." Hawthorne, the best observer of the
group, has left an account of some of the nightmare
originalities that were developed under the Concord influence.

We read of a certain character in one of Marivaux's
plays: "He is a man whose first impulse is to ask, not,
'Do you esteem me?' but, 'Are you surprised at me?'
His purpose is not to convince us that he is better than
other people, but that he resembles himself alone." The
comedy in which this eighteenth-century Bernard Shaw
figures was written a number of years before Rousseau
assumed the Armenian costume and began to agitate
Europe with his paradoxes. Since Rousseau the world
has become increasingly familiar with the man who
poses and attitudinizes before it and is not satisfied until
he can draw its attention to the traits that establish
his own uniqueness. The eccentric individualist not only

rejoices in his own singularity, but is usually eager to
thrust it on other people. His aim is to startle, or, as
the French would say, to *épater le bourgeois,* to make
the plain citizen "stare and gasp." Dr. Johnson said
of Lord Monboddo that if he had had a tail he would
have been as proud of it as a squirrel. Perhaps Rousseau was never more deeply hurt than by the lady who
said, on breaking with him, "you're just like other
men." This, as a French critic remarks, was a home
thrust that one of Molière's soubrettes could not have
improved upon. The claim of Rousseau and his earlier
followers was to be not simply unique, but unique in
feeling. This sentiment of uniqueness in feeling speed-
ily became that of uniqueness in suffering—on the familiar principle, no doubt, that life, which is a comedy
for those who think, is a tragedy for those who feel.
Hence arose in the romantic school a somewhat theatrical
affectation of grief. Byron was far from being the
first who paraded before the public "the pageant of
his bleeding heart." Chateaubriand especially nourished in himself the sense of fated and preëminent
sorrow, and was ready to exclaim at the most ordinary
mischance: "Such things happen only to me!" Sainte-
Beuve makes an interesting comparison between Chateaubriand and another native of Brittany, the author
of "Gil Blas." "A book like 'René'" says Sainte-
Beuve encourages a subtle spiritual pride. A man
seeks in his imagination some unique misfortune to which
he may abandon himself and which he may fold about
him in solitude. He says to himself that a great soul
must contain more sorrow than a little one; and adds in
a whisper that he himself may be this great soul. 'Gil
Blas,' on the other hand, is a book that brings you into
full contact with life and the throng of your fellow
creatures. When you are very gloomy and believe in

fatality and imagine that certain extraordinary things happen to you alone, read 'Gil Blas,' and you will find that he had that very misfortune or one just like it, and that he took it as a simple mishap and got over it."

The same contrast might be brought out by comparing Montaigne and Rousseau, the two writers who, in a broad sense, are the masters respectively of Lesage and Chateaubriand. This contrast is easily missed, because at first glance Montaigne seems an arch-egotist like Rousseau, and is almost equally ready to bestow his own idiosyncrasies on the reader. Yet in the final analysis Montaigne is interested in Montaigne because he is a human being; Rousseau is interested in Rousseau because he is Jean-Jacques. Montaigne observes himself impartially as a normal specimen of the genus homo. Rousseau, as we have seen, positively gloats over his own otherwiseness. Montaigne aims to be the average, or, it would be less misleading to say, the representative man; Rousseau's aim is to be the extraordinary man, or original genius. Rousseau is an eccentric, Montaigne a concentric individualist. The sentence of Montaigne that sums him up is, "Every man bears within him the entire image of the human lot." Rousseau is rather summed up in his phrase, "There are souls that are too privileged to follow the common path," with its corollary that he is himself one of these privileged souls.

The nineteenth century saw the rise of a race of eccentric individualists, especially in art and literature, who, like Rousseau, scorned the common path and strove to distinguish themselves from the bourgeois and philistine in everything, from the details of their dress to the refinements of their sensations. In this quest of the rare and the original they attained to a departure from the norm that was not only eccentric, but pathological. Every man was to have the right to express not only his own particular vision of life, but his own particular nightmare. We finally come to a writer like Baudelaire, who builds himself a "little strangely scented and strangely colored kiosk on the extreme tip of the romantic Kamchatka" and "cultivates his hysteria with delight and terror;" who, instead of being true to the human heart, as the old-fashioned classicist would say, makes it his ambition to create a "new shudder." All the modern writer cares for, says M. Anatole France, is to be thought original. In his fear of becoming commonplace he prides himself, like Victor Hugo, on reading only those books that other men do not read, or else he does not read at all, and so comes to resemble that eighteenth-century Frenchwoman who was said to have "respected in her ignorance the active principle of her originality." The danger of the man who is too assimilative, who possesses too perfectly the riches of tradition, is to feel that originality is henceforth impossible. It is related of a French critic that he used to turn away wearily from every new volume of poetry that was submitted to him, with the remark: "All the verses are written."

Genuine originality, however, is a hardy growth, and usually gains more than it loses by striking deep root into the literature of the past. La Bruyère begins his "Characters" by observing that "Everything has been said," and then goes on to write one of the most original books in French. Montaigne wrote a still more original book which often impresses the reader as a mere cento of quotations. An excessive respect for the past is less harmful than the excess from which we are now suffering. For example, one of our younger writers is praised in a review for his "stark freedom from tradition . . . as though he came into the world of letters without ever a predecessor. He is the expression in literary art of certain enormous repudiations." It is precisely this notion of originality that explains the immense insignificance of so much of our contemporary writing. The man who breaks with the past in this way will think that he is original when he is in reality merely ignorant and presumptuous. He is apt to imagine himself about a century ahead of his age when he is at least four or five centuries behind it. "He comes to you," as Bagehot puts it, "with a notion that Noah discarded in the ark, and attracts attention to it as if it were a stupendous novelty of his own."

We may be sure that the more enlightened of the Cave Dwellers had already made deeper discoveries in human nature than many of our modern radicals. Goethe said that if as a young man he had known of the masterpieces that already existed in Greek he would never have written a line. Goethe carries his modesty too far; but how grateful just a touch of it would be in the average author of to-day! With even a small part of Goethe's knowledge and insight, he would no longer go on serving up to us the dregs and last muddy lees of the romantic and naturalistic movements as originality and genius. He would see that his very paradoxes were stale. Instead of being a half-baked author, he would become a modest and at the same time judicious reader; or, if he continued to write, he would be less anxious to create and more anxious to humanize his creations. Sooner or later every author, as well as the characters he conceives, will have to answer the question that was the first addressed to any one who designed to enter the Buddhist church: "Are you a human being?" The world's suffrage will go in the long run to the writer or artist who dwells habitually in the centre and not on the remote periphery of human nature. Gautier paid a doubtful compliment to Victor Hugo when he said that Hugo's works seemed to proceed not from a man, but an element, that they were Cyclopean, "as it were, the works of Polyphemus." Hugo remained the original genius to the end, in contrast with Goethe, who attained humane restraint after having begun as a Rousseauist.

Romanticism from the very beginning tended to become eccentric through over-anxiety to be original; and romanticism is now running to seed. Many of our contemporary writers are as plainly in an extreme as the most extreme of the neo-classicists. They think that to be original they need merely to arrive at self-expression without any effort to be representative. The neo-classicist, on the other hand, strove so hard to be representative that he often lost the personal flavor entirely and fell into colorless abstraction. Both extremes fail equally of being humane. For, to revert to our fundamental principle, the humanist must combine opposite extremes and occupy all the space between them. Genuine originality is so immensely difficult because it imposes the task of achieving work that is of general human truth and at the same time intensely individual. Perhaps the best examples of this union of qualities are found in Greek. The original man for the Greek was the one who could create in the very act of imitating the past. Greek literature at its best is to a remarkable degree a creative imitation of Homer.

The modern does not, like the Greek, hope to become original by assimilating tradition, but rather by ignoring it, or, if he is a scholar, by trying to prove that it is mistaken. We have been discussing thus far almost entirely the originality of the Rousseauist or sentimental naturalist; but we should not fail to note the curious points of contact here as elsewhere between sentimental and scientific naturalism. The Baconian aims less at the assimilation of past wisdom than at the advancement of learning. With him too the prime stress is on the new and the original. Formerly there was a pedantry of authority and prescription. As a result of the working together of Rousseauist and Baconian there has arisen a veritable pedantry of originality. The scientific pedant who is entirely absorbed in his own bit of research is first cousin to the artistic and literary pedant who is entirely absorbed in his own sensation. The hero of modern scholarship is not the humanist, but the investigator. The man who digs up an unpublished document from some musty archive outranks the man who can deal judiciously with the documents already in print. His glory will be all the greater if he can make the new document a pretext for writing a book, for attempting a rehabilitation. The love of truth shades imperceptibly into the love of paradox; and Rousseauist and Baconian often coexist in the same person.

A royal road to a reputation for originality is to impugn the verdicts of the past,—to whitewash what is traditionally black or to blackwash what is traditionally white. Only the other day one of the English reviews published the "Blackwashing of Dante." A still better example is Renan's blackwashing of King David, which concludes as follows: "Pious souls, when they take delight in the sentiments filled with resignation and tender melancholy contained in the most beautiful of the liturgical books, will imagine that they are in communion with the bandit. Humanity will believe in final justice on the testimony of David, who never gave it a thought, and of the Sibyl, who never existed," etc. The whitewashings have been still more numerous. Rehabilitations have appeared of Tiberius, the Borgias, and Robespierre. A book has also been written to prove that the first Napoleon was a man of an eminently peace-loving disposition. Mr. Stephen Phillips undertakes to throw a poetical glamour over the character of Nero, that amiable youth, who, as the versifier in "Punch" observes,—

> "would have doubtless made his mark,
> Had he not, in a mad, mad, boyish lark,
> Murdered his mother!"

If this whitewashing and blackwashing goes on, the time will soon come when the only way left to be original will be to make a modest plea for the traditional good sense of the world. This traditional good sense was never treated with an easier contempt than at present. A writer named Bax, who recently published a volume rehabilitating the revolutionary monster Marat, says in his preface: "It is in fact a fairly safe rule to ascertain for oneself what most people think on such questions" (i.e. as the character of Marat), "and then assume the exact opposite to be true." Of most books of this kind we may say what FitzGerald said when Henry Irving made himself up in the rôle of Shylock to look like the Saviour: "It is an attempt to strike out an original idea in the teeth of common sense and tradition." Of course there are in every age and individual, as we have said elsewhere, elements that run counter to the main tendency. One of the regular recipes for writing German doctors' theses is to seize on one of these elements, exaggerate it, and take it as a point of departure for refuting the traditional view. Thus Rousseau says in one place that he has always detested political agitators. We may be sure in advance that some German will start from this to prove that Rousseau has been cruelly maligned in being looked on as a revolutionist.

Even our more serious scholars are finding it hard to resist that something in the spirit of the age which de-

mands that their results be not only just, but novel.
Even our older universities are becoming familiar with
the professor who combines in about equal measure his
love of research and his love of the limelight.   In public opinion, the perfection of the type is the Chicago
professor whose originality has become the jest of the
cheap newspapers.   Here are a few Chicago "discoveries," selected almost at random from the many that
have been announced from time to time in the daily
press:—

Kissing causes lockjaw.

The Pennsylvanians are turning into Indians.

A man does not need to take exercise after the age
of thirty-five.

Music is antiseptic.

A dog will not follow an uneducated man.

Marriage is a form of insanity.

Americans are incapable of friendship.

Boccaccio was a Swede.

John D. Rockefeller is as great a man as Shakespeare.

Some day a wounded or even worn-out heart of a human being may be replaced by a healthy heart from a
living monkey, etc.

The Chicago professors would say, and no doubt
rightly, that they are misrepresented by these newspaper statements.   But we are only giving the general
impression.   Even the utterance of Dr. Osler that at
once gave him such a start over all his academic rivals
in the race for notoriety becomes comparatively unsen-
sational when read in its context.   The professor with
an itch for the limelight has only to pattern himself on
Rousseau, the great master of paradox.   Rousseau's
method has been compared to that of a man who fires

off a pistol in the street to attract a crowd. When Rousseau has once drawn his crowd, he may proceed to attentuate his paradox, until sometimes it is in danger of dwindling into a commonplace.

Most good observers would probably agree that contemporary scholarship and literature are becoming too eccentric and centrifugal; they would agree that some unifying principle is needed to counteract this excessive striving after originality. For example, Professor Gummere, who is one of the most distinguished representatives of the scholarly tradition that ultimately goes back to Herder and the Grimm brothers, diagnoses our present malady with great clearness in a recent article on "Originality and Convention in Literature." The higher forms of poetry and creative art, he says, are being made impossible by the disintegrating influences at work in modern life, and by an excess of analysis. He suggests as remedy that we jettison this intellectual and analytical element, and seek to restore once more the bond of communal sympathy. This remedy betrays at once its romantic origin. It is only one form of Rousseau's assumption that an unaided sympathy will do more to draw men together than the naked forces of egoism and self-assertion will do to drive them asunder. Even in his studies of the beginnings of poetry Professor Gummere should, perhaps, have insisted more on communal discipline as a needful preliminary to communal sympathy. However that may be, our present hope does not seem to lie in the romanticist's attempt to revert to the unity of instinct and feeling that he supposes to have existed in primitive life. We need to commune and unite in what is above rather than in what is below our ordinary selves, and the pathway to this higher unity is not through sympathy, communal or otherwise, but through restraint. If we have got so far apart, it is because of the lack, not of sympathy, but of humane standards.

Without trying to enter fully into so large a topic as the impressionism of our modern society, its loss of traditional standards, and its failure as yet to find new, we may at least point out that education should be less infected than it is with a pedantic straining after originality. In general, education should represent the conservative and unifying element in our national life. The college especially must maintain humane standards, if it is to have any reason at all for existing as something distinct from university and preparatory school. Its function is not, as is so often assumed, merely to help its students to self-expression, but even more to help them to become humane. In the words of Cardinal Newman, the college is "the great ordinary means to a great but ordinary end"; this end is to supply principles of taste and judgment and train in sanity and centrality of view; to give background and perspective, and inspire, if not the spirit of conformity, at least a proper respect for the past experience of the world. Most of us have heard of Mrs. Shelley's reply when advised to send her boy to a school where he would be taught to think for himself: "My God! teach him rather to think like other people." Mrs. Shelley had lived with a man who was not only a real genius, but also an original genius in the German sense, and knew whereof she spoke. Now the college should not necessarily teach its students to think like other people, but it should teach them to distinguish between what is original and what is merely old and eccentric, both in themselves and others. According to Lowell, this is a distinction that Wordsworth could never make, and Wordsworth is not alone in this respect among the romantic leaders. We must insist, at the risk of causing scandal, that the college is not primarily intended to encourage originality and independence of thought as these terms are often understood. The story is told of a professor in one of our Eastern colleges that he invariably gave a high mark to the undergraduates who contradicted the received opinions in his subject; but the highest mark he reserved for the undergraduate who in addition to contradicting the traditional view set up a new view of his own. As this fact became known, the professor was gratified by a rapid growth among his students of independent and original thinking.

The college should guard against an undue stress on self-expression and an insufficient stress on humane assimilation. This danger is especially plain in the teaching of English composition. A father once said to me of a "daily theme" course that it had at least set his son's wits to working. But what if it set them to working in the void? The most that can be expected of youths who are put to writing with little or no background of humane assimilation is a clever impressionism. They will be fitted, not to render serious service to literature, but at most to shine in the more superficial kinds of journalism. It is still an open question whether any direct method of teaching English really takes the place of the drill in the niceties of style that can be derived from translation, especially the translation of Latin; whether a student, for example, who rendered Cicero with due regard for the delicate shades of meaning would not gain more mastery of English (to say nothing of Latin) than a student who devoted the same amount of time to daily themes and original composition. We must, however, be fair to our departments of English. They have to cope with conditions not entirely of their own making, of which the most serious is something approaching illiteracy in many of the stu-

dents that are forced upon them from the preparatory
schools. In practice they have to devote most of their
time to imparting, not the elegancies, but the simplest
decencies of the English language. Ultimately a great
deal of what goes on in the more elementary college
courses in English may well be relegated to the lower
schools,—and the home,—and the work that is done
in the advanced courses in composition will probably
either be omitted entirely, or else done, as it is in
France, in connection with the reading and detailed
study of great writers. Assimilation will then keep pace
as it should with expression.

Spinoza says that a man should constantly keep before his eyes a sort of exemplar of human nature (*idea
hominis, tamquam naturae humanae exemplar*). He
should, in other words, have a humane standard to which
he may defer, and which will not proscribe originality,
but will help him to discriminate between what is original and what is merely freakish and abnormal in himself and others. Now this humane standard may be
gained by a few through philosophic insight, but in most
cases it will be attained, if at all, by a knowledge of
good literature—by a familiarity with that golden chain
of masterpieces which links together into a single tradition the more permanent experience of the race; books
which so agree in essentials that they seem, as Emerson
puts it, to be the work of one all-seeing, all-hearing
gentleman. In short, the most practical way of promot-
ing humanism is to work for a revival of the almost lost
art of reading. As a general rule, the humane man
will be the one who has a memory richly stored with
what is best in literature, with the sound sense perfectly
expressed that is found only in the masters. Conversely,
the decline of humanism and the growth of Rousseauism
has been marked by a steady decay in the higher uses

of the memory. For the Greeks the Muses were not the daughters of Inspiration or of Genius, as they would be for a modern, but the daughters of Memory. Sainte-Beuve says that "from time to time we should raise our eyes to the hill-tops, to the group of revered mortals, and ask ourselves: What would they say of us?" No one whose memory is not enriched in the way we have described can profit by this advice. Sainte-Beuve himself in giving it was probably only remembering Longinus.

TRADITION

BY STUART P. SHERMAN

To LENGTHEN the childhood of the individual, at the same time bringing to bear upon it the influences of tradition, is the obvious way to shorten the childhood of races, nations, classes, and so to quicken the general processes of civilization. Yet in the busy hum of self-approbation which accompanies the critical activities of our young people, perhaps the dominant note is their satisfaction at having emancipated themselves from the fetters of tradition, the oppression of classical precedent, the burden of an inherited culture. By detaching the new literature from its learned past they are confident that they are assuring it a popular future. Turn to any one of half a dozen books which discuss the present movement, and you will learn that people are now discovering, for example, "often to their own surprise," that they can read and enjoy poetry. That is because poetry has been subjected to "democratization." The elder writers, such as Shakespeare, Milton, Emerson, and Longfellow, constantly gravelled them with strange and obsolete phrases, like "multitudinous seas incarnadine," and like "tumultuous privacy of storm." The ancient writers sent them to out-of-the-way reference books to look up obscure legends about Troy, not the city where collars are made, and old stuff about war in heaven, and the landing at Plymouth Rock. It is therefore a relief to countless eager young souls that Mr. Mencken has dismissed all this as "the fossil literature taught in colleges," and that Mary Austin insists that

58

native verse rhythms must be "within the capacity of the democratically bred." It is a joy to hear from Mr. Untermeyer that modern readers of poetry may now come out from the "lifeless and literary storehouse" and use life itself for their glossary, as indeed they may— or the morning's newspaper.

Those who encourage us to hope for crops without tillage, learning without study, and literary birth without gestation or travail are doubtless animated by a desire to augment the sum of human felicity; but one recalls Burke's passionate ejaculation: "Oh! no, sir, no. Those things which are not practicable are not desirable." To the new mode of procuring a literary renascence there may be raised one objection, which, to minds of a certain temper, will seem rather grave: all experience is against it. Such is the thesis recently argued by an English critic, Mr. H. J. Massingham, who reviews with mingled amusement and alarm the present "self-conscious rebellion against tradition." In the eyes of our excited young "cosmopolitans," whose culture has a geographic rather than an historical extension, Mr. Massingham's opinions will of course appear to be hopelessly prejudiced by his Oxford breeding, his acquaintance with the classics, his saturation in Elizabethan literature, and his avowed passion for old books in early editions, drilled by the bibliomaniac worm, "prehistoric" things, like Nares' *Glossary* and Camden's *Remains*. But it is not merely the opinion of our critic that is formidable: "The restoration of the traditional link with the art of the past is a conservative and revolutionary necessity." It is not the supporting opinion of Sir Joshua Reynolds: "The only food and nourishment of the mind of an artist is the great works of his predecessors." Sir Joshua, too, was prejudiced by his position as a pillar of the robust English classicism

of George III's time. It is not even the opinion of
Henry James, whom Mr. Massingham proclaims the pro-
foundest critic since Coleridge, and who even our own
irreverent youth seem to suspect should be mentioned
respectfully: "It takes an endless amount of history
to make even a little tradition and an endless amount
of tradition to make even a little taste and an endless
amount of taste, by the same token, to make even a little
tranquillity."

The formidable arguments against the radical engi-
neers of renascence are just the notorious facts of literary history. The fact that a bit of the "fossil literature
taught in colleges," the story of Arthur, written in
Latin by a Welsh monk in the twelfth century, has
flowered and fruited in poetry, painting, and music generation after generation pretty much over the civilized
world. The fact that Chaucer and his contemporaries,
in whom poetry had a glorious rebirth, had previously
devoured everything in what Mr. Untermeyer would
call the "lifeless and literary storehouse" of the Middle
Ages. The fact that the Elizabethans, to quote Mr.
Massingham's vigorous phrase, flung themselves on tradition "like a hungry wolf, not only upon the classics
but upon all the tradition open to them." The fact that
Restoration comedy is simply a revival of late Caroline
in the hands of men who had studied Molière. The fact
that the leaders of the new movement in the eighteenth
century, when they wished to break from the stereotyped
classicism, did not urge young people to slam the door
on the past, but, on the contrary, harked back over the
heads of Pope and Dryden to the elder and more central tradition of Milton, Shakespeare, and Spenser; and
sluiced into the arid fields of common sense, grown plati-
tudinous, the long-dammed or subterranean currents of
mediæval romance. The fact that "Childe Harold,"

"Adonais," "The Eve of St. Agnes," "The Cotter's Saturday Night," and "The Castle of Indolence" were all written by imitators of Spenser or by imitators of his imitators. The fact, to omit the Victorians, that Mr. W. B. Yeats, the most skilful living engineer of literary renascence, set all his collaborators to digging around the roots of the ancient Celtic tree before we enjoyed the blossoming of the new spring in Ireland. The fact that John Masefield, freshest and most tuneful voice in England, is obviously steeped to the lips in the poetry of Byron, Shakespeare, Spenser, and Chaucer.

Why is it that the great poets, novelists, and critics, with few exceptions, have been, in the more liberal sense of the world, scholars—masters of several languages, students of history and philosophy, antiquarians? First of all because the great writer conceives of his vocation as the most magnificent and the most complex of crafts. He is to be his own architect, master-builder, carpenter, painter, singer, orator, poet and dramatist. His materials, his tools, his methods are, or may be, infinite. To him, then, the written tradition is a school and a museum in which, if he has a critical and inventive mind, he learns, from both the successes and the failures of his predecessors, how to set to work upon his own problems of expression. As Mr. Yeats is fond of pointing out, the young poet may find Herbert and Vaughan more helpful to him than the work of his own contemporaries, because the faults in the elder poets, the purple patches that failed to hold their color, will not attract and mislead him.

But tradition is more than a school of crafts. It is a school of mood and manners. The artist who is also a scholar cannot fail to discover that what distinguishes all the golden periods of art, what constitutes the perpetual appeal of the masters, is a kind of innermost

poise and serenity, tragic in Sophocles, heroic in Michelangelo, skeptical in Montaigne, idyllic in Sidney, ironic
in Fielding.   This enviable tranquillity reigns only in
a mind that, looking before and after, feels itself the
representative of something outlasting time, some national ideal, some religious faith, some permanent human experience, some endless human quest.   Nothing
begets this mood and manner, the sovereign mark of
good breeding in letters, like habitual association with
those who have it, the majority of whom are, in the
vulgar sense of the word, dead.   Izaak Walton, a minor
writer in whose work there is a golden afterglow of the
great age, calls, in one of his Angler's Dialogues, for
"that smooth song which was made by Kit Marlowe,
now at least fifty years ago," and for the answer to it
"which was made by Sir Walter Raleigh in his younger
days."   If some of our modern imitators of the auc-
tioneer and the steam calliope would now and then,
instead of reading one another, step into the "lifeless
and literary storehouse" and compare these "fossils"
conscientiously with their own recent efforts to make
verse popular!   "They were old-fashioned poetry," says
Piscator apologetically, "but choicely good, I think
much better than the strong lines that are now in fashion in this critical age."

Out of the tranquillity induced by working in a good
literary tradition develops form.   The clever theorists
who insist that form alone matters, that form is the
only preservative element in literature, forget that form
is not "self-begotten" but a product of the formative
spirit.   Mr. Massingham is a bit fastidious in his use of
this word.   He denies form, for example, to Pope and to
Swinburne.   Though both have technique, that is another matter.   "Form," he declares, "is a vision contained and made manifest."   He attributes the unpro-

ductiveness of our age in the field of satire to a vision
without a traditional base, reeling and shifting in the
choppy waters of contemporary opinion. His remarks
on the deficiencies of Gilbert Cannan as a satirist and
novelist further elucidate his idea; and they may serve
also as a comment upon many of the younger writers
in America:

The works of Mr. Cannan seem to say, "That is what life is
—a surge of base and beautiful forces, intensified in the consciousness of man." But that is a fallacy. Life is like that to
the layman, but it is the business of the artist to see a clue
in it, to give it shape and order, to weld its particles into
congruity. Here is where his lack of a constructive or satiric
purpose growing out of and controlling the material tells to
his hurt. He knows life in the raw, but the satirist would
put it in the oven and dish it up. So he wanders in the dark,
and we blunder after him. But we want light, if it be only
from a tallow candle.

Now, many of the young writers in America are disposed to reject the English tradition as unserviceable
lumber. They scorn equally the greater part of the
American tradition as puritanical, effeminate, or over-
intellectualized. If they seek foreign allies, it is with
those who help them forget our national characteristics,
our native bent and purposes, our discovered special
American "genius." In what measure is the revolt due
to the conduct of the movement by writers whose blood
and breeding are as hostile to the English strain as a
cat to water? Whatever the answer, I suspect that the
young people who are being congratulated right and
left on their emancipation from tradition are rather
open to condolence than to felicitation. They have
broken away from so much that was formative, and
they suffer so obviously in consequence of the break.
Their poets have lost a skill which Poe had: though
they paint a little, and chant a little, and speak a great

deal of faintly rhythmical prose, they have not learned how to sing. Their novelists have lost a vision which Howells had: though they have shaken off the "moralistic incubus" and have released their "suppressed desires," they have not learned how to conceive or to present a coherent picture of civilized society. Their leaders have lost a constructiveness which a critic so laden with explosives as Emerson exhibited: though they have blown up the old highways they have not made new roads.

Am I doing the "young people" an injustice? I turn from their anthologies of verse, where I keep searching in vain for such music as the angler's milkmaid sang; and from the novels of Mr. Cabell, in whom I have not discovered that ascending sun heralded by the lookouts; to *A Modern Book of Criticism,* recently collected and put forth by Mr. Ludwig Lewisohn. The editor's desire is to show us that "a group of critics, young men or men who do not grow old, are at work upon the creation of a civilized cultural atmosphere in America." The idea resembles that, does it not? of Mr. Waldo Frank, who recently informed us that literature began in America in 1900—or was it 1910?—at Mr. Stieglitz's place in New York. It is related also to that recent comprehensive indictment edited by Mr. Harold Stearns and ironically entitled *Civilization in the United States.* The implication is clearly that the country which developed Bradford, Franklin, Emerson, Lincoln, Thoreau, Whitman, Mark Twain, here and there in villages and backwoods, had no "civilized cultural atmosphere" worth mentioning. It does not seem quite plausible.

But let us proceed with Mr. Lewisohn. His critics:— "Like a group of shivering young Davids—slim and frail but with a glimpse of morning sunshine on their foreheads—they face an army of Goliaths." The slim and shivering young Davids turn out on investigation to be Mr. Huneker, Mr. Spingarn, Mr. Mencken, Mr. Lewisohn, Mr. Hackett, Mr. Van Wyck Brooks, and Randolph Bourne. It is not a group, taken as a whole, however it may be connected with the house of Jesse, which should be expected to hear any profound murmuring of ancestral voices or to experience any mysterious inflowing of national experience in meditating on the names of Mark Twain, Whitman, Thoreau, Lincoln, Emerson, Franklin, and Bradford. One doesn't blame our Davids for their inability to connect themselves vitally with this line of Americans, for their inability to receive its tradition or to carry it on. But one cannot help asking whether this inability does not largely account for the fact that Mr. Lewisohn's group of critics are restless impressionists, almost destitute of doctrine, and with no discoverable unifying tendency except to let themselves out into a homeless happy land where they may enjoy the "colorful" cosmic weather, untroubled by business men, or middle-class Americans, or Congressmen, or moralists, or humanists, or philosophers, or professors, or Victorians, or Puritans, or New Englanders, or Messrs. Tarkington and Churchill. A jolly lot of Goliaths to slay before we get that "civilized cultural atmosphere."

By faithfully studying the writings of Mr. Mencken, Mr. Lewisohn, and other "shivering young Davids," I have obtained a fairly clear conception of what a "civilized cultural atmosphere" is not. It consists of none of those heart-remembered things—our own revenue officers probing our old shoes for diamond necklaces, our own New York newspapers, and Maryland chicken on the Albany boat—which cause a native American returning from a year in Europe to exclaim as he sails up the tranquil bosom of the Hudson and rushes by a standard steel Pullman, back to the great warm embrace of his own land, "Thank Heaven, we are home again." No, it is none of these things. If, without going to Munich, you wish to know what a "civilized cultural atmosphere" really is, you must let Mr. Lewisohn describe it for you as it existed, till the passage of the Volstead act, in one or two odd corners of old New York: "The lamps of the tavern had orange-colored shades, the wainscoting was black with age. The place was filled with a soothing dusk and the blended odor of beer and tobacco and Wiener Schnitzel. *I was, at least, back in civilization.* That tavern is gone now, swept away by the barbarism of the Neo-Puritans."

To the book from which this quotation is made, Mr. Lewisohn's recently published autobiographical record, *Up Stream,* students of contemporary critical currents and eddies are much indebted. The author, like many of the other belligerent young writers who have shown in recent years a grave concern for the state of civilization in America, has ostensibly been directing his attack against our national culture from a very elevated position. He has professed himself one of the enlightened spirits who from time to time rise above the narrowing prejudices of nationality into the free air of the republic of letters, the grand cosmopolis of the true humanist. From his watch-tower—apparently "in the skies"—he has launched lightnings of derision at those who still weave garlands for their Lares and Penates, at the nationalist with his "selective sympathies," at the traditionalist with his sentimental fondness for folkways. Those who feel strongly attracted, as I do myself, to the Ciceronian and Stoic conception of a universal humanity and by the Christian and Augustinian vision of a universal City of God, may easily have mistaken Mr. Lewisohn for a "sharpshooter" of the next age, an outpost from the land of their heart's desire. But in *Up Stream,* Mr. Lewisohn drops the mask and reveals himself, for all his Jewish radicalism, as essentially a sentimental and homesick German, longing in exile for a Germany which exists only in his imagination.

Even the purified and liberated mind of a Child of Light, living according to nature and reason, is unable to rid itself wholly of "selective sympathies." It betrays under provocation a merely "traditional emotion" for a cultural atmosphere compounded of the odors of beer, tobacco, and Wiener Schnitzel, with perhaps a whiff of Kant and a strain of Hungarian music floating through it, while two or three high philosophical spirits discuss what a poet can do when his wife grows old and stringy. I do not think it necessary to remonstrate with a man merely because his affective nature responds powerfully to a vision of felicity thus composed; but I think it a bit impractical to ask "a nation of prohibitionists and Puritans" to accept this vision as the goal of cultural efforts in America. It is a help to fruitful controversy, however, when a man abandons his absurdly insincere professions of "universal sympathy"—his purring protestation that he desires "neither to judge nor to condemn"—and frankly admits that he likes the German life, what he knows of it, and that he regards American life, what he knows of it, as "ugly and mean."

The militant hostility of alien-minded critics towards what they conceive to be the dominant traits of the national character is, on the whole, to be welcomed as provocative of reflection and as a corrective to national conceit. But the amendment of that which is really ugly and mean and basely repressive in our contemporary society is less likely to be achieved by listening to the counsels of exiled emancipators from Munich than by harking back to our own liberative tradition, which long antedates the efforts of these bewildered impressionists.

When we grow dull and inadventurous and slothfully content with our present conditions and our old habits, it is not because we are "traditionalists"; it is, on the contrary, because we have ceased to feel the formative spirit of our own traditions. It is not much in the American vein, to be sure, to construct private little anarchies in the haze of a smoking-room; but practical revolt, on a large scale and sagaciously conducted, is an American tradition, which we should continue to view with courage and the tranquillity which is related to courage. America was born because it revolted. It revolted because it condemned. It condemned because its sympathies were not universal but selective. Its sympathies were selective because it had a vision of a better life, pressing for fulfilment. That vision, and not a conception of life as a meaningless "surge of base and beautiful forces" liberated its chief men of letters. Thence their serenity, in place of that "gentle but chronic dizziness" which a critic of Young Germany, Hugo von Hofmannsthal, says, "vibrates among us." Thence, too, their freedom from ancestor-worship and bondage to the letter. Listen to Emerson:

> Ask not me, as Muftis can,
> To recite the Alcoran;
> Well I love the meaning sweet;
> I tread the book beneath my feet.

Thence, too, the traditional bent of the American spirit toward modernity, toward realism. It was nearly a hundred years ago that our then-leading critic wrote in his journal: "You must exercise your genius in some form that has essential life now; do something which is proper to the hour and cannot but be done."

Did he not recognize what was to be done? I quote once more from him a finer sentence than any of our impressionists has ever written: "A wife, a babe, a brother, poverty, and a country, which the Greeks had, I have." The grip and the beauty of that simple sentence are due to a union in it of an Athenian vision with Yankee self-reliance. It is the kind of feeling that comes to a man who has lived in a great tradition.

A PLEA FOR THE PLATITUDE

BY BRANDER MATTHEWS

I

IT IS greatly to be regretted that we do not know the name of the man who boldly declared that "Grover Cleveland was the greatest master of platitude since George Washington." It would be amusing to inquire whether he meant this for a compliment to Cleveland or for a reproof to Washington. It would be interesting to ask him also whether he was prepared to concede that a practical politician at the head of the commonwealth ought to be a master of platitude. If the unknown utterer of this pregnant saying was willing to admit this, he would find himself in the comfortable company of that shrewd student of affairs, Walter Bagehot, who held that a statesman was likely to be most useful to the community when he combined common ideas and uncommon ability.

One of Cleveland's more recent successors in the presidency of the United States was accused of talking about the Ten Commandments just as if he had received them as a direct personal revelation to himself. Now, there is no denying that Theodore Roosevelt was wont to talk in this fashion. And why not? As a matter of fact, the Ten Commandments had come to him as a direct personal revelation—for so they must come to every one of us who is ready to receive them and to take them to heart. In the case of Roosevelt, as in the case of Washington and Cleveland, that which was foolishly meant as a reproof turns out to be really a compliment. There can be no more imperative duty for the chief of state in a democratic republic than to reiterate the eternal verities. It is his privilege also to profit by the megaphone which destiny has put at his lips to cry aloud these imperishable truths and thus to force them upon ears that might otherwise refuse to listen. It may be charged that when a leader of men is insistent in asserting again and again that honesty is the best policy, he is lowering himself to the inculcation of the obvious. But if this is just what he believes to be needful at the moment, he has no right to shrink from saying once again what many have asserted before him. Stevenson hit the center when he suggested that "after all, the commonplaces are the great poetic truths."

Perhaps there is small risk in declaring that we Americans have a lust for novel ideas and that we listen with jaded credulity to those who get up in the market-place to proclaim a new gospel. Yet we are all aware that what is true is likely to be old. We all know this, and yet we are often impatient with those old fogies who abide by the ancient land-marks. We are prone to laugh at the mossbacks brave enough to risk the reproach brought against the katydid,—which has the habit of saying "an undisputed thing in such a solemn way." The undisputed things are always in danger of being neglected; and they need to be said afresh to every generation, in the special vocabulary of that generation and with whatever of solemnity we can command. The wisdom of the fathers must be restated for the benefit of the children, and yet again for the guidance of the grandchildren.

Just as it is a certain evidence of juvenility to shriek out an accusation of plagiarism whenever two plays happen to have a casual resemblance of situation or

whenever two poems chance to have a superficial identity of phrase or of cadence, so it is an assured sign
of immaturity to sneer at the political leader who re-
asserts the principles which he deems permanent and
essential for the common weal and to scoff at him as a
dealer in platitudes and as an expounder of commonplaces. "Commonplace," said Lord Morley (in words
that sound almost like an echo of Stevenson's), "after
all, is exactly what contains the truths which are indispensable."

The brief speech which Lincoln delivered at Gettysburg nearly sixty years ago is now accepted as one of
the masterpieces of English prose, withstanding comparison with the address on a similar occasion that
Thucydides put into the mouth of Pericles. It is as
perfect in its lofty dignity of sentiment as it is in its
lapidary concision of style. But there would be little
difficulty in proving that it contains nothing new, since
the thoughts that sustain it are as self-evident as they
are sincere. They are the ancient thoughts which demanded to be voiced again, then and there. The stones
of this sublime structure are commonplaces, recognized
as such long before Lincoln was born, long before Columbus set sail on the Western Ocean. These well-
worn blocks Lincoln chose for his own use with his
unerring tact; and he cemented them together once again
by his own personality.

Hamlet's soliloquy, "To be or not to be," is a mosaic
of sentiments and of opinions familiar to every one of
us from our youth up and already phrased in all sorts
of fashions in every tongue, living or dead;—nevertheless that monologue, compounded as it may be of commonplaces, bereft of all novelty, glows and burns with
the inner fire of Hamlet's soul at that awful crisis of his
fate. It propounds, once for all, the mighty questions

we cannot help putting to ourselves when we also find ourselves in the valley of the shadow. And when the time comes for any one of us to face those questions we shall not cavil at their antiquity, for then they will erect themselves in front of us with a new-born challenge.

II

It may be acknowledged frankly that the Gettysburg speech and Hamlet's soliloquy are extreme cases. The savor of a stimulating individuality is likely to be lacking from compositions as fundamentally unoriginal as these two are seen to be when they are reduced to their elements. A commonplace is effective and therefore not merely to be pardoned but even to be praised, only when it is a personal rediscovery of the speaker, when he unhesitatingly believes himself to be speaking out of the fulness of his own feeling. At the moment he may not know, and he surely does not care, whether or not the things he is called upon to speak have ever been uttered before; and he is well aware that this does not matter at all, since these things have come to him fresh from his own experience, hot from his own heart. Then the platitude is redeemed and transfigured by poignant personality,—as when the fabled Scotchman asseverated earnestly that "Honesty *is* the best policy," adding by way of explanation, "I hae tried baith." What can be more commonplace than "honesty is the best policy"? It is the tritest of truisms, but it came to the mouth of that man from the depth of his own soul. He had no doubt but that he was lighting a torch for the feet of those who wander in darkness.

Deprive commonplace of this note of rediscovery, by which the old is made new of its own accord, and it is the abomination of desolation. A sequence of platitudes peddled from a platform by an uninspired speaker who refuses to rely on his actual feelings, who never had an idea of his own and who is seeking to say only what nobody will dispute,—this cannot fail to be stale, flat and unprofitable, even if every single commonplace of which it is compacted may contain an immitigable truth. It is the prevalence of speechmaking of this sort, so threadbare and so colorless that it seems insincere, which revolts those who demand that a man shall reveal some evidence either of emotion or of cerebration before they will listen to him. This attitude is natural enough, but it brings with it a double danger. First of all, it tempts us to disregard the truth which may be clothed in the most offensively insipid commonplace; and second, it allures us into the primrose path of paradox.

The commonplace is not always to be accepted at its face value. It may not be true now, whatever it has been once upon a time; and it may even never have been true, but only plausible and specious. There is no virtue in the commonplace itself, and there may be vice in it. Its value resides wholly in the truth which it may contain and which each of us must appraise for himself. But as the truth is not necessarily inherent in a platitude, neither is it necessarily inherent in a paradox. Even Mr. Shaw and Mr. Chesterton, if pushed to the wall, would probably be willing to admit that there are some paradoxes which are not true. They might be ready even to accept the definition of a paradox as a truth serving its apprenticeship.

That is what a paradox may be, no doubt; it may be a peremptory challenge to a commonplace which has ceased to sheathe the verity, even if it has not yet worn out its welcome. The paradox of this quality, however, is not really a paradox; it is only a pseudo-paradox; it is a new shape of truth; and by that very fact it is condemned to become a commonplace in its turn, whenever it shall have ousted the platitude it is attacking. This pseudo-paradox, which sooner or later will inevitably issue from unthinking lips as an impregnable platitude, is never merely a commonplace reversed. To turn a truth upside down is not to turn it inside out. To stand a truism on its head is profitless; and there is no stimulus to clear thought in the glib suggestion that "Dishonesty is the best policy" or that "procrastination is the guardian of time." An infelicity of phrasemaking like this may have an evanescent glitter, yet it is but the flickering of thorns under a pot. It may amuse babes and sucklings for a little season to be told that the devil is not as black as he is painted, since he possesses at least the Christian virtue of perseverance. Verbal fireworks are attractive only to the very young. The writer whose pages corruscate with unexpected inversions of accepted beliefs and who exhibits himself as a catherine-wheel of multicolored paradox is likely soon to sputter out in darkness and in silence. If Mr. Bernard Shaw has any abiding value as a stimulating thinker this is in spite of his flamboyant method of expressing himself and not because of it.

A French critic has asserted that men may be grouped in three classes, so far as their attitude toward the truth is concerned. First of all, there is the immense majority assured that the wisdom of the past will be the wisdom of the future and glad always to hear again the accepted commonplaces. Second, there is a youthful minority, weary of these traditional statements and avidly relishing any paradox which seems to pierce the crust of convention. Third, there is the little knot of those who are in the habit of doing their own thinking and who are ever ready to receive a novel idea on probation, to weigh it cautiously and to test it thoroly with willingness to accept it ultimately and to make it their own thereafter if it approves itself. It is from this small company that new ideas come into being, and get into circulation. The members of this third group have to be won over before any novelty has a valid chance of acceptance; and when at last they have been taken captive, the members of the first group will slowly, very slowly, and after violent opposition, follow in their wake. The chosen few carry the flag to the front; and trailing after them comes the immense majority which gives solidity to the body politic, changing its mind only by almost imperceptible degrees. And the second group, the youthful minority, with its delight in disintegrating paradox, is almost negligible, because it lacks intellectual sincerity. Its puerile protests against the platitudes which buttress the social organization merely irritate the immense majority, while they evoke only tolerant contempt from wiser men. The youthful minority is puffed up with pride at its discovery that elementary truths are commonplace. But bread and beef are the commonplaces of diet, none the less wholesome, and indeed none the less welcome, because they lack the spice of novelty. Man cannot live by paradox alone. If the staff of life chances to be contained in any paradox, then this is not a true paradox and then also it is on the way in its turn to become a platitude. It was Boileau who remarked that "a new thought is a thought which must have come to many but which some one happens first to express," and this is perhaps the source of Pope's "What oft was thought, but ne'er so well expressed." If we insist on escaping from the fenced field of the commonplace we cannot complain if we find ourselves landing in the thorny hedge of freakish unreason.

BIBLIOMANIA

"Books," says Anatole France, "are the opium of the Occident. They devour us. A day is coming in which we shall all be keepers of libraries . . . and that will be the end." What a novel and wholly delightful outlook!

Since the days of Jeremiah all the best-trained prophets have clearly seen that the downfall of civilization could not be postponed much longer, but they have been unable to agree about the cause of this ever-impending downfall. They have insisted alternately that we are to be ruined by war and by peace, by race-suicide and by large families, by strong drink and by prohibition. Out of this welter of opinion it has been possible, of course, for the plain man to construct an eclectic pessimism, to capture and cage a private *bête noir* exactly to his own taste; but on the whole such disagreement among the prophets has not been for our souls' good. A little more and we should have begun to distrust all prophets whatsoever and to stray off into fools' paradises of facile optimism. But here comes M. France to the rescue, prognosticating a debacle so delightful that every man who has begun to pluck up hope for the world will now return gladly and at once to a decent and orthodox gloom. We are to die of books . . . of too many books, and, let us hope, too good. O blissful euthanasia!

"In Paris alone," he continues, "fifty books are published daily, and those who read them are like the eaters of hashish. They live in a dream. The subtle poison that penetrates their brains renders them insensible to the real world. It is a monstrous orgy. We shall emerge from it quite mad."

Is it even so? Then I defy you, stars! If I am to go mad from too much reading, I am determined to have a good time at it. The fact is that I have never yet been quite mad, and it can hardly fail to be an interesting experience. Yes, if it is at all possible to wrench a sunbeam out of this storm-cloud, I shall enjoy myself. Perhaps it would be well to itemize the compensations while I have some rays of reason left.

In the first place, then, there will be the good company. It would not be worth while to list the authors I shall read during my decline because I can't forsee what untoward effects the gradual dimming of reason may have upon my literary taste. Suffice it that there are going to be some noble ingredients in the potent drug that steals my wits away, and that Anatole France will be among them. Shakespeare, Shelley, Montaigne . . . but I will not name them. Have I not enough on my conscience already after these many years of concocting literary poisons of my own and forcing them upon a reluctant public? However, with such company as I can imagine—Hazlitt, Lamb, Thoreau, Bacon, Voltaire —all jingling merrily down the road to the everlasting mad-house, who would care to remain sane?

Secondly, I intend during the progress of my mental decay to learn something about life. "What! Just by reading books?" Well, why not? Isn't that a large part of what they are good for, to "ransack the ages, spoil the climes, gain me the gains of various men"? Brown, a banker, smiles benignly at this, preferring to look at life through the steel bars of his cage. Jones, a clergyman, is convinced that the only real view of the human scene is to be obtained from a pulpit. Smith thinks there is no place like a drawing room for getting acquainted with men and women. If they have good luck these friends of mine may get to know three or four people fairly well during a lifetime, although of course they will have to look at those three or four with the quite ordinary eyes God gave them. I shall think of Smith and Jones and Brown to-night when I roll my arm-chair toward the fire and take down my Shakespeare with his three hundred fully drawn characters, each seen by the deepest searcher of human hearts. My friends are convinced that I live in a world of shadows, while they are in touch with life itself. Somehow they remind me of Swinburne's words about the "dotage of dunce-dom which cannot perceive, the impudence of insignificance so presumptuous as to doubt that the elements of life and literature are indivisibly mingled one in another, and that he to whom books are less real than life will assuredly find in men and women as little reality as in his accursed crassness he deserves to discover." I have never quoted that gorgeous sentence to Brown, Jones, and Smith because I am afraid it might seem a bit too personal, although it would certainly have a quieting effect. But then of course poor Swinburne himself . . . we know what he was. Mad; quite mad.

Finally, I shall hope by the guidance and stimulus of books to do some hard thinking. This, I know, is even more dangerous than much reading and a greater weariness to the flesh. It is a sort of sister habit into which the other leads as tobacco does to drink. And here too, I am aware, my friends will be against me. Most of them are engaged, I am proud to say, in what they call "active life." That is, they are real estate agents, advertising men, vendors of patent pills—stern strugglers all. Thinking, they unanimously agree, is only one remove from plain loafing. What we need in order to avoid

universal catastrophe, in their opinion, is not to think
—good Heavens, no!—but to sell more land, to plaster
all the remaining landscape with soap ads, to make
people buy the proper quantities of pills. Behold the
stern struggler with his feet on the roll-top desk—the
vice-president, perhaps, of a pickle factory—how he
reads not, neither does he think, and yet he gives you
his candid opinion that he and his kind are about to bring
in the millennium. If we can only sell more pickles, says
he, we shall wipe away all tears. Heartily would he
agree, if you could make it clear to him, with M. France's
statement that books are a powerful poison and thought
a deadly drug distilled therefrom. He has always sus-
pected as much and acted upon the suspicion. It is true
that stern strugglers of this sort are greatly in the
majority just now, and it is also true—is it not?—that
in this democratic country the majority is always right.
. . . And yet, I don't know. In a time like this perhaps there is no more effective or necessary service than
that of simply sitting still and thinking things out. . . .
I forgot to mention that books, according to Anatole
France, are already bringing about a general paralysis.
This is not the least of their blessings to mankind. Complete paralysis of the entire race of stern strugglers is
a prospect that some of us could face with equanimity.
Then they would have to think.

But it is clear that my dementia is setting in sooner
than I had expected, and therefore I hasten to a conclusion. While I chew my literary hashish in the dark
years coming on, then, I shall be trying to know life,
to enjoy, and to understand it. Is this the road to
madness? How do I know, since, as I have admitted, I
have never yet been quite mad? If it were not for the
superior authority of M. France I should say that it
looks to me like the road to real sanity, but that is doubt-

less a symptom of the disease. M. France is a far wiser man than I am, has read many more books than I ever shall, and he ought to know. "You may believe me who adore them," says he, "and who have long given myself to them without reserve. Books slay us. Yes, books kill us." Very well then: so be it. We shall be buried like the titans of old under mountains—mountains of books. O Death, where is thy sting? O grave, where is thy victory?

PLATO AS A NOVELIST

BY VIDA D. SCUDDER

How far behind us seem the days when the future author of *Adam Bede* wrote sedately to a youthful friend that she read no novels, because "the weapons of the Christian warfare were never sharpened at the forge of Romance!" Whatever be true of Christian warfare and its weapons, novels are nowadays a necessary and wholesome part of everyone's daily life. Did they serve no other purpose, they afford an invaluable gymnastic of the sympathies. Reading them, we acquire with minimum effort a broadening of our affections, a liking for all sorts and conditions of people, including not a few —crooks, drunkards, fools, even—from whom in real life we should turn with disgust and distaste. If we moderns are growing more inwardly democratic, if we take life with more emotional versatility and humorous tolerance than our forbears, we owe the gain less to our political institutions than to our excellent habit of indiscriminate novel reading. Wiseacres may bid us devote our whole mind to Bergson. Him we should not neglect. But let us also insist on the advantage to our manners and our morals of familiarity with *Havoc, A Millionaire Baby,* and *The Tu-Tze's Tower.*

Yet there is a melancholy fact which we cannot escape. As people grow older, they get fussy about their fiction. Reproachfully, despondently, middle age finds that it has lost the delectable power of youth to enjoy anything in story form. The mysteries seem set in pattern, and flat when solved. The princesses of Graustein have no more attraction than summer girls in a tennis court. The latest flights of psychic aeroplanes lift us away from earth if you will, but into peculiarly vacuous mid-air. And the grim tales of mean streets revolt like a stroll through the slums in hot weather.

This I submit is the moment for Plato. Not Plato the philosopher. Such a gentleman may exist, spinning an intricate spider web of dialectic, along whose tenuous gossamers the daring intellect darts insecurely outward towards its elusive prey, a conclusion. This subtle personage is no hammock companion. Plato the novelist is our man; writer of fiction bathed in the immortal dew of the world's dawning; magician who evokes for us the moving-picture of the most fascinating society ever known; master delineator of the weaknesses and the loveliness of men. Tell me if you will of a Plato wise in archetypal ideas concerned with the relations of knowledge and virtue, keen on pursuit of the perfect state. Him I seek not in the summer noons,—nay, but the witty satirist, the lofty lover, the creator of that most vivid character in the world's fiction, who is the friend of Crito and Agathon, the adorer of Charmides, the beloved by Alcibiades. With this Plato I can keep delightful fellowship, whithersoever he may lead.

Nowhere shall I find more variety. Does my palate crave comic salt? Here is *Euthydemus,* bubbling over with pure mischief, which finally breaks into farce roaring as that of the *Pickwick Papers,* when the two Sophists, twisted up by Socrates to assert that everything is what it isn't, are greeted with a tumult of glee. Is high romance to my taste? Here it weaves spells true as in Shakespeare's sonnets; for these Dialogues abound with sentiment of every shade, and at the same banquet we may encounter passion most lofty and most base, listening at will to Diotima or to Alcibiades. Do we find light society sketches more to our mind than confidences so searching? The early Dialogues, *Lysis, Charmides, Laches,* and the rest, aim at nothing and hit it as inconclusively as modern realism, yet are felicitous as Jane Austen in echoing the chit-chat of the town and the evanescent moods of well-bred people. Where is a more amusing scene than the opening of the *Protagoras?* Where a sweeter idyll than the picture of Socrates in the *Phædrus,* dabbling his toes in the brook under the plane-tree, as he spins lazy yarns about that fair creature Psyche, and ends with an exquisite prayer to Pan? The aeroplane of the *Timæus* sweeps up into planetary space more effectively than that of Marie Corelli; *Phædo* and the *Apology* purify by pity and terror as only great tragedy can do.

The beauty of the art is that none of these types is produced mechanically after the modern fashion. Life in its entirety is in Plato behind each mode of life. Through the gayest persiflage plays suddenly high passion for the argument. Presto! Greek worldly wisdom inhibits with salutary jest some imaginative flight. Do not tell me that I am reading the man who has infected the generations with a microbe tempting them to prefer dream to fact. My Plato is obsessed by desire for experience, singularly alive to the concrete, fascinated by the stir and movement of very life. He is the match of Dickens for portraiture, of Meredith for dramatic dialogue, of Browning for situation. With Balzac or Tolstoi, he is competent to quicken us by the spectacle of existence, now to tragic passion, now to the laughter of the gods.

We may be pardoned for finding the dialectic stiff, and for offering our meek "Certainly" at intervals with Laches or Nicias, not quite sure to what we are assenting, but either because we want to please Socrates, or because the maddening old man will tease us worse if we contradict him. Let us forget the talk, think of the talkers, and give thanks for the men and manners that live for us in these pages. A sense of solid reality is the ultimate impression imparted to the literary mind by this greatest of the world's idealists.

Socrates is the centre of the group, of course, and we all think we know Socrates, though we are mistaken. But why ignore the Athenians who gather round him? How they stand out, the child and the citizen, the soldier and the actor, the academic dignitary, the plain man on the street! No dummies they, giving absent assent to the great teacher. Most are defined as to aspect with a few perfect touches, each speaks in character. In the dramatically vital dialogue, the very manner in which they take refutation, the quality of their agreement— now sullen, now eager, now careless, now thoughtful— sets them before us with high imaginative art. And how admirably are they introduced, in those love-settings which give us perhaps our most vivid knowledge of Greek life! Especially in the minor Dialogues, which are rather tentative *jeus d'esprit* than philosophical discussions, the argument does not pretend to get anywhere. It chases its own tail and drops like a tired kitten on the spot where it began. But meantime we are seeing life, we are meeting Greeks, and we do not care a rap whether or no we succeed in defining friendship or temperance or courage. It is more important to chat with the boy Charmides, to enjoy his choice manners and his rare beauty, and inhale the aroma of his delightful youth.

Socrates, in this Dialogue, is just back from military service at Potidæa, where he has borne hardship and danger stolidly, as Alcibiades shall one day tell us. Now he is hungry for civilization: the hum in the

palæstra is delectable to him. We listen for a few minutes to greetings, and the pleasant gossip of the town.
It must be acknowledged that Socrates asks about "the
present state of philosophy," as one might inquire into
politics after absence in foreign parts; but presently
with equal interest he is asking about the season's
"buds." These—we are in Greece—are the lads just
reaching manhood. Are any of them remarkable, he
wants to know, for beauty or sense? And just then the
merry troop appears, making a great din, one of them,
Charmides, easily the most beautiful. "I must admit,"
says Socrates, "that I was quite astonished at his beauty
and stature. All the world seemed to be enamored of
him. Amazement and confusion reigned when he entered. All the boys, even to the very least child,
turned and looked at him, as if he were a statue.
Chærephon called to me and said:

"'What do you think of him, Socrates? Has he not
a beautiful face? But you would think nothing of his
face if you could see his naked form.'

"'By Hercules,' I said, 'there never was such a para-
gon, if he has only one other slight addition.'

"'What is that?' said Critias.

"'If he has a noble soul; and being of your house,
Critias, he may be expected to have this.'

"'He is fair and good within as he is without,' said
Critias.

"'Shall we ask him, then,' I said, 'to show us, not his
body, but his soul? He is just of an age when he will
like to talk.'"

Hard to surpass in modern fiction, that bit of dialogue!
Here is full Greece: delight in beauty of form as of
countenance; swift courtesy; the Socratic love of loveliness within—"Is not the wiser always the fairer, sweet

friend?" asks the sage in another connection; and finally the unquenchable zest for conversation.

What interests Socrates just now is not an abstract question, but a charming boy. He proceeds to invent topics, that he may savor the soul of Charmides. First they talk a little about a headache that bothers the lad —ailments, then as now, forming a convenient introductory theme. And Christian Science would seem to be less original than it supposes, for we find Socrates remarking that Charmides can get rid of his headache easily if he will cure his soul "by the use of certain charms, and these charms are fair words." All very well, but they soon grow bored over Charmides' headache, and cast about for another subject. Temperance will do; what does Charmides think of temperance? He is a remarkably temperate lad, by the way, remarks his relative, Critias, taking no pains to lower his voice.

Charmides blushes—his blushes come readily—at this blatant praise. Then, after some hesitation he feels his way till he says that temperance is quietness. Not a bad answer, surely—one well befitting a young Greek gentleman. Socrates, however, though pleased, points out that a sluggish man is not necessarily a temperate one, and that energetic actions are usually better than slow, quiet ones; in a word, that scientific efficiency does not preclude temperance. Greek standards are not so far from modern, we perceive. Charmides tries again, frank ingenuousness and good breeding in his every word: May not temperance be modesty? Then Socrates, with Critias to help, gets seriously to work: the trail may lead in a circle, but to pursue it is great sport, and his object, the enjoyment of Charmides in his lovely youth, has been fully attained.

Lysis is younger than Charmides; he and his chum, Menexenus, are little fellows, hardly beyond childhood.

A bigger lad, one Hippothales, has what in college par-
lance would be termed a "crush" on Lysis; we are in
that Greek world where romance lives from man to
man. Socrates will show Hippothales the best way to
win the boy's affections. At least so he pretends; what
he is really after is the pleasure of converse with an
awakening mind. How to get at Lysis? Hippothales
says that if only Socrates will sit down and begin
to talk, the boy will be sure to come, and so it happens.
There has been a sacrifice, and all the boys are dressed
in white. They are playing a game, taking their dice
out of little wicker baskets; small Lysis, crowned with
a wreath and fair as a vision, is looking on. Presently
he begins to glance around, timidly but wistfully, at
Socrates chatting in his quiet corner. Soon his friend
Menexenus joins the group, and then Lysis picks up
courage to come too—sentimental Hippothales, whom
the lad evidently does not like, hiding out of the way.
It is a pretty scene, and the talk is equally pretty, though
desultory enough on the surface. Anyone who wants an
example of grown-up mind adapting itself wisely and
tenderly as to childhood, might well turn to it:

"I dare say, Lysis, that your father and mother love
you very much?"

"That they do," he said.

"And that they would wish you to be perfectly
happy?"

"Yes."

"But do you think that anyone is happy who . . .
cannot do as he likes?"

"I should think not, indeed," he said. . . .

"Do your father and mother, then, permit you to do
what you like, and never rebuke or hinder you?"

"Yes indeed, Socrates, there are a great many things
which they hinder me from doing."

So Lysis has to tackle some hard thinking—yet thinking within the compass of a little chap. He enjoys the talk hugely, and wants his friend to share it. "In a childish and affectionate manner," he whispers in Socrates' ear: "Do, Socrates, tell Menexenus what you have been telling me." Once he interrupts: "I am sure that we have been wrong, Socrates." "And he blushed at his own words, as if he had not intended to speak: but the words escaped him involuntarily in his eagerness." Before the talk is over, all concerned know a good deal more than they did about friendship and other important matters—though as for definitions, on which Socrates is daft, they have not reached any. Is friendship based on contrast or similarity of temperament? they wonder, and we are wondering yet. Who knows? They might have decided, or even have reached a definition, had it not been for the tutors. But these break in "like an evil apparition," very cross because it is so late; and though the talkers drive them off, they keep on shouting at their charges till they force them to start for home.

Endearing and beautiful youths like Charmides and Lysis hold a position of central importance throughout the Platonic tales. We know how Socrates loved them, and remember that his fascination over them was a cause of his death. Yet if the Dialogues breathe his ecstatic joy in youth for youth's sake, they are also full of sly delight in noting the humors of grown men. Crito, Socrates' special friend, is an old man, wealthy, dignified, not at all clever. One wonders what he got from life-long converse with the deepest mind in Greece. Socrates is fond of his company, tells him merry tales like that of the Euthydemus; it is to Crito that he addresses his last words. The figure is always respectfully and tenderly touched. So is that of gentle old Lysi-

machus, who has never heard of Socrates, but has a
high regard for Socrates' father. Another old man is
Protagoras the Sophist, an academic type cleverly
sketched: honest, weighty, a copious lecturer, presenting
with facile sonority the truth of the past, and a little
fussed and cross under the impact of the truth of the
future.

Plato gives us men of action, too. There are the soldiers, Laches and Nicias, who seek a just idea of courage
to impart to the rising generation. Laches is a blunt
man, annoyed that he cannot express himself: "I fancy
I do know the nature of courage," he complains, "but
somehow or other she has slipped away from me, and
I cannot tell her nature." He considers privately that
"the examination of such niceties" as definitions is no
suitable employment for a statesman or a soldier. Still
he gets a little way when, from satisfaction with the
remark that a courageous man is one who does not run
away, he discovers with hardly any help that "courage
is the endurance of the soul." However, Nicias has to
give him yet more hints—ill-fated Nicias, who is shown
as one of the most thoughtful people in Plato, hardly
inferior to Socrates himself in insight. Was the reflective
turn of mind, such an asset to the man, a disadvantage
to the soldier?

Other types are the broad-minded physician Eryxi-
machus and Ion the actor—the purely emotional man,
this last, a-quiver over his own recitations. Socrates is
particularly felicitous with Ion, who avows that there
is no part of Homer on which he does not speak well,
and that he feels rapt out of himself when he recites,
but strange to say, is inclined to be sleepy when anyone
else recites from another poet. Socrates, who depreciates
himself pleasantly as "a common man who only speaks
the truth," treats him gently; tells him that he is quite

mad, and when Ion, though acquiescent, is a little subdued, proceeds to say that Homer and all the great
imaginations were mad likewise, and that inspiration is
none the worse for being irrational, but rather the better;
and we leave Ion as pleased and bewildered as M. Jour-
dain. It is a very amusing dialogue.

Some of Plato's *dramatis personae* are dull, some slow,
some simple-minded; yet on the whole they are amazingly
attractive. He shows us no villains. Nevertheless there
are shadows, firmly if delicately touched, in his picture.
No fierce denunciation—that was not the style of Plato,
or his master—but an inexorable trick of letting the
shallow, fanatical or cruel man speak for himself. There
is Anytus, for example, in the *Meno*. It is worth while
to study Anytus, for he is to be one of Socrates' chief
accusers. His inimitable responses, few and brief, illuminate him forever.

Socrates praises him warmly when he first appears:
"There is Anytus sitting by us; he is the person whom
we should ask. In the first place, he is the son of a
wealthy and wise father, and he is a well-conditioned,
modest man, not insolent or overbearing or annoying;
moreover, he has given his son a good education." All
this appears to be true; it is persons like Anytus who
usually put to death Socrates and Jesus. Anytus gives
placid acquiescence to the course of the argument till it
touches the concrete; then he flares up. This happens
to be at a mention of the Sophists. Socrates is mildly
surprised; he reasons with Anytus; Can the men whom
everyone considers so wise be really out of their minds,
as Anytus hints? But Anytus is not a reasoning being.
"Out of their minds!" he cries. "No, Socrates, the
young men who gave their money to them are out of
their minds, and their relatives and guardians who entrusted them to their care were still more out of their

minds." What irony, that Socrates should have first incurred this man's suspicions and rage on behalf of the Sophists! For we know that Socrates was not overfond of the Sophists himself. But how human it all is, and how prone Anytus still is to raise the angry cry. "Out of their minds!" against those with whom he disagrees!

"Has any of the Sophists wronged you, Anytus?" . . .

"No, indeed; neither I nor any of my belongings has ever had, nor would I suffer them to have anything to do with them." . . .

"Then, my dear friend, how can you know whether a thing is good or bad, of which you are wholly ignorant?"

"Quite well. I am sure that I know what manner of men these are, whether I know them or not."

Anytus is quite sure still, and he writes for almost every newspaper in the country; his violent talk, charged with prejudice and animosity, greets us in every haunt of men. For Anytus is a "stand-patter"—modest, well-conditioned Anytus, who educates his sons so carefully. "If you won't trust the Sophists, to whom do you look for guidance?" asks Socrates; and Anytus gives the unvarying answer of his caste: "Any Athenian gentleman" taken at random will, so he asserts, do perfectly well. But these gentlemen—did they grow of themselves? Socrates must know; and Anytus, impatiently satisfied, returns the immortal answer: "I imagine that they learned of the previous generation of gentlemen."

It is of no use, Socrates; you might as well leave Anytus alone. But Socrates does not leave him alone, thereby, were safety dear, making a vast mistake. He plays gadfly till he stings the poor, comfortable man past endurance. So Anytus breaks into open rage; accuses Socrates—and again the stand-patter's complaint of the radical sounds queerly familiar—of "speaking evil of men," and utters a veiled threat, sinister enough in the light of the outcome. Socrates dismisses him with a touch of cool contempt, unusual in the suavest of adversaries, who generally coaxes his most irritated antagonists back into the trail of the argument; then turns to point out to the more responsive Meno the unconventionality of virtue, and its immediate character, derived from no tradition, not even that of the gentlemen of Athens. For with subtle instinct for dramatic contrast, Plato includes in this Dialogue that famous scene in which the independent intuition of truth is illustrated by the power of Meno's boy-slave to prove a geometric proposition.

Nothing could be more natural, more unstudied, than all this talk. It has the desultory wavering of life itself. Of conversation, that crux of the novelist, Plato is past-master; one must turn to Meredith or Anatole France to find his equal. His dialogue makes the ordinary talk, say of the people in Mrs. Humphry Ward, appear soggy with the curse of art, the obvious. There is never too much flour in Plato's baking; and his deft touch is one reason why we rank him among the poets, "light, winged, and holy." He catches the words as they fly, and though they seem to flutter vaguely like butterflies, they are really driving straight like a flight of migrating birds for a goal beyond the horizon.

However, it is to be remembered that Plato had an advantage over modern writers, for he had Greece to present and Athenians for his characters. The fine art of social intercourse is here brought to its last point of perfection. Men are thinking—everybody, except perhaps Anytus, is thinking in Plato—though, being human, they tend to think overmuch the thoughts of other people; but they are never thinking alone. The intellectual life in Greece is a social and not a solitary pursuit. That is why Plato is a great novelist as well as a philosopher. This society is worth reading about, moreover, quite apart from its brains, for the mere charm of its manners, a charm unsurpassed. When Aristodemus appears uninvited at the banquet, how graciously does Agathon put him at his ease! What pretty compliments they pay one another, how generously they admire each other's excellencies, what capital and witty jokes they crack! Never do we pass our time in vulgar company; we are aristocrats in every sense. We move on principle only in the best circles—and how very good they are!

Socrates revels in this society, for he, too, is the most sociable of men. Like Dr. Johnson, whom he much resembles, he takes unfeigned interest in all the little affairs of the town; especially is he quite at home in that perennial topic of conversation, the psychology of the affections. He likes a gossip as well as any man, and has a marvellous catholic taste in his choice of associates. It is entertaining to study him through his reaction on people. Browning did not invent the oblique method of showing character in *The Ring and the Book*. Courteous old Lysimachus, who does not move in intellectual circles, invites Socrates to call because he is the son of his father. The soldier Laches knows him only as a man of action, and has sincere regard for him. Bit by bit, we get a feeling for the man himself. A quick man, intolerant of stupidity, yet helped to patient self-control by the rare, the divine instinct of the teacher; taking his revenge in that irony that baffles and allures the ages, an irony of which his successors—Rabelais, Swift, Arnold—have never quite caught the secret. He never lays down the law, he never loses his grip. Yet one sees that people have one trick that tries him almost past endurance, the inveterate habit of defining the concrete instance. "Courage is not running away from your post," says Laches. "Temperance is doing things orderly," says Charmides. And Euthyphro, whom we shall meet presently, caps the climax of this kind of definition when he gravely announces: "Virtue is doing as I am doing." But Socrates never snubs one of them; with infinite forbearance he leads them on. Terrible tease, superb old man, who loves the argument, as argument, tenaciously, yet is capable of turning round with splendid inconsistence and "believing where he has not proved"! What a picture! But if we talk of Socrates we shall never stop. The portrait is literally incomparable; nothing has ever approached it.

So is Plato realist of the realists. Yet at times we leave Greece behind us and below. We watch the soul putting forth her wings, or the chariot of humanity thundering on its perilous way, or the strange life of "earth-born men"; and find ourselves at the fountainhead of the imaginative literature of Europe. Plato the myth-maker gives us more direct narrative than Plato the realist; and his myths, whether in the *Timæus,* the *Phædrus,* or the *Symposium,* are in purest romantic tone. All dreamers have dreamed these dreams after him. Yet from the starry flights through which he bears us we return with pleasure to Greek life. We are glad to know that Socrates held high converse on the passions with Diotima, the priestess, in those mysterious interviews that suggest the very quintessence of romance; for our part, we are well content with the society of the pompous Protagoras, and the absurd Euthydemus, of Euthyphro the prig, and fair Agathon, most winning of hosts, of little Lysis, and the rest; with the walk, the palæstra, the beloved scenes through which moves a spirit in Silenus mask, at once their representative and their destroyer. Even in Plato, realism wins out in the long run.

Mastery over dialogue, over characterisation, setting, romantic invention—these are great assets for a novelist. Plato has one more, perhaps greater: unfailing instinct for the dramatic. True, there is as little formal plot as in those admirable intimations concerning M. Bergeret; but there is an immense amount of drama, so to speak, in solution. In the undercurrent of the dialogue, things are constantly happening to people. Relations of affection and hate develop, mature, decay; minds are brought into ever-shifting connections with each other and with ideas. If there is no plot, at least the feeling for situation is strong. Who can forget that dining-hall where Socrates is found at dawn prophesying Shakespeare to the sleepy Aristophanes and Agathos; or the prison where disciples gather around an old man chafing his leg; or the judgment hall, where Socrates, far from keeping august silence as did a Greater brought to judgment, pours forth marvellous words for the last time?

Perhaps the most poignant situation just precedes these last. Socrates, awaiting trial in that familiar porch to the temple of King Archon, near which he had once held pleasant converse with young Charmides, encounters Euthyphro the pious soothsayer, to whom he begins to talk with his usual friendly cheer. Socrates is accused by one Meletus, a young man he hardly knows, who "has a beak," it seems, and "long, straight hair, and a beard that is ill-grown." Euthyphro, on the contrary, is an accuser; the man whom he accuses is his own father, arraigned by him on a charge of murder. Socrates' spontaneous start of shocked surprise, his horrified remarks on the complacent Pharisee clinging to the letter of the law, reveal with flashing clarity, as they were meant to do, the deep devoutness and innate reverence for the

past of the man to be put to death by respectable Athens
for a free-thinker and a corrupter of youth. "Virtue
is doing as I am doing"! Or, if you please, men learn
their standards "from the preceding generations of
gentlemen"! "Neither," says Socrates sternly. Between the arrogant self-confidence of Euthyphro and
the conventionality of Anytus, he holds sensitive balance, difficult and just.

Socrates was executed, of course. The *Euthyphro*
serves as prelude to the sure tragedy towards which the
undercurrent has been setting from the first. For here is
the final greatness of Plato's superb historic romance;
one tense conflict is in progress from first to last. We
discover this gradually, and do not quite understand
the situation till all is over. Then, ah! then, looking
back, we realize that there has been a plot after all.
Over that exquisite youth on which the high lights carefully fall, that youth so delicately presented, so passionately wooed, the world of Athens wedded to its smooth
tradition, and the man intent upon the naked truth, must
wrestle to the death. These protagonists are shown with
a composed mastery of art. The artist's dispassionate
sympathy reveals without partisanship the animus of
both, as well as that of the onlookers, who are presented
with unrivalled finesse.

For there is no mechanical villainy about this Athenian
world that kills Socrates. It is admirable in its way.
Its conception of a gentleman has never been equalled.
Its sense of *noblesse oblige* is strong. We have noted
its perfect manners, its gracious charm. Moreover, it is
far from being consciously materialised. These noble
citizens have the personal beauty and the delight in
physical activities of Arnold's barbarians; but show at
first sight none of the imperviousness to ideas which he
attributes to the class. Quite the contrary. They pre-

fer after-dinner speeches to music and wine; and their speeches are concerned, not with programmes, as too often befalls us moderns, but with ideas. They think they want to think, these supple-minded Greeks. "Let us follow the argument," they are always blithely saying, "whithersoever it may lead us." As Hippothales says, "Their entertainment is conversation," and the zest of this good talk lives down the ages. It touches with impartial cheer on social justice, philology, military tactics, mysticism, ethics, poetry, small quibbles, and large issues. How well, as a rule, good breeding checks their eagerness, how anxiously they consider the best methods of education, how solicitous they are about the beautiful-and-the-good! And how enthusiastic about great minds! When Protagoras comes to Athens, Hippocrates rushes before daybreak to announce the event, has to feel around in the dark for Socrates' truckle-bed; and Socrates has all the trouble in the world persuading him to wait for light before they seek the presence of the sage. He is quite in the fashion, if we may judge from the cross servant who bangs the door in their faces, he is so tired of opening it to seekers. In breadth of outlook, in culture, in lively charm and noble seriousness, this is the very society in which we should all like to live.

And Socrates? Well, Socrates is certainly exasperating to a degree. There is that Silenus aspect of him, when he jeers with such gusto at things we hold sacred. And then we never know whether he is in earnest or not. And he is for ever putting us in the wrong, when he knows that we are in the right. A horrid habit! It undermines our good practical pragmatism, and prevents us from getting a living. Society is bound to put the man to death who allows it no assumptions. It is morally immodest, so Anytus is convinced, to insist

like that on pulling off Truth's last garment. Then
he is always so maddeningly good-natured! And the
vicious fascination of the man! There is youth, adorable, expectant youth, wistfully waiting to be led in
that appointed way of honorable, safe tradition in which
we are its precursors and natural guides: and there is
Socrates, always luring it into untried trails! Can we
allow his anarchical force to have its way? Oh, we remember it too well! We are older now, but we too have
felt that magic. We know how that voice lured us, how
we were be-spelled by the keen wit, the merry word,
the ironic play that so easily put our elders to the blush,
the delusive sympathy with our interests; how we had
glimpses of a far skyey country where the eternal were,
which made the streets of Athens flat and dull. Nor
have we ever been quite satisfied since, grave citizens
though we be, in our function of carrying on the state
with due regard to the proprieties. It is all the fault of
Socrates! Away with this agitator, this impious person,
this corrupter of youth!

For Socrates had been teaching in Athens a long time,
and the youths whom he had charmed and wooed, con-
nived when they grew up at killing him. Unlike Jesus,
whose ministry was brief, though we do not know its
exact duration, Socrates has his full, free chance at
winning men. And he made a failure of it. Some of his
most important pupils—Alcibiades, Charmides, Critias
—turned out badly, and the Athenians did not forget it.
Most of the others deserted him. Was it that he was
on the wrong tack, after all, in trying to make man
cultivate virtue by the means of knowledge? Was it
that the times were not ripe? At all events, he was much
alone at the last. Besides old, faithful Crito, there was
a very small group in that prison. Youth had deserted
him: tradition had won the day. So he drank his poison

—not sorry, one surmises, despite all his cheery love of this good world, to try the great adventure; and the proprieties were left in possession of youth, the forever desired. They usually are, for that matter: this dogged struggle for possession of the future is actual to-day as in Athens, renewed from generation to generation, never lost, never won. Socrates is among us still; always worsted, never disposed of, albeit it our democratic days his spirit is diffused, and must be sought at diverse points of collective experience, rather than in one great figure. And the compositions which show him in his Greek dress moving through that vital and charming society are immortal fiction, not only because they have such rare power to enlarge our sympathies, but because at bottom they present persistent fact.

THE BOOK OF BOOKS

BY HENRY VAN DYKE

AN APOLOGUE

THERE was once an Eastern prince who was much enamoured of the art of gardening. He wished that all flowers delightful to the eye, and all fruits pleasant to the taste and good for food, should grow in his dominion, and that in growing the flowers should become more fair, the fruits more savoury and nourishing. With this thought in his mind and this desire in his heart, he found his way to the Ancient One, the Worker of Wonders who dwells in a secret place, and made known his request.

"For the care of your gardens and your orchards," said the Ancient One, "I can do nothing, since that charge has been given to you and to your people. Nor will I send blossoming plants and fruiting trees of every kind to make your kingdom rich and beautiful as by magic, lest the honour of labour should be diminished, and the slow reward of patience despised, and even the living gifts bestowed upon you without toil should wither and die away. But this will I do: a single tree shall be brought to you from a far country by the hands of my servants, and you shall plant it in the midst of your land. In the body of that tree is the sap of life that was from the beginning; the leaves of it are full of healing; its flowers never fail, and its fruitage is the joy of every season. The roots of the tree shall go down to the springs of deep waters; and wherever its pollen is drifted by the wind or borne by the bees, the gardens shall put on new beauty; and wherever its seed is carried by the fowls of the air, the orchards shall yield a richer harvest. But the tree itself you shall guard and cherish and keep as I give it you, neither cutting anything away from it, nor grafting anything upon it; for the life of the tree is in all the branches, and the other trees shall be glad because of it."

As the Ancient One had spoken, so it came to pass. The land of that prince had great renown of fine flowers and delicious fruits, ever unfolding in new colours and sweeter flavours the life that was shed among them by the tree of trees.

I

Something like the marvel of this tale may be read in the history of the Bible. No other book in the world has had such a strange vitality, such an outgoing power of influence and inspiration. Not only has it brought to the countries in whose heart it has been set new ideals of civilization, new models of character, new conceptions of virtues and hopes of happiness; but it has also given new impulse and form to the shaping imagination of man, and begotten beauty in literature and the other arts.

Suppose, for example, that it were possible to dissolve away all the works of art which clearly owe their being to thoughts, emotions, or visions derived from the Bible, —all sculpture like Donatello's "David" and Michelangelo's "Moses"; all painting like Raphael's "Sistine Madonna" and Murillo's "Holy Family"; all music like Bach's "Passion" and Handel's "Messiah"; all poetry like Dante's "Divine Comedy" and Milton's "Paradise Lost,"—how it would impoverish the world!

The literary influence of the Bible appears the most wonderful when we consider that it is the work of a race not otherwise potent or famous in literature. We do not know, of course, what other books may have come from the Jewish nation and vanished with whatever of power or beauty they possessed; but in those that remain there is little of exceptional force or charm for readers outside of the Hebrew race. They have no broad human appeal, no universal significance, not even any signal excellence of form and imagery. Josephus is a fairly good historian, sometimes entertaining, but not comparable to Herodotus or Thucydides or Tacitus or Gibbon. The Talmuds are vast storehouses of things new and old, where a careful searcher may now and then find a legendary gem or a quaint fragment of moral tapestry. In histories of mediæval literature, Ibn Ezra of Toledo and Rashi of Lunel are spoken of with respect. In modern letters, works as far apart as the philosophical treatises of Spinoza and the lyrics of Heinrich Heine have distinction in their kind. No one thinks that the Hebrews are lacking in great and varied talents; but how is it that in world-literature their only contribution that counts is the Bible? And how is it that it counts so immensely?

It is possible to answer by saying that in the Old Testament we have a happily made collection of the best things in the ancient literature of the Jews, and in the New Testament we have another anthology of the finest of the narratives and letters which were produced by certain writers of the same race under a new and exceedingly powerful spiritual impulse. The Bible is excellent because it contains the cream of Hebrew thought. But this answer explains nothing. It only restates the facts in another form. How did the cream rise? How did such a collection come to be made? What gives it unity and coherence underneath all its diversity? How is it that, as a clear critic has well said, "These sixty books, with all their varieties of age, authorship, literary form, are, when properly arranged, felt to draw together with a unity like the connectedness of a dramatic plot?"

There is an answer, which if it be accepted, carries with it a solution of the problem.

Suppose a race chosen by some process of selection (which need not now be discussed or defined) to develop in its strongest and most absolute form that one of man's faculties which is called the religious sense, to receive most clearly and deeply the impression of the unity, spirituality, and righteousness of a Supreme Being present in the world. Imagine that race moving through a long and varied experience under this powerful impression, now loyal to it, now rebelling against it, now misinterpreting it, now led by the voice of some prophet to understand it more fully and feel it more profoundly, but never wholly losing it for a single generation. Imagine the history of that race, its poetry, the biography of its famous men and women, the messages of its moral reformers, conceived and written in constant relation to that strongest factor of conscious life, the sense of the presence and power of the Eternal.

Suppose, now, in a time of darkness and humiliation, that there rises within that race a prophet who declares that a new era of spiritual light has come, preaches a new revelation of the Eternal, and claims in his own person to fulfil the ancient hopes and promises of a divine deliverer and redeemer. Imagine his followers, few in number, accepting his message slowly and dimly at first, guided by companionship with him into a clearer understanding and a stronger belief, until at last they are convinced that his claims are true, and that he is

the saviour not only of the chosen people, but also of
the whole world, the revealer of the Eternal to mankind. Imagine these disciples setting out with incredible courage to carry this message to all nations, so
deeply impressed with its truth that they are supremely
happy to suffer and die for it, so filled with the passion
of its meaning that they dare attempt to remodel the
life of the world with it. Suppose a human story like
this underneath the writing of the books which are gathered in the Bible and you have an explanation—it seems
to me the only reasonable explanation—of their surpassing quality and their strange unity.

This story is not a mere supposition: its general outline, stated in these terms, belongs to the realm of facts
which cannot reasonably be questioned. What more is
needed to account for the story itself, what potent and
irresistible reality is involved in this record of experience, I do not now ask. This is not an estimate of the
religious authority of the Bible, nor of its inspiration
in the theological sense of that word, but only of something less important, though no less real—its literary
influence.

II

The fountain-head of the power of the Bible in literature lies in its nearness to the very springs and sources
of human life—life taken seriously, earnestly, intensely;
life in its broadest meaning, including the inward as well
as the outward; life interpreted in its relation to universal laws and eternal values. It is this vital quality
in the narratives, the poems, the allegories, the medita-
tions, the discourses, the letters, gathered in this book,
that gives it first place among the books of the world
not only for currency, but also for greatness.

For the currency of literature depends in the long run upon the breadth and vividness of its human appeal. And the greatness of literature depends upon the intensive significance of those portions of life which it depicts and interprets. Now, there is no other book which reflects so many sides and aspects of human experience as the Bible, and this fact alone would suffice to give it a world-wide interest and make it popular. But it mirrors them all, whether they belong to the chronicles of kings and conquerors, or to the obscure records of the lowliest of labourers and sufferers, in the light of a conviction that they are all related to the will and purpose of the Eternal. This illuminates every figure with a divine distinction, and raises every event to the nth power of meaning. It is this fact that gives the Bible its extraordinary force as literature and makes it great.

Born in the East and clothed in Oriental form and imagery, the Bible walks the ways of all the world with familiar feet and enters land after land to find its own everywhere. It has learned to speak in hundreds of languages to the heart of man. It comes into the palace to tell the monarch that he is a servant of the Most High, and into the cottage to assure the peasant that he is a son of God. Children listen to its stories with wonder and delight, and wise men ponder them as parables of life. It has a word of peace for the time of peril, a word of comfort for the day of calamity, a word of light for the hour of darkness. Its oracles are repeated in the assembly of the people, and its counsels whispered in the ear of the lonely. The wicked and the proud tremble at its warning, but to the wounded and the penitent it has a mother's voice. The wilderness and the solitary place have been made glad by it, and the fire on the hearth has lit the reading of its well-worn page. It has woven itself into our deepest affections

*and coloured our dearest dreams; so that love and friend-
ship, sympathy and devotion, memory and hope, put on
the beautiful garments of its treasured speech, breathing
of frankincense and myrrh.*

*Above the cradle and beside the grave its great words
come to us uncalled. They fill our prayers with power
larger than we know, and the beauty of them lingers
on our ear long after the sermons which they adorned
have been forgotten. They return to us swiftly and
quietly, like doves flying from far away. They surprise
us with new meanings, like springs of water breaking
forth from the mountain beside a long-trodden path.
They grow richer, as pearls do when they are worn near
the heart.*

*No man is poor or desolate who has this treasure for
his own. When the landscape darkens and the trembling
pilgrim comes to the Valley named of the Shadow, he
is not afraid to enter: he takes the rod and staff of
Scripture in his hand; he says to friend and comrade,
"Good-by; we shall meet again"; and comforted by that
support, he goes toward the lonely pass as one who walks
through darkness into light.*

It would be strange indeed if a book which has played
such a part in human life had not exercised an extraordinary influence upon literature. As a matter of fact,
the Bible has called into existence tens of thousands of
other books devoted to the exposition of its meaning, the
defense and illustration of its doctrine, the application
of its teaching, or the record of its history. The learned
Fabricus, in the early part of the eighteenth century,
published a *catalogue raisonné* of such books, filling
seven hundred quarto pages.* Since that time the length

---

* *Syllabus Scriptorum Veterum Recentiumque qui Veritatem
Religious Christianæ Asseruerunt:* Hamburg, 1725.

of the list has probably more than trebled. In addition, we must reckon the many books of hostile criticism and contrary argument which the Bible has evoked, and which are an evidence of revolt against the might of its influence. All this tangle of Biblical literature has grown up around it like a vast wood full of all manner of trees, great and small, useful and worthless, fruit-trees, timber-trees, berry-bushes, briers, and poison-vines. But all of them, even the most beautiful and tall, look like undergrowth, when we compare them with the mighty oak of Scripture, towering in perennial grandeur, the father of the forest.

Among the patristic writers there were some of great genius like Origen and Chrysostom and Augustine. The mediæval schools of theology produced men of philosophic power, like Anselm and Thomas Aquinas; of spiritual insight, like the author of the *Imitatio Christi*. The eloquence of France reached its height in the discourses of Bossuet, Bourdaloue, and Massillon. German became one of the potent tongues of literature when Martin Luther used it in his tracts and sermons, and Herder's *Geist der hebräischen Poesie* is one of the great books in criticism. In English, to mention such names as Hooker and Fuller and Jeremy Taylor is to recall the dignity, force, and splendour of prose at its best. Yet none of these authors has produced anything to rival the book from which they drew their common inspiration.

In the other camp, though there have been many brilliant assailants, not one has surpassed, or even equalled, in the estimation of the world, the literary excellence of the book which they attacked. The mordant wit of Voltaire, the lucid and melancholy charm of Renan, have not availed to drive or draw the world away from the Bible; and the effect of all assaults has been to leave it more widely read, better understood, and more intelligently admired than ever before.

Now it must be admitted that the same thing is true, at least in some degree, of other books which are held to be sacred or quasi-sacred: they are superior to the distinctively theological literature which has grown up about them. I suppose nothing of the Mussulmans is as great as the "Koran," nothing of the Hindus as great as the "Vedas"; and though the effect of the Confucian classics, from the literary point of view, may not have been altogether good, their supremacy in the religious library of the Chinese is unquestioned. But the singular and noteworthy thing about the influence of the Bible is the extent to which it has permeated general literature, the mark which it has made in all forms of belles-lettres. To treat this subject adequately one would need to write volumes. In this chapter I can touch but briefly on a few points of the outline as they come out in English literature.

III

In the Old-English period, the predominant influence of the Scriptures may be seen in the frequency with which the men of letters turned to them for subjects, and in the Biblical colouring and texture of thought and style. Cædmon's famous "Hymn" and the other poems like "Genesis," "Exodus," "Daniel," and "Judith," which were once ascribed to him; Cynewulf's "Crist," "The Fates of the Apostles," "The Dream of the Rood"; Ælfric's "Homilies" and his paraphrases of certain books of Scripture—these early fruits of our literature are all the offspring of the Bible.

In the Middle-English period, that anonymous masterpiece "Pearl" is full of the spirit of Christian mysticism, and the two poems called "Cleanness" and "Patience," probably written by the same hand, are free and spirited versions of stories from the Bible. "The Vision of Piers the Plowman," formerly ascribed to William Langland, but now supposed by some scholars to be the work of four or five different authors, was the most popular poem of the latter half of the fourteenth century. It is a vivid picture of the wrongs and sufferings of the labouring man, a passionate satire on the corruptions of the age in church and state, an eloquent appeal for a return to truth and simplicity. The feeling and the imagery of Scripture pervade it with a strange power and charm; in its reverence for poverty and toil it leans closely and confidently upon the example of Jesus; and at the end it makes its ploughman hero appear in some mystic way as a type, first of the crucified Saviour, and then of the church which is the body of Christ.

It was about this time, the end of the fourteenth century, that John Wyclif and his disciples, feeling the need of the support of the Bible in their work as reformers, took up and completed the task of translating it entirely into the English tongue of the common people. This rude but vigorous version was revised and improved by John Purvey. It rested mainly upon the Latin version of St. Jerome. At the beginning of the sixteenth century William Tindale made an independent translation of the New Testament from the original Greek, a virile and enduring piece of work, marked by strength and simplicity, and setting a standard for subsequent English translations. Coverdale's version of the Scriptures was published in 1535, and was announced as made "out of Douche and Latyn"; that is to say, it was based upon the German of Luther and the Zurich Bible, and upon the Vulgate of St. Jerome; but it owed much to Tindale, to whose manly force it added a certain music of diction and grace of phrase which may still be noted in the Psalms as they are rendered in the Anglican Prayer-Book. Another translation, marked by accurate scholarship, was made by English Puritans at Geneva, and still another, characterized by a richer Latinized style, was made by English Catholics living in exile at Rheims, and was known as "the Douai Version," from the fact that it was first published in its complete form in that city in 1609-1610.

Meantime, in 1604, a company of scholars had been appointed by King James I in England to make a new translation "out of the original tongues, and with the former translations diligently compared and revised." These forty-seven men had the advantage of all the work of their predecessors, the benefit of all the discussion over doubtful words and phrases, and the "unearned increment" of riches which had come into the English language since the days of Wyclif. The result of their labours, published in 1611, was the so-called "Authorized Version," a monument of English prose in its prime: clear, strong, direct, yet full of subtle rhythms and strange colours; now moving as simply as a shepherd's song, in the Twenty-third Psalm; now marching with majestic harmonies, in the book of Job; now reflecting the lowliest forms of human life, in the Gospel stories; and now flashing with celestial splendours in the visions of the Apocalypse; vivid without effort; picturesque without exaggeration; sinewy without strain; capable alike of the deepest tenderness and the most sublime majesty; using a vocabulary of only six thousand words to build a book which, as Macaulay said, "if everything else in our language should perish, would alone suffice to show the whole extent of its beauty and power."

The literary excellence of this version, no doubt, did much to increase the influence of the Bible in literature and confirm its place as the central book in the life of those who speak and write the English tongue. Consider a few of the ways in which this influence may be traced.

IV

First of all, it has had a general effect upon English writing, helping to preserve it from the opposite faults of vulgarity and affectation. Coleridge long ago remarked upon the tendency of a close study of the Bible to elevate a writer's style. There is a certain naturalness, inevitableness, propriety of form to substance, in the language of Scripture which communicates to its readers a feeling for the fitness of words; and this in itself is the first requisite of good writing. Sincerity is the best part of dignity.

The English of our Bible is singularly free from the vice of preciosity: it is not far-sought, overnice, elaborate. Its plainness is a rebuking contrast to all forms of euphuism. It does not encourage a direct imitation of itself; for the comparison between the original and the copy makes the latter look pale and dull. Even in the age which produced the authorized version, its style was distinct and remarkable. As Hallam has observed, it was "not the English of Daniel, of Raleigh, or Bacon." It was something larger, at once more ancient and more modern, and therefore well fitted to become not an invariable model, but an enduring standard. Its words come to it from all sources; they are not chosen according to the foolish theory that a word of Anglo-Saxon origin is always stronger and simpler than a Latin derivative. Take the beginning of the Forty-sixth Psalm:

"God is our refuge and strength, a very present help in trouble. Therefore will not we fear, though the earth be removed, and though the mountains be carried into the midst of the sea; though the waters thereof roar and be troubled, though the mountains shake with the swelling thereof."

Or take this passage from the Epistle to the Romans:

"Be kindly affectioned one to another with brotherly love; in honour preferring one another; not slothful in business; fervent in spirit; serving the Lord; rejoicing in hope; patient in tribulation; continuing instant in prayer; distributing to the necessity of saints; given to hospitality."

Here is a style that adapts itself by instinct to its subject, and whether it uses Saxon words like "strength" and "help" and "love" and "hope," or Latin words like "refuge" and "trouble" and "present" and "fervent" and "patient" and "prayer" and "hospitality," weaves them into a garment worthy of the thought.

The literary influence of a great, popular book written in such a style is both inspiring and conservative. It survives the passing modes of prose in each generation, and keeps the present in touch with the past. It preserves a sense of balance and proportion in a language whose perils lie in its liberties and in the indiscriminate use of its growing wealth. And finally it keeps a medium of communication open between the learned and the simple; for the two places where the effect of the Bible upon the English language may be most clearly felt are in the natural speech of the plain people and in the finest passages of great authors.

V

Following this line of the influence of the Bible upon language as the medium of literature, we find, in the next place, that it has contributed to our common speech a great number of phrases which are current everywhere. Sometimes these phrases are used in a merely conventional way. They serve as counters in a long extemporaneous prayer, or as padding to a page of dull and pious prose. But at other times they illuminate the sentence with a new radiance; they clarify its meaning with a true symbol; they enhance its value with rich associations; they are "sweeter than honey and the honeycomb."

Take for example such phrases as these: "a good old age," "the wife of thy bosom," "the apple of his eye," "gathered to his fathers," "a mother in Israel," "a land flowing with milk and honey," "the windows of heaven," "the fountains of the great deep," "living fountains of waters," "the valley of decision," "cometh up as a flower," "a garden enclosed," "one little ewe lamb," "thou art the man," "a still, small voice," "as the sparks fly upward," "swifter than a weaver's shuttle," "miserable comforters," "the strife of tongues," "the tents of Kedar," "the cry of the humble," "the lofty looks of man," "the pride of life," "from strength to strength," "as a dream when one awaketh," "the wings of the morning," "stolen waters," "a dinner of herbs," "apples of gold in pictures of silver," "better than rubies," "a lion in the way," "vanity of vanities," "no discharge in that war," "the little foxes that spoil the vines," "terrible as an army with banners," "precept upon precept,

line upon line," "as a drop of a bucket," "whose mer-
chants are princes," "trodden the wine-press alone,"
"the rose of Sharon and the lily of the valley," "the
highways and hedges," "the salt of the earth," "the burden and heat of the day," "the signs of the times," "a
pearl of great price," "what God hath joined together,"
"the children of light," "the powers that be," "if the
trumpet give an uncertain sound," "the fashion of this
world," "decently and in order," "a thorn in the flesh,"
"labour of love," "a cloud of witnesses," "to entertain
angels unawares," "faithful unto death," "a crown of
life."   Consider also those expressions which carry with
them distinctly the memory of some ancient story: "the
fleshpots of Egypt," "manna in the wilderness," "a mess
of pottage," "Joseph's coat," "the driving of Jehu,"
"the mantle of Elijah," "the widow's mite," "the elder
brother," "the kiss of Judas," "the house of Martha,"
"a friend of publicans and sinners," "many mansions,"
"bearing the cross."   Into such phrases as these, which
are familiar to us all, the Bible has poured a wealth of
meaning far beyond the measure of the bare words.
They call up visions and reveal mysteries. . . .

VI

The largest and most important influence of the Bible
in literature lies beyond all these visible effects upon
language and style and imagery and form.   It comes
from the strange power of the book to nourish and inspire, to mould and guide, the inner life of man.   *"It
finds me,"* said Coleridge; and the word of the philosopher is one that the plain man can understand and repeat.

The hunger for happiness which lies in every human
heart can never be satisfied without righteousness; and

the reason why the Bible reaches down so deep into the breast of man is because it brings news of a kingdom which *is* righteousness and peace and joy in the Holy Spirit. It brings this news not in the form of a dogma, a definition, a scientific statement, but in the form of literature, a living picture of experience, a perfect ideal embodied in a Character and a Life. And because it does this, it has inspiration for those who write in the service of truth and humanity.

The Bible has been the favourite book of those who were troubled and downtrodden, and of those who bore the great burden of a great task. New light has broken forth from it to lead the upward struggle of mankind from age to age. Men have come back to it because they could not do without it. Nor will its influence wane, its radiance be darkened, unless literature ceases to express the noblest of human longings, the highest of human hopes, and mankind forgets all that is now incarnate in the central figure of the Bible,—the Divine Deliverer.

THE PRACTICAL VALUE OF POETRY

BY MAX EASTMAN

Every little while the members of a young men's society debate the question whether poets or statesmen have had the greatest effect upon history. They decide in favor of the poets, and then go and devote themselves to politics and practical affairs. If meanwhile a poet arises among them, he has attributed to him an unusually liquid and ineffectual character. It appears that a poet in history is divine, but a poet in the next room is a joke. Nobody demurs at our attributing power to Shakespeare, the supreme greatness of Anglo-Saxon life. Few feel that Bacon could uphold such greatness. And the farther into history we look, the more the statesmen dwindle and the poets shine. Lincoln's word of praise gives final honor to Walt Whitman, but poets are the very fame of Pericles.

This mixture of veneration with distrust toward poetry is not colloquial. It is the world's attitude. There are savages of Africa who give beads of wealth and honor to the singers that entertain them, but they bury them upside down in a hollow tree, to show that the honor is not unmixed with contempt. I sometimes think the singers of our own day have a similarly compounded attitude toward themselves. For while they consider a life of realization so self-justifying as to warrant their renouncing for it every aspiration of an acting man, they still descend from this to complain that they are not appreciated by others, as though they had not their own reward. Even the greatest have been affected by some double current of feeling, for they have been moved to defend poetry and write apologies for her, as though she were in contempt of men, but these apologies when they were written gave her such character as would make apology an impertinence. They defended her by declaring that she is above the need or possibility of defence, she is life and mind itself.

One supreme man in literature is reputed to have renounced poetry altogether. But he did in fact only dwell with especial emphasis upon each side of this paradox. Plato is magnificent both in scorn and adoration of the poetic gift. Poets, he declares, are foolish, they are an outrage upon the moral understanding, so insidious in their arts that he is all but ready to banish the whole tribe from his ideal Republic. For what are they engaged in? They are engaged in presenting to the affections, not ideas, but mere things, and these generally the most blood-heating kinds of things, over which they work us up into a wholly inconsequent madness. Nay, it is worse than that, for these things of theirs are not even real, they are not there at all, they are only imagined things! So why should we sacrifice our equilibrium to them? Have we not enough to exercise us in the conduct of genuine life according to intelligent principles? Such is the great question as to poetry. And I think that every poetic person who is well equipped for life, has in him this platonic and vulgar contempt of conscious realization, and can taste the anathema in the term poet. "He who cannot rise above his writings that he has been long patching and piecing together, adding some and taking away some, may be justly called Poet!" says Plato, in high scorn of his own pursuits.

It seems as though a man ought to have something

to do. Sitting in a hammock with a book of rhyme, realizing the intrinsic being of something, perhaps the west wind, when he ought to trim a windmill, and be starting up to the pump—this is a poor picture of a hero. So poor is it, that it will probably bring those who adore poetry, if they have not been brought already, into open conflict with our opinion that it is essentially a realization. They will declare that poetry does promote achievement, does concern itself with practical truth and meaning. A man unacquainted with the "Book of Poems," according to Confucius, is not only unable to see, but also unable to advance—he is face to face with a stone wall. According to Philip Sidney, effective instruction is almost the definitive function of poetry. For Shelley all life's idealism, all progress of the spirit, all hope of high action, is contained in the word. And no one of these enthusiasts exceeds Plato himself, who declares, with royal inconsistency, that the character of a people depends so much more upon their songs than upon anything else, that we ought to make these the chief forces in education. Give them great poetry and the state will flourish. Did he say that poetry is madness? Yes—but the madness of poets is the most efficacious state of being that this world offers. Madmen are strong. They mould history and the earth. Is it not a kind of madness that the world exists at all, a kind of infatuation with the idea of being? And is not the madness of Homer more akin to divinity than the sanity of all our politicians? Would you not even rather join yourself with Homer, who so loved reality, and begot with her such children as the *Iliad* and the *Odyssey,* than be a husband and the father in respectability of a whole family of industrious citizens? Such is the other judgment of Plato, and his enthusiasm when

he speaks upon the brighter side of this universal paradox.

We cannot but conclude that poetry is of high practical value; it is of value to purposive conduct and adjustment for the future. And yet we know that in
some way it is also not practical, and of no value beyond
itself. I think there would be no inconsistency here, if
we were not too eager to generalize—if we were content
to say that some poetry is of high practical value, and
that other poetry is of no such value at all. Then we
should be separating the general definition of poetry
from the estimation of particular poems, as heretofore
none of its lovers have been willing to do, and we could
resolve that ancient paradox and subject it to the demands of rationality.

The poetic as such is not concerned with conduct or
the conveyance of meaning. But when one who is concerned with conduct and desires to convey a meaning,
conveys it poetically, he adds to his speech a great and
separate power. He not only gives to our mind the
indication, or the general information that he wishes,
but he gives to our bodies an acute impression less easy
to forget. To read in practical language is to be told,
but to read in poetry is to learn by experience. And
it is because of this, because imaginative realization can
enhance the statement of a meaning and augment its
practical effect, that poetry has become identified with
meaning, and with truth, and wisdom, and morality, and
all those things that look greatly into the future. Poetry
but lends itself to them. It is of its own nature foreign
to them all.

Suppose we say that life and danger and death are a
great adventure, and it is best to know them and enter
into them heartily—we should put into that statement

almost all the meaning of this poem, but we should leave
out the living realization of its meaning:

> "Give me a spirit that on life's rough sea
> Loves to have his sails fill'd with a lusty wind
> Even till his sail-yards tremble, his masts crack,
> And his rapt ship run on her side so low
> That she drinks water and her keel ploughs air;
> There is no danger to a man that knows
> What life and death is—there's not any law
> Exceeds his knowledge."

Does not such poetry add itself and its own efficacy,
entirely new, to the meaning which we had expressed?
And furthermore, if poetry can add efficacy to such a
meaning, will it not also add efficacy to false or impractical meanings? I think that we should as rigor-
ously condemn a poet for touching the torch of realization to an unheroic idea, such as this,

> "'T is not what man Does which exalts him, but what man
> Would do!"

as we should extol him for giving illumination to a great
concept. But in either case the illumination is not the
concept, and if opinions are ever to be consistent upon
this subject, it must be distinguished from it by the
understanding. No meaning properly so called has ever
been expressed with poetry, which could not conceivably
be severed from its poetry and set forth in practical
language.

Perhaps this judgment does not give to poetry as such
the most commanding place in men's esteem. For while
they all respect the expression of a meaning destitute
of poetry, calling this a culmination of their scientific
spirit, but few give honor to any poetry that is unre-
lated to a meaning. Reading pure poetry is like gazing
on the moonlight long. We wish we could receive it,

but we cannot—a final proof that we are sadly practical at heart. We are but driven pilgrims through the world, the children of its evolution, and we must be going on. Pure being is too much for us. The best that we can ask of moonlight is that it shall shine upon our occupation. Perhaps the best that we can ask of poetry is that it shall attend the statement of a truth with glory. And yet there are great poems, poems universally called great, which are pure realizations. There is Keats's "Ode to Autumn." Let it be held a supreme achievement of his genius. For with all the world intent upon a future, eager for the word that indicates, it is not easy to withhold it and be noble. It is not possible for those mere lovers of their moods who oftenest elect to try it. But for those whose character and thought are deep, determined onward with the world, and who arrest us as the world itself sometimes arrests us for a moment only with the wonder of its being, it is possible. Pure poetry upon their lips seems even more divine than truth, more ultimate, more universal.

There is indeed, for those who recognize its aim, a value in such poetry that goes beyond the present. There is a value toward a goal not yet attained. Even the mere realization of autumn in its absence—unattended though it be by any moral or true meaning—looks somewhat to a future end. It looks to autumn. It is not only an imagination, but a preperception, and its value culminates in the more full experience of the very hours it dreamed of. Thus the poetry of words may be regarded as a means toward the poetry of life. It is to that end practical. It nourishes the waking spirit, nourishes the gift of vision, and the tendency to issue from the bondages of habit and receive the world. We recognize this value in our kindergartens, where we seek to train the mind in childhood for keeping awake dur-

ing a lifetime. But poetry continues and renews this
training always. We do not read Shelley and then
return to the world, but we see the world through Shelley's eyes. Creative vision of the specific actual throughout all time—creative vision kindled by that flaming
language, is an onward and immortal value of his songs.

The poetry of books prepares, and also it restores.
To us the world grows stale, because in proportion as
we become accustomed to a thing we are estranged
from it. In proportion as we win the daily presence of
our friends, we lose them. We come to regard life as a
dry package of facts. We want the spirituous refreshment of another's vision. We want to have our eyes
reopened, and our souls made naked to the touch of
being.

This is the priesthood of art—not to bestow upon
the universe a new aspect, but upon the beholder a new
enthusiasm. At our doors every morning the creation is
sung. The day is a drama, the night as an unfolding
destiny within whose shadowy arena impetuous life
shall still contend with death. A world laughs and
bleeds for us all the time, but our response in this me-
teoric theatre we suffer to be drugged with business and
decorum. We are born sleeping, and few of us ever
awake, unless it be upon some hideous midnight when
death startles us, and we learn in grief alone what bit
of Olympian fire our humid forms enwrapped. But we
could open our eyes to joy also. The poet cries
"Awake!" and sings the song of the morning. He that
hath eyes let him see! Even now all around us the
trees have arisen, and their leaves are tongues of the air
in song—the earth swings on in drastic revolution—
and we laugh and love perpetually—and the winds enlarge our goings and our comings with a tune.

The poet, the restorer, is the prophet of a greater

thing than faith. All creeds and theories serve him, for he goes behind them all, and imparts by a straighter line from his mind to yours the spirit of bounteous living. His wisdom is above knowledge. He cries to our sleeping selves to come aloft, and when we are come he answers with a gesture only. In him we find no principle; we find ourselves re-born alive into the world.

So far from being past, or on the wane, this wisdom of the soul of poetry looks for the first time joyfully into the future. Man is now returning to his rights as an animal. He has now learned that morals are not meant for a scourge and a dry medicine, and that joy is its own reason. Existence was not perpetrated in malice or benevolence, but simply is, and the end of our thinking is that here we are, and what can we make of it. We have a planet to act upon, a sense of the drama. We will not squat and argue, nor balk, and try to justify God, but we will make with high hearts of abandon our entrance and our exit before the congregation of the stars.

THE EXTIRPATION OF CULTURE

BY KATHARINE FULLERTON GEROULD

It is odd how words recur. There has been more talk about culture, among educated people in America, during the last months, than there had been for years. To be sure, the culture discussed since August, 1914, has been German Kultur; but that does not matter. We have actually been talking about culture once more; rehabilitating it, if only for the sake of denying that the Germans, by and large, have a monopoly of anything so good. To some of us, this recurrence of a word so long *tabu* is welcome—and as side-splittingly funny as it is welcome. For the fact is that for twenty years—ever since Matthew Arnold went out of fashion—to speak of culture has meant that one did not have it. The only people who have talked about it have been the people who have thought you could get it at Chautauqua. To use the word damned you in the eyes of the knowing. Now I have always, privately and humbly, thought it a pity that so good a word should go out of the best vocabularies; for when you lose an abstract term, you are very apt to lose the thing it stands for. Indeed, it has seemed only too clear that we were doing all in our power to lose both the word and the thing. I fancy we ought to be grateful to the Germans for getting "culture" on to all the editorial pages of the country; though I admit it sometimes seems as if the Germans bore out the rule that only those people talk about it who have it not. I should really like to make a plea for the temporary reversal of the rule. Indeed,

125

I think we are getting to a point where we are so little "cultured" that we can really afford to talk about it. When the plutocrat goes bankrupt, he may once more, with decency, mention the prices of things. Culture has ceased to be a passionate American preoccupation. Perhaps we shall not offend modesty if we use the word once more.

Now there are some who, believing that all is for the best in the best of possible worlds, and that to-morrow is necessarily better than to-day, may think that if culture is a good thing we shall infallibly be found to have more of it than we had a generation since; and that if we can be shown not to have more of it, it can be shown not to be worth seeking. Having, myself, a congenital case of agoraphobia, I habitually say nothing to the professional optimists in the public square. The wilderness is a good place to cry in; the echoes are magnificent. So I shall not attempt to deprive any one of Candide's happy conviction. If any person is kind enough to listen, I will simply ask him to contemplate a few facts with me. No one will be too optimistic, I fancy, to grant that there are *proportionately* fewer Americans who care about culture—and who know the real thing when they see it—than there were one or two generations ago. Contact with "the best that has been thought and said in the world" is not desired by so large a proportion of the community as it was. That there are new and *parvenu* branches of learning, furiously followed, I, on my part, shall not attempt to deny. But culture is another matter. Perhaps the sociologists can show that this is a good thing. I do not ask any one to deplore anything. I only ask the well-disposed to examine the change that has come over the spirit of our American dream.

If I were asked to give, off hand, the causes of the

gradual extirpation of culture among us, I should name the following:

1. The increased hold of the democratic fallacy on the public mind.

2. The influx of a racially and socially inferior population.

3. Materialism in all classes.

4. The idolatry of science.

Only one of these is purely intellectual; two might almost be called political. In point of fact, all four are interwoven.

I should be insultingly trite if I proceeded here to expound the fallacy of the historic statement that all men are born free and equal. We have all known for a long time that individual freedom and individual equality cannot co-exist. I dare say no one since Thomas Jefferson (and may I express my doubts even of that inspired charlatan?) has really believed it. No one could believe it at the present day except the people who are flattered by it; and of people who are flattered by it, it is obviously not true. The democracy of the present day—like the aristocracy of another day—is fostered by the people whom it advantages; and the people whom it advantages are adding themselves, at the rate of a million a year, to our census lists. When even democracy has to reckon with the fact that its premises are all wrong, and that men are not born equal—that hierarchies are inherent in human kind regardless of birth or opportunity—it proceeds to do its utmost to equalize artificially; it becomes Procrustes. But will any one contend that Procrustes left people free?

Now, what has this to do with culture? Simply this: that culture is not a democratic achievement, because culture is inherently snobbish. Contact with "the best that has been thought and said in the world" makes people intellectually exclusive, and makes them draw distinctions. Those distinctions, seriously speaking, are not founded on social origins or great possessions; they are founded on states of mind. So long as democracy is simply a political matter, culture is left free to select its groups and proclaim its hierarchies. But it is characteristic of our democracy that political equality has not sufficed to it; the "I am as good as you are" formula has been flung out to every horizon. The people with whom it has become a mania insist that their equality with every one else in their range of vision is a moral, an intellectual, a social, as well as a political, equality. Let that formula prevail, and culture, with its eternal distinction-drawing, will naturally die. For contact with the best that has been thought and said in the world induces a mighty humility—and a mighty scorn of those who do not know enough to be humble before the Masters. They are an impersonal humility and an impersonal scorn—attitudes of the mind, both, not of the hearth. But humility and scorn are both ruled, theoretically, out of the democratic court.

The pure-bred American once cared for culture, and no longer—to the same extent, at least—does. If any one asks why America (I use the word loosely, as meaning our United States), having always, since the Revolution, been a democracy, can have cared for so undemocratic a thing, the answer is simple. The democracy of our forefathers was a purely pragmatic affair. The Declaration of Independence was framed by men living in a world where it was almost true enough to be workable. Roughly speaking, in pioneer and colonial days—wherever and whoever the pioneers and colonists may be—the community is a democracy because it is an aristocracy. In those grimmer worlds, the fittest do survive because there is no incubator process to keep the feeble going. A pioneer and colonial group, moreover, is apt to be like-minded; people do not exile themselves in each other's company unless they want the same things. Minor differences of opinion are swallowed up in like major needs: you form coalition governments against savages and famine or a specially detested tyranny. In the modern "I am as good as you are" sense, our ancestors were not democratic at all. They were democratic for their own special group, and a pragmatic truth misled them—as, because we admire them, we are permitting it to mislead us. They were Brahminical in their attitude to learning; they thought it supremely valuable, and they did not believe in—no Brahmin wants to believe in—a royal road to it, any more than they believed in a royal road to the salvation of the soul. They believed in intellectual, as much as they did in spiritual, election; and they certainly did not think that politics could influence either. Up to the last generation or two, they looked upon the cultured man as a peculiarly favored person; and because culture (unlike beauty, let us say) depended to some extent on the effort of the individual, they thought it fit to mention.

Now there is this about a pragmatic truth: like any other invention of the devil, it smooths the road for the lazy. If it did not smooth the road, it would not be, by pragmatic definition, truth. And the great bulk of us have found the "free and equal" statement such a help that, though we cannot pretend for a moment that it is true, we stick to it. The schoolboy sticks to it because it greases his oratory; the politician sticks to it because his constituents like the sound of it; the detrimental sticks to it because it is his only apology. And, just as you cannot suppress a word without eventually suppressing the thing it stands for, so you cannot utter a

statement forever without imbibing some of its poison.
Even as our reasonable national pride turned into the
spread-eagleism that Dickens and Mrs. Trollope carica-
tured, so the "free and equal" shibboleth turned into the
"I am as good as you are" formula. Why trouble about
anything, if you were already lord of the world? At
first, it was Europe we defied. What were the ancient
oligarchies, to impose on us their standards, intellectual, social, or moral? We set up our own standards,
because we were as good as any one else—and also because it was a little easier.

Let me say before going further, that I am not blaming the lower classes alone for the extirpation of culture among us. The upper classes are equally responsible—if, indeed, not even more to blame. We have
become materialistic: our very virtues are more materialistic than they were. It is forgivable in the poor man
to be materialistic; for unless he has bread to keep his
body alive, he will presently have no soul to cherish.
Materialism is less pardonable in the man who always
knows where his next meal is coming from. He, if you
like, does have time to worry about his soul. None
the less, he worries about it very little. There used to
be a good deal of fun poked at settlement-workers who
tried to read Dante and Shakespeare to slum-dwellers. I
am not sure that those misguided youths and maidens
who first carried Dante and Shakespeare into the slums
were not right as to substance, however wrong they were
as to sequence. The only morally decent excuse for
wanting to have a little more money than you actually
need to feed and clothe your family, is your ambition
to have a little mental energy to spend on things not of
the body. The ultimate tragedy of the slums is that, in
slum conditions, one can scarcely think, from birth to
death, of anything but the body. The upper-class peo-

ple who think of pleasing their palates instead of relieving hunger, of being in the fashion instead of covering their nakedness, are no more civilized than the slum-dwellers. They are apt, it is true, to become more so; for it is a strange fact that a family can seldom be rich through several generations without discovering some æsthetic truths. And æsthetic truths lead to moral perceptions. You cannot with impunity fill your ears with good music, your eyes with good painting and sculpture and architecture. Something happens to you, after a time, no matter how vulgar you may be. But wealth is very fluctuating in our country; and several generations of it are not often seen. The people who are now rich are generally people whose grandfathers and great-grandfathers were fighting for sheer existence. So we have the spectacle of the dominant plutocrats (no one will deny that plutocracy is the order of the day, both here and in Europe) either mindful themselves of the struggle for existence, or in a state of having only just forgotten it. They are not going to push their children into a race for intangible goods. And the more we recruit from immigrants who bring no personal traditions with them, the more America is going to ignore the things of the spirit. No one whose consuming desire is either for food or for motor-cars is going to care about culture, or even know what it is. And it is another misfortune of our over-quickened social evolution that the middle classes do not stay middle-class. They climb to wealth, or sink to indigence. Neither that quick rise nor that quick fall is a period in which to cherish their own or their children's intellects.

Both from above and below, then, our colleges and schools have felt the hostile pressure. Colleges are, on the one hand, jeered at for doing their business badly, and, on the other, accused of being too difficult. We are always hearing that college is of no earthly use to a man except as he learns there to rub up against other men. We are always hearing, also, that the college curriculum is a cruel strain on the average boy or girl. On one score or another, the colleges are always being attacked; and the attack usually includes the hint that the real test of a "college education" is not the intrinsic value, but its success or failure in preparing the youth for something that has nothing to do with learning. Will it be of social or financial use to him? If not, why make sacrifices to get it? Far be it from me to assert that the intellectual flame never burns in the breast of collegiate youth! But I do believe it provable that there is far less tendency to regard learning as a good in itself, and far more tendency to cheat scholarship, if possible, in the interest of some other thing held good, than there was two generations ago. Ignorance of what real learning is, and a consequent suspicion of it; materialism, and a consequent intellectual laxity—both of these have done destructive work in the colleges.

The education of younger children is in like case. We put them into kindergartens where their reasoning powers are ruined; or, if we can afford it, we buy Montessori outfits that were invented for semi-imbeciles in Italian slums; or we send them to outdoor schools and give them prizes for sleeping. Every one knows what a fight the old universities have had to put up to keep their entrance standards at all. With the great new army of state universities admitting students from the public schools without examination, because they themselves are part of the big public-school system, how can it be otherwise?

Now the patriotic American may see—and rightly enough—in the public-school system which includes a college training, a relic of the desperate desire of our forefathers that education, as a major good, should be within the reach of all and sundry. But even the patriotic American must see another impulse at work: the impulse to put the college intellectually, as well as financially, within the reach of all. The colleges must not set up standards for themselves that the average boy or girl, from the ordinary school, cannot reach without difficulty, because that is undemocratic.

Now I know as well as other people that it is positively harder to get into our old universities to-day than it was in our fathers' day. But granted the enormously increased facilities for preparation all over the land, it is not relatively anything like so hard. Certainly, once in, it is possible to get through the college course with less work than ever before. In the first place, there is a much wider choice of subjects on which a boy can get his degree: his tastes are consulted as they never used to be. If he does not want to endure the discipline of Greek, he can get an A.B. at every college in the country —except Princeton—without knowing a word of Greek. Even at Princeton, he can take a Litt.B. and let Greek forever alone.* He can study sociology, or Spanish, or physical culture, or nearly anything he likes. I have even heard that in one of our state universities there is a department of hat-trimming, which contributes its quota to the courses for a (presumably feminine) academic degree.

It may be objected at this point that the fluctuations

* I have been told, since writing this essay, that the University of Chicago demands a modicum of Greek for the A.B. degree. The Catholic University does the same. And it is only fair to say, also, that, since this essay was written, Princeton has abdicated her well-nigh unique position. It will hereafter be possible to acquire the Princeton A. B. without knowing *alpha* from *omega*.

of colleges have nothing to do with our standards of
culture. I think they have, a great deal. No one will
deny that culture can be got elsewhere, or that colleges
do not suffice in themselves to give it. But if colleges
do not consider themselves custodians of culture, warders,
and cherishers of the flame, they have no reason for
existence. It is a platitude that business men consider
college a worthless preparation for business life—save
as a young man may have laid up there treasure for
himself in the shape of valuable "connections." Even
the conception of college as a four years' paradise intervening before the hell of an active struggle for existence, does not touch upon the original reason for
universities' being at all. Universities were invented
for the sake of bringing their fortunate students into
contact with the precious lore of the world, there gar-
nered and kept pure. There was no idea on the part of
their founders that every one would or could partake
of academic benefits. The social scheme would not
originally have allowed that; still less would the conception of the public intellect have admitted the notion.
Every one was not supposed to be congenitally qualified
for intimacy with the best that has been thought and
said in the world. They had no notion, until very recently, of so changing the terms of that intimacy that
every one might think he could have it. Learning, culture, were not to be adulterated so that any mental
digestive process whatsoever could take them in.

But now, in America, there is a tendency that way.
If a boy does not feel a pre-established harmony between his soul and the humanities, then give him an
academic degree on something with which his soul will
be in pre-established harmony. And if there is no pre-
established harmony between his soul and any form of
learning, then create institutions that will give him a

degree with no learning to speak of at all. I do not
mean to deny that many of our virtually valueless colleges were founded in the pathetic inherited conviction
that learning and culture were too great goods not to be
accessible to all who cared passionately for them. But
I do believe that the reverence for learning and culture
has been largely replaced by a conviction that anything
which has so great a reputation as a college degree must
be put within the reach of all, even at the risk of making
its reputation a farce. The privileged have been unwilling that their children should be made to work; the
unprivileged have been unwilling that their children
should see anything of good repute, anything with a prestige value, denied to them. We have all demanded a
royal road to a thing to which there is no royal road.
The expensive schools lead their pupils from kinder-
garten to nature-study and eurhythmics, with basket-
work and gymnastics thrown in; the public schools follow them as closely as they can. Of real training of
the mind there is very little in any school. The rich
do not want their children overworked; the poor want
a practical result for their children's fantastically long
school hours. So domestic science comes in for girls, and
carpentering for boys. Anything to make it easy, on the
one hand; anything to make a universal standard possible, on the other.

Take one example only: the attitude towards Greek.
There are two arguments against teaching our children
Greek: one, that it is too hard; the other, that it is
useless. The mere fact that public opinion has drummed
Greek out of court as an inevitable part of a college
curriculum shows that these arguments have been potent. No person who could be influenced by either has
the remotest conception of the meaning or the value of
culture. Culture has never renounced a thing because

it was difficult, or because it did not help people to make money. And the mere fact that Greek is no longer supposed by the vast majority of parents to be of any "use" —even as a matter of reputation—to their sons, shows that the old standards of culture have changed. The larger number of our public schools no longer teach Greek at all; a great many private schools have to make special arrangements for pupils who wish to study it. And the attitude towards Greek is only a sign of our democratic, materialistic times.

Now I have done with the colleges. I have dealt with them at all only by way of hinting that they have been so democratized that culture means, even to its avowed exponents, something different from what it has ever meant before. May I speak for one moment explicitly of the public schools? For we must trace all this back to the source—must begin with the ostensible homes of "culture" and follow up the stream to the latent public consciousness. Each class that comes into college has read fewer and fewer of what are called the classics of English literature. An astonishing number of boys and girls have read nothing worth reading except the books that are in the entrance requirements. An increasing proportion of the sons and daughters of the prosperous are positively illiterate at college age. They cannot spell; they cannot express themselves grammatically; and they are inclined to think that it does not matter. General laxity, and the adoption of educational fads which play havoc with real education, are largely responsible. In the less fortunate classes, the fact seems to be that the public schools are so swamped by foreigners that all the teachers can manage to do is to teach the pupils a little workable English. Needless to say, the profession of the public-school teacher has become less and less tempting to people who are really fit for it.

It is not only in the great cities that the immigrant population swamps the schoolroom. An educated woman told me, not long since, that there was no school in the place where she lived—one of our oldest New England towns—to which she could send her boy. The town could not support a private school for young children; and the public school was out of the question. I had been brought up to believe that public schools in old New England towns were very decent places; and I asked her why. The answer made it clear. Three-fourths of the school-children were Lithuanians, and a decently bred American child could simply learn nothing in their classes. They had to be taught in English, first of all; they approached even the most elementary subjects very slowly; and—natural corollary—the teachers themselves were virtually illiterate. Therefore she was teaching her boy at home until he could go to a preparatory school. Fortunately, she was capable of doing it; but there are many mothers who cannot ground their children in the languages and sciences. A woman who could not would have had to watch her child acquiring a Lithuanian accent and the locutions of the slum.

An isolated case is never worth much. But one has only to consider conditions at large to see that this has everything to make it typical. One has only to look at any official record of immigration, any chart of distribution of population by races, to see how the old American stock is being numerically submerged. If you do not wish to look at anything so dull as statistics, look at the comic papers. A fact does not become a stock joke until it is pretty well visible to the average man. Our forefathers cared immensely for education; they felt themselves humble before learning; and their schools followed, soon and sacredly, upon their churches. They stood in awe of the real thing; and they had no illusions as to the ease of the scholar's path. They legislated for their schools solemnly, and if not with complete wisdom, always at least with accurate ideals. Educational (like all other) legislation nowadays is largely in the hands of illiterate people, and the illiterate will take good care that their illiteracy is not made a reproach to them. If any one chooses to say that culture must always be in the hands of an oligarchy, and that the oligarchy has not been touched, I will only ask him to consider the pupils and the teaching in most private schools. In the end, prestige values are going to tell; and the vast bulk of our population will see to it that the prestige values are not absolutely unattainable to them. The great fortunes have made their way to the top—yes, really to the top. In many cases there has been time for a quick veneer of grammar to be laid over their original English. In many cases there has not; and no one cares. The custodians of culture cannot afford to care; for their custody must either be endowed or be forsaken.

Oh, yes, there are a few Brahmins left; but one has only to look at the marriages of any given season to see what is becoming of the purity of the Brahmin caste. The Brahmins themselves are beginning to see that they are lost unless they compound with the materialists, and make or marry money—or increase, by aid of the materialists, what they have inherited. In what New England village, now, is the minister or the scholar looked up to as a fount of municipal wisdom because he is a learned man? Is he a "good mixer"? That is what they ask: I have heard them. Once it was possible in America for a poor man to hope to gain for his children, if they deserved it, the life of the intellect and of the spirit. Now it no longer is; for the poor themselves have defiled the fount. They are a different kind of poor, that is all; and they have become an active and discontented majority, with hands that pick and steal. When they no longer need to pick and steal, they carry their infection higher and give it as a free gift. And they have been aided by the Brahmins themselves; who, having dabbled in sociology *pour se désoeuvrer,* and then for charity's sake, are now finding that sociology is a grim matter of life and death, and endow chairs of it—as if one should endow chairs of self-preservation. But self-preservation is not culture and never will be; and no study of the manners and customs of savages or slums can call itself "contact with the best that has been thought and said in the world."

We owe, too, I think, a great deal of our cultural deterioration (which I admit is a villainous phrase) to science. Science has come in with a rush, and is at present—why deny it?—on top. "Scientific" is a word to charm with, even though it has already had time to be degraded. If Mrs. Eddy had called her bargain-counter Orientalism anything but "science," would she have drawn so many followers? Science has done great things for us; it has also pushed us hopelessly back. For, not content with filling its own place, it has tried to supersede everything else. It has challenged the super-eminence of religion; it has turned all philosophy out of doors except that which clings to its skirts; it has thrown contempt on all learning that does not depend on it; and it has bribed the skeptics by giving us immense material comforts. To the plea, "Man shall not live by bread alone, but by every word which proceedeth out of the mouth of God," it has retorted that no word proceeds authentically out of the mouth of God save what it has issued in its own translations. It is more rigorous and more exclusive than the Index of the Roman Church. The Inquisition never did anything so oppressive as to put all men, innocent or guilty, into a laboratory. Science cares supremely for physical things. If it restricted itself to the physical world, it would be tolerable: we could shut ourselves away with our souls in peace. But it must control the soul as well as the body: it insists on reducing all emotions, however miraculous and dear, to a question of nerve-centres. There has never been tyranny like this.

Now I do not mean to say that all scientists despise culture. That would be silly and untrue. But the "scientific" obsession has changed all rankings in the intellectual world. The insidiousness of science lies in its claim to be not a subject, but a method. You could ignore a subject: no subject is all-inclusive. But a method can plausibly be applied to anything within the field of consciousness. Small wonder that the study of literature turns into philology, the study of history into archæology, and the study of morals and æsthetics into physical psychology. With the finer appeals of philosophy and poetry and painting and natural beauty, science need not meddle; because about their direct effect on the thought and wills of men it can say nothing valuable. You cannot determine the value of a Velasquez by putting your finger on the pulse of the man who is looking at it; or the value of Amiens Cathedral by registering the vibration of his internal muscles; or of the Grand Cañon of the Colorado by declaring that all perception of beauty is a function of sex. Nor does it matter very much, at the moment, to the enraptured reader or observer that such and such a work of art was the logical result of a given set of conditions. The point is that it is there; and that it works potently upon us in ways which we can scarce phrase. Culture puts us disinterestedly in communication with the distilled and sifted lore of the world. Science is in comparison a prejudiced affair—prejudiced because it seeks always to bring things back to literal and physical explanations. Far be it from me to deny that geology, biology, physics, have given us unapprehended vistas down which to stray —only, strictly speaking, it forbids the straying. The moment the layman's imagination begins to profit, begins to get real exhilaration from scientific discoveries, it contributes something unwelcome to science. Science has its own stern value; in the end we are all profoundly affected by its gains in the field of fact. One's quarrel is not with science as such, but with science as demanding an intellectual and spiritual hegemony. With nothing less than hegemony, however, will science be content.

Now if it is not yet clear what effect all this must have on culture, a few words may make it clearer. The great danger of the scientific obsession is not the destruction of all things that are not science, but the slow infection of those things. If the laboratory is your real test, then most philosophies and all art are no good. The scientists are not good philosophers, and they are not good artists; and if science is to rule everywhere, we must shelve philosophy and art, or else take them into the laboratory. I need not point out what has become of literature under a scientific régime. We all know the hopeless fiction that is created by the scientific method; fiction that banks on its anecdotal accuracy and has in it no spiritual truth. Literature is simply a different game: you do not get the greatest literary truth by the laboratory method. Art is not reducible to science, because science takes no account of the special truth which is beauty, of the special truth which is moral imagination.

It is not only by the laboratory method that our fiction has been ruined: a great many of our writers of fiction are not up to the laboratory method. But all our fiction has been harmed by the prevalent idea that no fiction is any good which is not done according to the laboratory method, and that even fiction which attempts that method is of little value in comparison with a card-catalogue. There were some snobs who were not affected by the democratic fallacy; but even the snobs have been affected by scientific scorn.

I may have seemed to be showing rather the reasons for the extirpation of culture among us than the fact of the extirpation. Perhaps that is not the best way to go to work. But the actual evidence is so multitudinously at hand that it was hardly worth while beginning with solemn proofs of the fact. In all branches of art and learning we have a cult of the modern. Modern languages rank Latin and Greek in our schools and colleges; practical and "vocational" training is displacing the rudiments of learning in all of our public and many of our private institutions for the teaching of the young; the books admitted to the lists of "literature" include many that never have been and never will be literature. I found, a few years ago, the following books on a list from which students of English were allowed to choose their reading for the course—this, in one of the old and respectable high schools of Massachusetts, not twenty miles from Boston: *Soldiers of Fortune, Pushing to the Front, Greifenstein, Doctor Latimer, The Prisoner of Zenda, The Honorable Peter Stirling, The First Violin,* and "any of the works of Stewart Edward White." These, and many others, may be, in their way, good reading, but there is no excuse for offering them to the young student of English as examples of "literature."

Standards of beauty and truth are no longer rigidly held up. In philosophy we have produced pragmatism; in art we have produced futurism—and what not, since then?—in literature we have produced the pathologic and the economic novel, and no poetry worth speaking of. The "grand style" has gone out; and the classics are back numbers. Our children do not even speak good English; and no one minds. They cannot be bored with Scott and Dickens; they cannot be bored with poetry at all. And why should they, when their fathers and mothers are reading *Laddie* and *The Sick-a-Bed Lady,* and their clergymen are preaching about *The Inside of the Cup*—or the latest work dealing with the slums by some one who was slum-born and slum-bred and is proud of it? You can be slum-born and slum-bred and still achieve something worth while; but it is a stupid inverted snobbishness to be proud of it. If one had a right to be proud of anything, it would be of a continued decent tradition back of one. The cultured person must have put in a great many years with nothing to show for it; his parents have usually put in a great many years, for him, for which they have nothing to show. There is nothing to show, until you get the complex result of the disciplined and finished creature. "Culture" means a long receptivity to things of the mind and the spirit. There is no money in it; there is nothing striking in it; there is in it no flattery of our own time, or of the majority.

Ours is a commercial age, in which most people are bent on getting money. That is a platitude. It is also, intellectually speaking, a materialistic age, when most of our intellectual power is given either to prophylaxis, or to industrial chemistry, or to the invention of physical conveniences—all ultimately concerned with the body. Even the philanthropists deal with the soul through the body, and Christianity has long since become "muscular." How, in such an age, can culture flourish

—culture, which cares even more about the spirit than about the flesh? It was pointed out not long ago, in an *Atlantic* article, that many of our greatest minds have dwelt in bodies that the eugenists would have legislated out of existence. Many of the greatest saints found sainthood precisely in denying the power of the ailing flesh to restrict the soul. There is more in the great mystics than psychiatry will ever account for. But science, in spite of its vistas, is short-sighted. It talks in æons, but keeps its eye well screwed to the microscope. The geologic ages are dealt with by pick and hammer and reduced to slides, and the lore of the stars has become a pure matter of mathematical formulæ. Human welfare is a question of microbes. Neither pundit nor populace cares, at the present day, for perspective. The past is discredited because it is not modern. Not to be modern is the great sin.

So, perhaps, it is. But every one has, in his day, been modern. And surely even modernity is a poor thing beside immortality. Since we must all die, is it not perhaps better to be a dead lion than a living dog? And is it not a crime against human nature to consider negligible "the best that has been thought and said in the world"? It is only by considering it negligible that we can consent to let ourselves be overrun by the hordes of ignorance and materialism—the people (God save the mark!) of to-morrow. Let us stand, if we must, on practical grounds: the bird in the hand is worth two in the bush. As if our only guaranty that to-morrow would be tolerable were not precisely that it is sprung from a past that we know to have been, at many points, noble! It is pathetic to see people refusing to learn the lessons of history; it is a waste that no efficiency expert ought to permit. All learning is a text-book which would save much time to him who works for the perfection of the world. But I begin to think that our age does not really care about perfection; and that it would rather make a thousand-year-old mistake than learn a remedy from history. So much the worse for to-morrow!

But meanwhile let us—those of us who can—see to it that the pre-eminent brains of other ages shall not have passed away in vain. M. Anatole France, in *La Révolte des Anges,* has a good deal to say about the absurdity of a Jehovah who still believes in the Ptolemaïc system. Well, the Ptolemaïc system did not prevent the ancient world from giving us Greek theatres and Roman law, or England from giving us Magna Charta. We are still imitating Greek theatres (rather badly, I admit) in our stadia; Roman law is still, by and large, good enough for such an enlightened country as France; and Magna Charta—or its equivalent—had to be there before we could have a Declaration of Independence. Our superior scientific knowledge has not given us our standards of beauty or justice or liberty. Let us take what the present offers—airplanes and all. But let us not throw away what other men, in other ages, have died for the sake of discovering. If the lore of the past is useless, there is every chance—one must be very overweening indeed not to admit it—that the lore of our generation will be useless, too. Culture—whether you use the word itself or find another term—means only a decent economy of human experience. You cannot improve on things without keeping those things pretty steadily in mind. Otherwise you run the risk of wasting a lot of time doing something that has already been done. Any one, I think, will admit that. And it is not a far step to the realization that on the whole it is wise not to lose the past out of our minds. There is no glory in being wiser than the original savage; there is glory in being wiser than the original sage. But in order to be wiser than he, we must have a shrewd suspicion of how wise he was. By and large, without culture, that shrewd suspicion will never be ours.

OUR FEAR OF EXCELLENCE

BY MARGARET SHERWOOD

IN THIS age crying out for democracy there come, even to loyal Americans, ardent believers in America and the potentialities of America, moments of questioning as to whether it is not possible to carry democracy too far. On the street, in railway trains, in market place and lecture hall, misgivings creep into the minds of the stoutest-hearted among us; and the printed word does not always reassure. Liberty, equality, fraternity, are for us a glorious heritage, a privilege, a responsibility, but the haunting sense will not down that there may be an excess of liberty, equality, and fraternity.

The hard and cutting blows that, from time to time, strike at the very root of our political faith, do not always concern political matters; it is increasingly apparent that great and beneficent movements may have, as by-products, wholly disconcerting results. A remark, heard long ago on a steamer deck, of a fellow-passenger who declared to admiring listeners, that, in her recent visit to the continent, she had seen many famous pictures, at Antwerp, Paris, Florence, and elsewhere, but that nothing she had seen abroad could at all compare in excellence with those exhibited a year before at Pebble, Colorado, the work of local talent, comes back to me now and then as a suggestion of the influence of our civic faith upon our ways of thinking, as a possible foreshadowing of the goal toward which our feet are set.

Among the various aspects of a triumphing democracy, none is more distressing than this tendency of a consciousness of liberty, equality, and fraternity to creep into the wrong place, this fatal confusion of liberty, equality, and fraternity with intellectual and æsthetic ideals. The remark, and others like it, which float in our buoyant American air, could hardly come from any country but our own. Reading the records of early days, of the endeavor, the aspirations of the founders of our country, and watching innumerable manifestations of life, east, west, north, and south, we are forced to realize that our national creed has had wholly unexpected, and not always happy, results. Urged on by a desire to secure rightness of conditions for the many, justice among men, our ancestors looked forward to a fairer commonwealth where no man should be oppressed. They hardly foresaw the effect of their doctrine in a new attitude toward men's feeling, judgment, or dreamed for the future anything so disastrous as the triumphant conviction prevalent today that one man's opinion is as good as another's, with the threatened loss of standards inherent in this belief.

Doubtless out of the struggle for liberty and equality has come our sheep-like tendency, our longing to be gathered into one æsthetic or intellectual fold. One must not protest, of course, against the desire of the young to look alike, act alike, dress alike, resulting in so precise a similarity in thousands upon thousands of the new generation that one might imagine them a manufactured product, turned out with a stamp by some gigantic machine. Fashion lays all low in whatsoever country, and the passion for sameness in dress is not so extraordinary nor so deplorable as a curious levelling tendency manifest here in standards of thought and of action. The desire shown, the country over, to be alike in ways of thinking and of appreciation would suggest that one article in our national creed had defeated another, and that, however far we may have gone in achieving equality, we are far, very far from achieving liberty. In the community at large, in schools, in colleges we are slaves to the fear of being unlike the others, and no Clarkson, no Wilberforce rises to break the fetters of the human soul, as the fetters binding the human body were broken. The country over, we thrill to the same cheap oratory; the standardized prettiness of our magazine covers triumphantly sweeps the land; best sellers delight us because they are best sellers.

Even in institutions of learning, if I may so designate our colleges, the young are, as a rule, ashamed of intellectual distinction, concealing any unusual interest in things of the mind, feeling that they have disgraced their families if they win Phi Beta Kappa, hiding artistic ability as if it were a sign of shame. There is certainly an idea abroad among us in America, and especially astir in the hearts of the young, that to see a bit farther, to hold one's standard a bit higher than one's fellows, is not being a good sport, as if some advantage were being taken in the great game. He who betrays finer appreciation or unusual insight is as one playing with marked cards.

Undoubtedly this is, in part, the effect of a new generosity. When we take our place in the long list of the prehistoric, in line with the Stone Age, the Age of Bronze, and other ages which have had their day, as we are having ours, we shall doubtless be known as the Chemical Age. Yet if periods were named, not for the weapons which men used, or the material for fashioning household equipment, but for their inner trend of life, this would perhaps be known as the Age of Sympathy. For that vast awakening to the needs, the suffering of others, in progress for a century and a half, no one can be too grateful. It is almost as limitless, as many-sided as human life itself, this new discernment of another's woes, this penetrative understanding of another's need, this swift effort to help. Everywhere is a literature of sympathy, pleas for the oppressed in mine and in factory; sympathy of working man for working man, of pal for pal, of criminal for criminal, even of good man for good man. It is, pre-eminently, the mark of our advance, this extension of one's interest beyond the narrow bounds of one's own, this ability to put oneself into another's place. So great is our pride in the breaking of the old Puritan sternness, when cruelty often masqueraded as righteousness, that one hesitates to speak questioningly, yet there is cause for fear in this extreme, possibly as great as the other.

All great gifts have peril in their holding. Sympathy is almost the most beautiful thing in the world, but it is also the most dangerous, to be cherished with prayer and fasting and heart searching. All lofty places are fraught with hazard; standing on them it may be well to remember the depth to which we must plunge. The greater the height, the greater the possible fall, and this supreme human attribute carries with it a supreme menace. Hearts of great saints meet in this great accord, but sympathy for one another, loyalty to one another is also one of the most marked characteristics of thieves. With one's brother, yes, our whole modern hope is here, but with one's brother on the downward path is a different story. Keeping step is highly desirable, but one has to remember not only the union, but the direction of the step. Triumphant democracy will do well to recall that ancient, picturesque, yet accurate statement of spiritual truth, that broad is the path leading to destruction, and many feet in unison go down it together. Are we forgetting entirely the direction of our step in the feeling that all will be well because we are all together?

Narrow the way,—just as narrow as ever,—that leadeth unto life, and few there be that find time to look for it: we have so many engagements now-a-days!

One welcomes this new sympathy, much of it at least; one recognizes it as, in part, a consequence of that determination toward justice in which our civic history began. Increasingly we thrill to the finer hope of a liberty, equality, and fraternity, wherein all human beings shall have their rights and their privileges, yet, looking the country over, observing the present condition of things, we are aware of something subtly wrong. The new generosity in spirit is not matched in practice; our deeds limp haltingly behind our facile emotions. That likeness, kinship, sameness of which we are aware in listening to public speakers, reading the printed word, hearing the conversation of our fellows in mart, market place, and on the street, this one stamp of idea and manner, reaching from Maine to California, disappears when we fix our attention on material things. Turning from the intangible to the tangible, from men's thoughts and feelings to their possessions, the similarity vanishes; one is aware in the spectacle of life in our land of hideous contrasts, of a something, in spite of the vast increase in human sympathy, unfulfilled in the hope of the world. No royalty-ridden country of Europe can show more appalling differences between wealth and poverty, more appalling inequalities in the matter of food, clothing, and material things. The question inevitably arises as to whether the levelling has not been in the wrong place, whether the sharing has not been of the wrong things, whether we have not become free and equal in the wrong way. We have pooled our ideas, our standards, and have clung fast to our material possessions; that which should be kept sacred and individual, our ideals and aspirations, we have tossed into the general store, while we have clung tightly to that which should have been shared. Our only communism is a commonness of thought and of belief, a lack of standards. Men and women who pride themselves on the exclusive foods they eat, on the individual distinctiveness of the cut of their clothing, yet thrill to the same cheap eloquence of the stump orator, and are content, by way of diversion, with the crude emotional appeal and the distorted lines of the same moving pictures. In matters where there should be differences, constant personal effort to work out standards, to bring to bear upon the mass the impress of higher endeavor, thought, feeling,— that right development of individuality which is the goal of democracy, and the hope at the heart of Christianity,—mass opinions are substituted for finer individual judgments; mob psychology invades our standards. It is not the unique jewels, the priceless fur coats, the automobiles that cannot be duplicated, but souls that are thrown into the melting pot.

All this is sad, but undeniable; who can tell the reasons? Perhaps it means that we are but following the line of least resistance; it is easier to give up standards than it is to give up bodily comforts and luxuries; moreover, the excellent is more difficult to discern in the world of thought and of spiritual endeavor than in the "emporium." The truth is that we have grown to have a certain fear of standards, both of thought and of action, because they are above the comprehension of the many; while we delight in outstripping Brown, Jones, and Robinson in the matter of wearing apparel, and glory in getting the better of them, even through a little trickery, in business, we do not want to have any ideas or ideals which these fellow human beings do not share.

We are shamefaced in owning a loftier aspiration, a finer insight, and hide the better man within us under a hail-fellow-well-met manner, and bluff Yankee speech, preferably slangy, or a bit ungrammatical. There are moments when one wonders whether we have not wholly mistaken the point of that great endeavor in which our country had its birth; our forefathers struggled to break the rule of force, so that spirit might be free to rule. I cannot believe that they wished to eliminate leadership; rather, they severed bonds in order to let real leaders emerge and take their rightful places. In our deification of the average man we defeat their high intent, and prevent the future. We must outgrow our naïve and childish fear,—whether it means recognition in others or cultivation in ourselves,—of that which is beyond the mass, if we are ever to achieve anything of value, morally, politically, or in the world of art and of letters. When liberty and equality get into our intellectual and aesthetic standards, the result is intellectual and aesthetic chaos. All men's judgments may be free, but they can never, please God, be equal.

Whether or not our present condition is the inevitable result of democracy we do not know; historians have suggested that it is by way of democracies that civilizations go out. If democracy is, as we believe, a glorious opportunity, the best solution that has been found for the problem of human rule, it is also a great and perilous experiment for the human soul, full of a fatal impulsion toward levelling down. Its watchword may be a golden thread leading us to the very heart of God, or a trail ending in a quicksand where aspiration, endeavor, higher hope go down. Its subtle menace was as apparent in ancient as in modern times. We should pause, in our triumphant praise of democracy, to recall the fact that an ancient democracy put to death its greatest philosopher, Socrates, for proclaiming, in an age enchanted with the sophist conviction that this man's idea and that man's idea were the measure of things, and all that men could know of truth,—a belief in the existence of universal standards of excellence, standards of truth, of conduct, objective, enduring, different from the mere subjective judgment, the momentary whim, conviction, impulse, of this person or that.

Thinking of our period, thinking of our own country, one realizes that, in our present self-complacence is the measure of our failure, in our persistent belief that a deeper faith, a higher conviction cannot be true, because our neighbors do not believe them to be true. We are tolerant of our fellow sophist, and gladly grant him a freedom as great as our own, but there is something lacking in the programme of both of us. Tolerance is undoubtedly a virtue, but not sufficient as the sole basis of a civilization, into which, if it is to endure, must be mortised not only negative but positive virtues, knowledge, wisdom, faith, and unshrinking conviction as to the difference between right and wrong.

As for the future, it is fairly evident where we are going to get tolerance, where we are going to get sympathy, but where are we going to get standards to guide mind and soul? The young *are* the future, and, in the unwillingness of the young to admit a gift or to confess an aspiration not shared by the crowd, we see the most menacing aspect of our contemporary tendency. Full of generosity to one another, of desire not to be conspicuous, they yet betray, these children of triumphant democracy, a certain spiritual shortsightedness. Perhaps the trouble comes from thinking too much in terms of things, of confusing intellectual superiority and high inner endeavor with delicacies pleasing to the palate at the human banquet, with choice bits of sweet, in regard to

which the young are perhaps more scrupulous than their
elders as to claiming more than their share.   There is
a mistake here, for there is a fundamental difference
between standards of life, intellectual, moral, spiritual,
artistic, and chocolate creams.   In any assembled company one does not want more than one's share of these;
so should it be with all material things.   But generosity
in matters of mind and spirit is a different thing; it is
a very energy of life, showing itself in search for hid
treasure, the finder, the darer, being under stern obligation to seek out and share with his fellows what perhaps he only could discover; it may be a lone search
for lost trails, for the higher trail, that others may follow after.

He who shirks the responsibility of the greater gift,
the keener insight, betrays a species of mental obliquity,
a lack of vision.   In striving toward excellence, winning
it, there is something impersonal; aspiration is not necessarily vanity, genuine aspiration never; the attainment
of the fine and high in thought and in conduct should
be for the sake of that ever clearer discernment of the
better whereby the race measures its inner growth.
Refusing to try to win, because all may not win together, may not the very conception of the fine and high
vanish?   In this scruple, this hesitation to put forth
one's utmost, there is fallacy, subtle and insidious, a
thinking about people, rather than about intellectual or
spiritual excellence.   The quest of the greater, the un-
attained, represents no selfish claim; absolute self-for-
getfulness may come in winning toward the goal;
honestly facing the greatest, one loses sight of the
ego.   It is a mistaken sympathy which means thinking
of oneself and the other man, rather than of that which
draws attention from both to something higher.   Here

is failure to discover the presence of anything but individuals in our cosmos, the many, not the One.

Stern is the obligation to search beyond one's self and one's neighbor, in order to find stepping stones leading to high places. One must do more than understand one's brother, and put oneself in his place; one must love him deeply enough to hurt him, if necessary, by failing to acquiesce in his present programme. It is a duty, not only to keep step with one's fellow, but to try to hasten that step. One must understand his possibilities, help keep quick and alive the principle of growth in him, help him discern a something beyond his or one's own present attainment. There must be something deeper than surface sympathy with the lesser self which holds potential menace, cutting off the future; there must be sympathy at times like a keen-edged, naked sword, piercing to the very heart of his lack or limitation, as self-scrutiny pierces to one's own, cutting off all that hampers or keeps back. Without this higher sympathy one does not, in truth, understand one's brother at all.

The business of a true citizen of a democracy is to search out continually better and better standards of thought and of conduct, to carry on, worthily, in the face of new challenge, the effort of our forefathers, to justify the open road of freedom. The impact of mind on mind, of soul on soul, in a land where thought and speech are free, ought to mean, not a levelling down but a levelling up, each individual soul doing its utmost, by stern endeavor, by searching the ways of truth and beauty through life, to render its own individual interpretation, a something no other human soul could do, of possibilities of higher existence.

If mediæval saint and Indian mystic of today err on the side of too exclusive contemplation of the Principle of Excellence,—too steady a gaze meaning, perhaps, a blinding of the eyes; if, thus, human sympathies shrivel, and one deep path of wisdom and understanding, knowledge of the human heart, of the facts of life, of human experience, the way of the Lord through human lives, be closed,—this excess is still no excuse for our closing our eyes to that other glorious way of the Lord, the long and splendid dream of human aspiration, the unwearied striving toward the best, the contemplation of the beauty of the Lord our God.

Of the great behests, Love the Lord thy God with all thy heart and soul and mind, and love thy neighbor as thyself, the former was given first.

There is one simple, but absolute condition of growth, after the soul has become conscious of itself, the stern and constant measuring of oneself by something higher than oneself, rather than the excusing of one's defects and limitations because one's neighbors also have theirs. Our chief human business is, in truth, a discerning of values, all life being but a process of selection and refusal.   Life without constant challenge of the higher is not life at all, nor subject to the laws of physical and spiritual development, as ancient intuition and modern logic have revealed them.

We must search out excellence, through great personalities, great artistic achievements, great faiths, gaining, by contemplation of the highest reach of thought and conduct of individuals, in different times and different places, a constantly enlarging intellectual and spiritual apprehension.   Working on the stuff that human life has wrought out, the best that the long struggle, the undying creative impulse have evolved, gaining acquaintance with great thought, great feeling, great men, we shall be constantly revising our idea concerning that which is excellent.   Thus, measuring by great personalities, great deeds, great faiths, we shall at last discern more clearly the white light of truth, of which these are the breaking. Following the ways of those other neighbors of other times and other countries, thinkers, statesmen, creators of any kind, we shall learn some measure for our own self-assertion. Pebble, Colorado, must learn to make obeisance to the Ufizzi and the Louvre.

It is in contemplating human life and human thought at their greatest that we realize how inadequate our new standard of sympathy proves as a statement of the whole human case. This kindliness, this feeling for humanity which we are achieving, means great gain, but, in the very measure of our preoccupation with our contemporary fellow-man, there is danger, grave cause for fear lest, in learning to understand my brother, I lose desire or power to understand anything else. There may be farther reaches of the human soul than are manifest in my brother. This making the individual, the mere human characteristic, the measure of excellence, putting the personality, the qualities of this man or that in place of a loftier conception, to whose formation all high thought and great deeds contribute, is a dangerous process; this great gust of common thinking may be the wind that blows civilization out. Another loyalty is necessary, loyalty to a higher ideal, a something beyond and above you, me, and those about us.

Fear-God-Barebones could do great good among us now.

We are, in truth, face to face with the old problem of the many and the one, the need of the single, the perfect, the one to strain toward. Unless we take heed, in our content with present achievements and present ideas, we shall lose the challenge of the forever unsatisfied within us, the sense of something, in every aspect of thought and conduct, yet to be attained. We must not

forget, for no aspect of modern development can com-
pensate for this loss, the search of the religious instinct
out of the worship of many gods toward the One; the
search of the philosopher for the secret, the one, that
will explain the manifold, that which the Greek Plato
conceived as the Idea of Perfect Beauty, the Hebrew
in his reverential thought of the Lord our God.

To tell the truth, we are in the throes of a new polytheism, forgetting the conception of oneness, which is
the fundamental basis of belief of religious teacher,
prophet, and philosopher. It is a new and dangerous
polytheism, this worship of Brown, Jones, and Robinson; one misses in it something of the spirituality of
one's father's faith; Brown, Jones, and Robinson after
all go only so far.

The young say that the spiritual sense is as strong as
ever, that it has gone into good works, the desire to
serve. This is undoubtedly good, yet we need something
to cut through our present complacency in our own good
works, our tendency to look the country over and con-
gratulate the age on having arrived, now when everything is being done for everybody who suffers, as if we
all, in devoting ourselves to some measure or other of
physical relief, had wholly met our eternal obligations.
Yet surely we need something beyond; the manifold
ideas and ideals regarding service,—this too a polytheism,—cannot fill the human heart and soul, direct and
hold the human spirit, any more than the many gods of
Greece could permanently hold the human spirit. In
all their beauty, their manifold beauty, they failed.

This ethical polytheism, though it goes a bit farther
than the worship of our contemporaries, is too many-
sided to afford the necessary knitting up and central-
izing of human thought and aspiration. Nor can self-
engendered and self-directed ideas of duty, of service,

fine, high, admirable though they may be, ever content us. There is that within the human soul which yearns for something beyond; only the Infinite can satisfy. For the true fulfillment of life we must find something better to worship than our own immediate neighbors, or our own Good Deeds.

RED-BLOODS AND MOLLY-CODDLES

BY G. LOWES DICKINSON

I AM staying at a pleasant place in New Hampshire. The country is hilly and wooded, like a larger Surrey; and through it flows what, to an Englishman, seems a larger river, the Connecticut. Charming villas are dotted about, well designed and secluded in pretty gardens. I mention this because, in my experience of America, it is unique. Almost everywhere the houses stare blankly at one another and at the public roads, ugly, unsheltered, and unashamed, as much as to say, "Every one is welcome to see what goes on here. We court publicity. See how we eat, drink, and sleep. Our private life is the property of the American people." It was not, however, to describe the country that I began this letter, but to elaborate a generalization developed by my host and myself as a kind of self-protection against the gospel of "strenuousness."

We have divided men into Red-Bloods and Mollycoddles. "A Red-blood man" is a phrase which explains itself; "Mollycoddle" is its opposite. We have adopted it from a famous speech by Mr. Roosevelt, and redeemed it—perverted it, if you will—to other uses. A few examples will make the notion clear. Shakespeare's Henry V is a typical Red-Blood; so was Bismarck; so was Palmerston; so is almost any business man. On the other hand, typical Mollycoddles were Socrates, Voltaire, and Shelley. The terms, you will observe, are comprehensive, and the types very broad. Generally

speaking, men of action are Red-Bloods. Not but what
the Mollycoddle may act, and act efficiently. But, if so,
he acts from principle, not from the instinct for action.
The Red-Blood, on the other hand, acts as the stone
falls, and does indiscriminately anything that comes to
hand. It is thus he that carries on the business of the
world. He steps without reflection into the first place
offered him and goes to work like a machine. The ideals
and standards of his family, his class, his city, his
country and his age, he swallows as naturally as he
swallows food and drink. He is therefore always "in
the swim"; and he is bound to "arrive," because he has
set before him the attainable. You will find him everywhere in all the prominent positions. In a military age
he is a soldier, in a commercial age a business man. He
hates his enemies, and he may love his friends; but he
does not require friends to love. A wife and children
he does require, for the instinct to propagate the
race is as strong in him as all other instincts. His
domestic life, however, is not always happy; for he can
seldom understand his wife. This is part of his general
incapacity to understand any point of view but his own.
He is incapable of an idea and contemptuous of a principle. He is the Samson, the blind force, dearest to
Nature of her children. He neither looks back nor looks
ahead. He lives in present action. And when he can
no longer act, he loses his reasons for existence. The
Red-blood is happiest if he dies in the prime of life;
otherwise, he may easily end with suicide. For he has
no inner life; and when the outer life fails, he can only
fail with it. The instinct that animated him being dead,
he dies too. Nature, who has blown through him, blows
elsewhere. His stops are dumb; he is dead wood on the
shore.

The Mollycoddle, on the other hand, is all inner life.

He may indeed act, as I said, but he acts, so to speak, by accident; just as the Red-blood may reflect, but reflects by accident. The Mollycoddle in action is the Crank; it is he who accomplishes reforms; who abolished slavery, for example, and revolutionized prisons and lunatic asylums. Still, primarily, the Mollycoddle is a critic, not a man of action. He challenges all standards and all facts. If an institution is established, that is a reason why he will not accept it; if an idea is current, that is a reason why he should repudiate it. He questions everything, including life and the universe. And for that reason Nature hates him. On the Red-blood she heaps her favors; she gives him a good digestion, a clear complexion, and sound nerves. But to the Mollycoddle she apportions dyspepsia and black bile. In the universe and in society the Mollycoddle is "out of it" as inevitably as the Red-blood is "in it." At school, he is a "smug" or a "swat," while the Red-blood is captain of the Eleven. At college, he is an "intellectual," while the Red-blood is in the "best set." In the world, he courts failure while the Red-blood achieves success. The Red-blood sees nothing; but the Mollycoddle sees through everything. The Red-blood joins societies; the Mollycoddle is a non-joiner. Individualist of individualists, he can only stand alone, while the Red-blood requires the support of a crowd. The Mollycoddle engenders ideas, and the Red-blood exploits them. The Mollycoddle discovers, and the Red-blood invents. The whole structure of civilization rests on foundations laid by Mollycoddles; but all the building is done by Red-bloods. The Red-blood despises the Mollycoddle; but, in the long run, he does what the Mollycoddle tells him. The Mollycoddle also despises the Red-blood, but he cannot do without him. Each thinks he is master of the other, and, in a sense, each is right. In his lifetime the

Mollycoddle may be the slave of the Red-blood; but after his death, he is his master, though the Red-blood know it not.

Nations, like men, may be classified roughly as Red-blood and Mollycoddle. To the latter class belong clearly the ancient Greeks, the Italians, the French, and probably the Russians; to the former the Romans, the Germans, and the English. But the Red-blood nation *par excellence* is the American; so that, in comparison with them, Europe as a whole might almost be called Mollycoddle. This characteristic of Americans is reflected in the predominant physical type,—the great jaw and chin, the huge teeth, the predatory mouth; in their speech, where beauty and distinction are sacrificed to force; in their need to live and feel and act in masses. To be born a Mollycoddle in America is to be born to a hard fate. You must either emigrate or succumb. This, at least hitherto, has been the alternative practised. Whether a Mollycoddle will ever be produced strong enough to breathe the American atmosphere and live, is a crucial question for the future. It is the question whether America will ever be civilized. For civilization, you will have perceived, depends on a just balance of Red-bloods and Mollycoddles. Without the Red-blood there would be no life at all, no stuff, so to speak, for the Mollycoddle to work upon; without the Mollycoddle, the stuff would remain shapeless and chaotic. The Red-blood is the matter, the Mollycoddle the form; the Red-blood the dough, the Mollycoddle the yeast. On these two poles turns the orb of human society. And if, at this point, you choose to say that poles are points and have no dimensions, that strictly neither the Mollycoddle nor the Red-blood exist, and that real men contain elements of both mixed in different proportions, I have no quarrel with you except such as one has with the man who states the obvious. I am satisfied to have distinguished the ideal extremes between which the Actual vibrates. The detailed application of the conception I must leave to more patient researchers.

THE DICTATORSHIP OF THE DULL

BY ALEXANDER BLACK

THE biographer of Philip II described the Inquisition as a "heavenly remedy, a guardian angel of Paradise." No despotism can be so galling as to quench every apologist. Naturally the despot has a good word for himself, and it is a part of his business to prod his press agent. Quite as naturally the press agent completes the calamity. On one of those days when we feel the presence of Mr. Conrad's two veiled figures, Doubt and Melancholy, "pacing endlessly in the sunshine of the world," the press agent does the trick. The right rhapsody finishes that which oppression began. We bear an oppression because it may have enveloped us gradually with the seeming unavoidableness of a changed temperature, or, if it comes a bit suddenly, like the contact of a shrinking shoe, we may try adjusting ourselves as to an inevitable annoyance; but when some one drives in the nail of the enabling adjective, philosophy fails.

We should, of course, cultivate with regard to life what Montaigne cultivated with regard to books—"a skipping wit." But one can't skip a despotism unless it is distant enough. We can be academic about those that are far enough off. We can look at Russia and decide that the dictatorship of a proletariat is good or bad, according to our ideals, and especially, perhaps, according to our information. Perhaps, too, we may decide, with regard to a dictatorship in Russia, that it gets a good deal of attention not because it is a dictatorship, but because it is different.

All of us who are governed live under some sort of dictatorship. The benevolent despotism of democracy can be like a padded cell in which one is supposed not to be able to hurt himself. Mostly radicalism expresses consolation equivalent to a hunger strike. And all dictatorship is not political. The doctrine of supply and demand sets up a mighty dictatorship. So does all dogma for all who accept. So do fashion and family. There is dictatorship in science's word "normal." The prefix "ab" builds an inquisitorial spiked chair for rebel or genius.

There are moments when a sense of individual security may reach so nearly the dimensions of an individual serenity as to remind us that it takes two to make a dictatorship. There are other moments when we feel sharply impelled to go out and look for the dictators and have the thing done with. In our evenest mood, one in which we feel most assured of being balanced, and reasonably if not fanatically forbearing, we can scarcely hope to escape consciousness of that widest and most permeative of all dictatorships, the dictatorship of the dull.

The dull. . . . Not the frail who have never begun, but the free who have finished; not the stupid who cannot think, but the dull who object to thinking; not the submerged, the thwarted who have never had a chance, but the mediocre who admire themselves, the complacent who have fixed the final mold—all who make up the legion of self-halted men and the sisterhoods of smugness. These have an immensity of numbers. They swarm to the horizon, though they never seem to recognize that there is a horizon. There is no thinkable situation in which they do not impinge. In our arrogant moments we think of them all as Barrier. In our weak moments we may wonder in the matter of the vast, sticky obstacle, whether we are not ourselves entangled and have not begun to belong to the hopelessly finished.

Of course only a mood in which we can quite securely feel that we do not belong can be effective for attack. A plunge into the past is a great help in effecting a sense of detachment. History makes it plain enough that sinister cleverness could not have succeeded without the support of the dull, but it seldom shows how steadfastly dullness itself has stabilized the uncomfortable, how its sheer pervasiveness has affected the eternal conflict between idealism and the forces supporting inertia. Inertia is often confused with dullness. Inertia is, in fact, merely dullness's operating weight. It gives it the formidable displacement that helps block the way. Inertia does not intrude. It has no passion to prohibit, for example. It lets everything alone, good and bad. It giggles or whispers, and subsides. But dullness can have qualities. It can be both obstinate and aggressive. It can assert. Intrusion is indispensable to certain of its moods, because it has its pride, its sense of responsibility, its recognition of a common enemy—the creative.

How definitely dullness represents a mental condition rather than a class, yet quite surely assembles its class, in all ages and in all places, is echoed in every creative adventure, whether the adventure be political, industrial, social, educational, or artistic. It mingles in every group. It hates the radical more than it hates the reactionary, but it shadows both. If liberality cannot be trusted to respect dullness, neither can conservatism. When dullness can see nothing else it can see its duty. It is the most active censor.

Of course, all criticism is a form of censorship. When it is creative criticism we are in the habit of saying that it fills a high office. When it is dullness in action we ought to have no trouble in recognizing the source, yet furies of resentment often lead us to forget that dullness did not invent criticism nor introduce censorship. Doing away with criticism because it is so frequently stupid would be like abandoning any other useful implement because the foolish or vicious many misuse it.

But dullness's worst offense is not giving any good implement a bad name. Its worst offense is the benumbing influence of its presence. It casts a pall over the creative. It perverts the acoustics of the world. It tramples the gardens of invention; not always by any wish to destroy, as exasperation is every ready to conclude, yet with all the destructive effects of its weight and pervasiveness. The odd thing is that with so much of mass it is frequently and violently contemptuous of "the masses." It is willing to be the Public. But it is never willing to be Crowd. It is as glib about "mobs" as about morality.

Thus all creative effort encounters dullness as the foreground obstacle, and since creative effort can have its bigotries, deadlocks are repeated. One sees this again and again in the matter of audiences. It is to be read in myths like that of the Tired Business Man. Dullness's dislike of thinking leads it to use all sorts of evasions to escape admitting the trait; such, for example, as the familiar plea as to having thought so much that it wants a rest. People who are annoyed by intelligent plays or intelligent books do not turn away because they are tired, but because they care more for something else. They may not always be dull. They may only have been dulled. Life has extraordinary diverse effects on people who live through it. Some people learn to want life to be livelier. Others want it to be quieter. It hurts their eyes and ears. Some people are sharpened by life.

Others are blunted by it. Dislike of thinking can emerge from all experience with its prejudice unimpaired. It is a sturdy growth. By an effort it can "set and think," but it can "just set" with a more normal facility. And it can "just set" in a legislature quite as definitely as in a dooryard.

So that to ask thinking is in many situations to ask a sacrifice. It is true that audiences which protest against being asked to think are often able to make out a fairly plausible case against art. Artists are sometimes caught in the act of maintaining that art must not think, but must only feel. If, as Mr. Max Eastman has reminded us again, art must be "playful" to be successfully creative, if it must be "very free and irresponsible," it is hard to see how audiences can be denied the right to be playful and to watch or to listen or to read in a very free and irresponsible mood. The paradox is, of course, that a playful thing, representing pure response to emotion, is often saturated with thought, and that a joyous response is not denied the right to be intelligent. We have to remember, too, that an audience in a given place is handicapped in thinking where it is not handicapped in feeling. Mass accentuates emotion where it retards thought. With a reader the case is different. Except for the infectious influence of ballyhooing about a book, the reader is left to be kindled by the writer's direct action. Maybe there is for the writer some advantage in this. Yet without the help of spectacle the writer must begin with a larger assumption as to thinking, or at least with a larger assumption as to attention, and the total must count as a handicap in the earning of response. To challenge closeness of attention is the beginning of a request for thinking, and the writer who asks for prolonged concentration asks for something that narrows his audience automatically. He must first lose all who cannot think or who object to thinking, then all who are good only for a spurt. In time he may come to have the pathetic satisfaction of sharply recognizing the dividing line between people who really read and people who only own set.

The motion-picture hall has been called a haven for the dull. Certain complaints against the motion picture have been grotesquely severe. Though it begins at zero and can entertain without asking more than mere consciousness, the cinema has an almost unlimited range so far as its possibilities go. I have seen the *Odyssey* and *Macbeth* on the screen. Both were admirably done. But they had a short life. The cinema, by the conditions of its present distribution, cannot appeal to special groups, and always to appeal to general groups is to pass under the censorship of the dull. No official censorship could be so relentless. An official censorship can be diagrammed because it starts with a diagram. The censorship of the dull is immeasurable. The one arouses shrieks of protest. The other is accepted as a phenomenon of sale. The strong probability that the preferences of dullness will be translated by another dullness, or by a bewildered producer who is pretty well dulled by the pressure, accounts for the feeble average of merit, and repeated failure to please even the dull.

Education knows the dictatorship. It knows how often education bleeds between the two millstones. It knows how completely prodigious dullness in school committees and university trustees may reflect the dullness that sentinels and selects. It knows the penalty of offending dullness. It learns to prefer the lockstep of conformity to the strait-jacket in solitary. It knows why, among all the things that are taught, early or late, thinking is most inconvenient and most frequently hazardous. To teach thinking is to teach individuality, and the original is the enemy of the curriculum—and the committee. The efficiency theory of education is of a machine with standardized parts. If any teacher breaks, it is convenient to be able to pick up a machine-punched duplicate at any service station. The theory makes a profound appeal to dullness, because it avoids contact with originality— because it doesn't disturb the finished. When dullness starts out to buy an education for its boy it wants the efficiency kind. It wants standard goods, not the sort that puts ideas into his head.

A *liberal* education! Suppose it *should* happen! Suppose the boy came home with new notions about Rome or the Pilgrims; suppose he came home not with the proper impress of machine-made parts, but with a new feeling about history and life, a new sense of personal privilege, a new impulse as to what he was going to do with himself and the world. What is dullness then to conclude about the system? What is it to conclude as to that bunch of "dangerous radicals" down there? Are the trustees asleep? Somebody ought to be disciplined. Dullness didn't raise its boy to be a Bolshevik.

To dullness, thinking is a radicalism. If you begin by being disrespectful as to your grandfather everybody knows that you are likely to end by being seditious as to your Congressman. If you use your pulpit for talk about life and growth instead of sticking to Jeremiah; if you preach about poverty as a living fact instead of being content to quote it as a literary illustration of a strictly theological compassion; if you forget that revelation is historic, that religion is finished; if you turn from the labor in a biblical vineyard to the labor in your own town factories, dullness will find a way of reminding you that it is no part of a preacher's business to meddle in "politics."

When I wrangled with Emma Goldman about "social pressure," we reached no disagreement as to the reality of that phenomenon. The anarchist thought such pressure was all-sufficing. I thought it needed its written wishes and its committee. But there was no escape, by either logic, from the enormous, enveloping, and unconquerable reality of the pressure itself. I emerged with an impression that the anarchist saw the great force as reaching a kind of unity, like gravitation, and she could call to her support the formidable philosophy of monism. Yet I saw groups rather than a group—I saw oneness as a destination or an ideal rather than as a working fact, and felt that the anarchism which wanted no law, and any antipodal theory which wanted more law, both were ignoring the persistent diversity that disturbs the oneness of the world. I saw the inert (in all "classes") who go after nothing; the "winged creatures without feet," their eyes fixed on infinity; the real creators and pathfinders; the mothering people who ask least and give most; the herders, the procurers, and the leeches; and I saw the dull who dominate the Middle and think they are Stability because they are a weight.

As a stabilizer dullness always feels itself to be the appointed custodian of respectability. It finds war respectable, and a boxing match an infamy. It is not the sole supporter of war nor the sole objector to the boxing match. But it is a mainstay to both contentions. It is the mainstay of jails. Plenty of jails here and hereafter becomes a concomitant of the dull brand of righteousness. The comfort of being out of jail assumes the presence of a substantial proportion of the duly padlocked. A dull heaven is predicated on a populous hell. Of all the arguments used to keep a dreamer like Eugene Debs in a cell, there has been, naturally, none that could stress the disappointment to dullness that must result from letting him out.

Yet dullness loves to save if it may discriminate. It saves cats, but is inclined to find the saving of babies as rather messy. In fact, it indicates that babies, by and large, are an indelicacy. Babies suggest sex, and sex—well, you know what sex is. Dullness hasn't been able effectively to rebuke nature's invention of sex, but it has done all it can. It is still respectable to belong to one sex or the other. Beyond that you are in danger.

The dull get themselves divorced, but they dislike divorce as too frequently noisy. They take here the same position they occupy in an apartment house. It isn't the landlord who dislikes children. His discomfort is occasioned not by the children, but by the complaints of the dull tenants who resent the ill-advised fecundity of those who have yet to learn that it is bad form to breed in captivity.

Moreover, to the dull, children are likely to seem an economic error, an error frightfully expensive as well as complicating. Perhaps this is why dullness, after its first violent attack on birth control propaganda, attained an equally violent silence. The offense of reproducing seems to be mitigated by avoidance of the plural. If one child expressed the idea, why be tautological? Theory, in this instance, is illustrated by the story of the practical man whose wife first had twins, then triplets. When, on the third adventure, she produced a single baby, the husband remarked that he was glad she had at last got down to a good business basis.

The dull are profound believers in "prosperity." They believe in holding the thought. To face toward prosperity one must turn his back on the opposite. It is well enough to see a slum from a sight-seeing bus, but if you contact it too closely, if you admit it fully, you are letting it influence you, and if you let it influence you how can you give single-minded attention to prosperity? How can you "get on" if you stop to listen to all the blind, or maimed, or sick, or ill-treated that line the path? There was a Galilean who stopped repeatedly. Dullness crucified him.

Where "Society" has a capital S, dullness is in charge. American "Society" is accused of being the dullest in the world because it alone leaves out the intellectuals. We cannot deny that it omits certain elements indispensable to a European social group, but it might be inaccurate to contend that it has not tried to get these elements in. It is possible that American intellectuals are less perfectly house-broken than the European sort. And it would be foolish to assume that scientists, writers, and political pretenders cannot, when rightly selected, add a harmonious dullness to a society anywhere. It is sufficient to note that the organized emptiness called "Society" is utterly congenial to dullness. To be free of any of these people with ideas, to dodge books and paintings, to dismiss with a stale adjective some play dullness has interrupted by coming in late, to shake off the horror of "labor troubles," to talk a jargon, dance nakedly, devour filigrees of food, and fatten in limousines, appeal to dullness as an inexhaustible resource.

Yet dullness is so sensitive as to any frivolity in which it may not happen to join, that one of its most persistent activities of intrusion is in demonstrating that an indecent levity is the other fellow's amusement. In avoiding an issue that might be convicting to itself it is fertile in devices of segregation, and is equally fertile in ways of breaking in upon situations its own cowardice has invented. Wicked gambling is the kind it does not practice or has not agreed to overlook. Naturally it seeks to hold the copyright on all definitions of sin, and particularly to guarantee that no sinners shall be amused. Macaulay supplied the classic characterization when he said of the Puritans that they objected to bear baiting not so much because it hurt the bear as because the spectators got too much fun out of it.

The sarcasm of Macaulay has been useful to modern exasperation. The berating of the Puritans has sometimes been stupid and sometimes brilliant. The Puritans cartoon well. They are a wonderful theme, and not the least serviceable contribution of Puritanism has been that of a label for anything we don't like. Giving to the divagations of dullness the label of Puritanism seems to me altogether too much of a compliment. The Puritans may be responsible for Puritanism, but they are not responsible for all that in our haste for a handle we fasten upon the name. The Puritans were suspicious of beauty, and openly hostile to joy; they believed in a solemn God, a God disappointed and jealous, and they saw duty in the gray light of that belief; but they were hard thinkers if not good thinkers; they had no antipathy to thinking in itself. Critics of the Puritans will protest that they had a very clear idea of the directions in which thinking must not go, but this cannot disturb the contention that they were essentially a thinking lot. They thought their way out of Europe. They had pluck and punch, and any dull descendants or other members of the breed of the dull in general do not deserve the glamour of their mantle.

It is equally plain that the dull do not deserve the distinction implicit in the cries of savage irritation which are always being wrung from those who feel challenged. A thousand confessions prove that this rage can become a preoccupation. "We begin to live," says Mr. Yeats, "when we have conceived life as a tragedy." Who shall say how much this sense of the woeful may be due to that overlaid irritant of dullness? One of the ablest of American literary artists turned to me, in the midst of a social adventure of an eminent pleasantness, and quite as if the thing had flashed to him out of nowhere, to remark that all great art is created in a state of acute exasperation toward life. I was reminded afterward (when we are reminded of most things) that a conspicuous absence of dullness in the occasion had doubtless given twist to the thought. Perhaps Flaubert and others who have flung out parallel acerbities have reached incandescence at times when relief from pressure reminded them, in a piercing degree, of its essential unendurableness.

In any case, getting the thing said is evidently a relief. To conceal irritations is to germinate another complex. There is, of course, no assumption that the dull will hear. "It is not by insulting the Neapolitans," said Cavour, "that you will modify them." But modifying the dull is an inconceivable undertaking, as inconceivable as a dullness that is not modified, that does not undergo changes in form and expression. It is change of form and expression which is always leading to misplaced labels and to failures in identification of the eternal traits that lie underneath.

THE ARISTOCRATIC SPIRIT

BY HANFORD HENDERSON

AT SUCH a critical moment as the present, when turmoil prevails everywhere, and the earth itself seems palpitating with violence, it is a strange situation, and somewhat sinister, that the one thing which would bring tranquillity and an almost passionate return to the beautiful arts of peace, is the very thing which on all sides is now being flouted and defamed—I mean the aristocratic spirit.

Those who were born to this spirit, or who have, by adoption, made it their own, must always marvel that its inspiration and devout rule of life have not been seized upon with greater eagerness and by larger numbers. It must be that in the hurry of every-day life its claims have been overlooked by some, and misunderstood by others. There are, I think, three specific reasons why the aristocratic spirit has not made headway against the more popular currents of the hour. They may properly be called the three antagonisms.

The most obvious and most excusable antagonism is also the most wide-spread. It is, like so many other antagonisms, the direct result of a quite complete misunderstanding. Men have been called aristocrats who were entirely untouched by anything so beneficent as the aristocratic spirit. Societies have been classed as aristocratic when in reality they were doing violence to the very fundamentals of that spirit. The term aristocracy has been made a term of reproach as the imputed possessor of the very qualities which it would itself be the first to repudiate. To answer the first antagonism, one has only to define the aristocratic spirit, but one must do it carefully. In reality, this spirit is subtle, pervasive, penetrating, but it is not complex. It is as delicately simple as a child, and as easily understood, provided, of course, that one has not oneself wandered too far from the kingdom. I should define the aristocratic spirit as the love of excellence for its own sake, or even more simply as the disinterested, passionate love of excellence. The aristocrat, to deserve the name, must love excellence everywhere and in everything; he must love it in himself, in his own beautiful body, in his own alert mind, in his own illuminated spirit, and he must love it in others; must love it in all human relations and occupations and activities, in all things in earth or sea or sky. And this love of his must be so passionate that he strives in all things to attain excellence, and so tireless that in the end he arrives. But not even the hope of Heaven may lure him. He must love and work disinterestedly, without the least thought of reward, enamored only of the transcendent beauty of excellence, and quite unregardful of himself. It is this impersonal requirement which makes salvation at once so simple and so paradoxical, for it is literally true that to save one's soul, one must lose it; one must go back to the kingdom of the child, where subject and object are one, and the unique reality is absorption in a universe.

If one accepts this simple and true definition of the aristocratic spirit, it becomes quite obvious that aristocracy is an attitude of mind, a religion, and not a social group. Aristocrats do not constitute a social class in the concrete sense that laborers, or artisans, or professional men, or capitalists do. At most, aristocrats may be said to make up a party, since they are found in all classes of society. To be an aristocrat one must be the unselfish devotee of excellence, and happily such devotees are found in every walk of life, from the humblest to the most exalted. It is a grave mistake to confound aristocracy with social station, or with any other outer trapping. In the hot crucible of events, tinsel withers, while gold refines. The Great War has been such a crucible and it has put kings as well as commoners to the test. To love excellence, not the appearance of excellence, and to love it disinterestedly, and not for the sake of the loaves and fishes—this is the whole creed of the aristocrat.

When it is urged against the so-called aristocracies of the past that they were the class of privilege and prided themselves upon their exclusiveness, the criticism is perfectly just, but it is not a criticism of the aristocratic spirit; it is evidence that this high spirit was sadly lacking. Greed, arrogance, snobbishness, cruelty can never be the qualities of an aristocrat, for the excellence which he seeks in the great outer world, he seeks still more passionately in himself. It is a contradiction to say that aristocracy asks privilege or seeks exclusiveness. Such a policy is contrary to the doctrine of perfection. What the aristocrat wants, and wants passionately, is that all the world shall come into that same love of excellence which makes his own life such a profound delight. He may accept nothing which others may not have upon precisely the same terms, and the terms are unremitting, passionate effort. The injunction, *Be ye perfect,* was not addressed to any class or any group—it was addressed to mankind. To strive without thought of reward, to love the good, the true, the beautiful for their own sake—the man who does that is an aristocrat. He may be a day-laborer, an artisan, a shop-keeper, a professional man, a writer, a statesman. It is not a matter of birth, or occupation, or education. It is an attitude of mind carried into daily action, that is to say, a religion. Aristocrats form a world-wide party, a party with wide-open doors, but they do not constitute a social class. And if at times they seem to be exclusive, it is simply because they decline to call excellent the things that are not excellent. They demand of others what they demand of themselves, obedience to a difficult and severe discipline.

The second antagonism to the aristocratic spirit is the antagonism of antithesis. Democracy is set over against aristocracy. They are commonly presented as the opposite poles of the social creed. It is quite natural, therefore, that the current over-praise of democracy should involve, by implication, a corresponding dispraise of aristocracy. At the present moment it does not seem to occur to anyone to defend or even indeed to define democracy. Its merits and its nature are alike taken for granted. For many it sums up all that is most desirable in human affairs. When one wishes to praise a man, whether he be king or commoner, landlord or tenant, one has only to call him democratic and the praise is bestowed. When Mr. Wilson coined his now famous phrase, "to make the world safe for democracy," the poor old world went quite wild with enthusiasm. The phrase has been repeated by such multitudes, and so ceaselessly that even its friends have grown a bit sick of it. It is no longer a phrase to conjure with. Yet the poor old world still insists that democracy is what it believes in, and what it wants, and still takes it for granted that democracy needs neither defense nor definition. There is something strangely touching in this simple faith in the saving power of democracy, and something actually pitiful in the current ignorance of what democracy really is. It sounds like a passionate, heart-broken cry to the unknown gods, and the pity of it is that the unknown gods do not answer, and the hungry multitudes show signs of bitterness and disillusionment. All human terms are vague, for they must be defined in terms of other terms. Our most precise language is only approximate. This is one of the many reasons why emotion transcends in validity the nicest academic phrase; why our swift intuition eternally outvalues the most labored statement. We can genuinely share another man's feeling, while at best we can only approximate his language. In the matter of vagueness, the term "democratic" is particularly unfortunate. It has two quite different meanings, one social and one political, and to the masses at least it has a third and confusing connotation as the name of an active political party which may in reality be more or less democratic than its several rivals. To the man in the street, all this is certainly confusing, and when he shouts for democracy and to have the world made safe for democracy, he is, for the most part, simply making a noise.

Bearing in mind the unlimited praise of democracy that one hears on all sides from persons important and unimportant, one would naturally expect it to offer some rule of life which would satisfy a universal aspiration of the human heart. But in reality this very natural expectation is never realized. The result of any effort to get at the inner heart of democracy is amazingly disappointing. One finds indeed that strictly speaking it has no inner heart, no genuine content, no sufficient ground on which to build either creed or ideal. It offers no rule of life that the earnest seeker after righteousness can lay hold of and apply. Whether one use the term democracy in its social or its political sense, it offers no discernible goal. The amazing, disquieting thing which such a penetrating scrutiny reveals is that a democratic society is totally without compass. It may face in any direction whatsoever, toward heaven or toward hell. And a democratic state is equally at the mercy of chance tides. One finds in democracy no goal either expressed or implied. What one does find is simply a method. I am not arguing that this method, when applied to suitable goals, is not extremely valuable, but what I am pointing out is that democracy itself does not supply these goals. It supplies merely a highly generalized method. When, therefore, one offers democracy to a grief-smitten, heart-broken world as a panacea for its mortal pain, and such empty phrases as "to make the world safe for democracy" as the slogan for its effort, one offers a stone instead of life-giving bread.

What then is the method of democracy? I should say in a large way that the method of democracy is the method of the whole. Its major characteristic is that everybody shall be included. This is the wholly admirable element in democracy, and one can hardly over-praise it, for this inclusiveness is at least the beginning of justice. But mischief enters almost as soon as the method begins to be used, for this is commonly done without discrimination, and ends by setting up a quite hopeless confusion of values. Once more I am tempted to quote those wise words of the blessed Bhagavad-Gîtâ, that he who loses discrimination, loses everything. The composite whole for which democracy so resolutely and so loyally stands may be complete and all-inclusive without the false assumption that its component parts are either alike or equal. But democracy makes this false assumption in practically every case, and so vitiates an otherwise admirable method.

It is this curious lack of discrimination which has made the social method of democracy so conspicuous a failure. The method presupposes a similarity of taste and an equality in spiritual and intellectual development not borne out by the most rudimentary social experience. As Miss Etchingham remarks, people are only amused by what amuses them. Happily for the world, they are amused by very different things; and it is one step in toleration when I realize that my neighbor has as valid a right to his amusements as I have to mine, provided of course that neither one of us interferes with the other. The democratic ideal of having everybody join in would make for an excessively dull time, for half of the players would not know what the other half were up to, and the game would fall very flat. When I was a small boy I noticed that certain of my relatives always bored me, but having a well developed family conscience I still felt it my duty at stated intervals to go to see them. One day, however, I had an illuminating thought. It was simply this, that if they bored me so persistently, in all probability I bored them equally or even more, and after that my conscience was quite clear. The same obvious principle applies, I think, to larger groups and more serious affairs.

Even more mischievous than this insistence upon an alikeness which does not exist is the democratic insistence upon an equality which is also unreal. That all men are created free and equal is a sufficiently inaccurate statement of our actual experience of human quality. It requires very slight reflection to see that large numbers of men are distinctly inferior to one's self, and that goodly numbers are superior. But one need not go outside of one's self for the material of such a comparison. One has only to contrast the man of today with the same man, ten, twenty, thirty years ago to be acutely aware of their inequality. And it would be profoundly discouraging if these long, arduous years of effort brought no result. The doctrine of equality calls in question the whole evolutionary process, the Pauline doctrine of growing in grace, the heroic individual struggle for perfection, all the forces that press men on towards righteousness. If after all is done and said, the man who tried is no better than the man who didn't, the whole process of human life is a ghastly tragedy. One would be quite justified in saying that the game is not worth the candle.

That social democracy makes for a sense of brotherhood, and a friendly, human intercourse among all sorts and conditions of men is its one practical glory, but it is not unique in this. Common sense, mere every-day decency, the most elementary good breeding make for an equally gracious intercourse. Certainly no true aristocrat falls short in this respect, for the idealizing of all human relations forms an integral part of his passionate quest of excellence. As a matter of fact, equality among men is mere eighteenth-century theorizing. The observed fact is a profound, inescapable, much-to-be-desired inequality. It is the very condition of progress. It would be a poor world without leadership, and leadership implies a larger vision and a greater power.

In politics, the democratic method is the method of the whole carried to the extreme. Its doctrine of equality, denied social expression by the common sense of all concerned, finds political expression in universal suffrage, and harms even those whom it is supposed to benefit. To give every man and woman a vote, and to declare these votes equally important and significant is both unsound and mischievous. The man who has no property stake in the community, who assumes no duties for the maintenance and defense of the state, who is ignorant of its history and institutions and literature, who does not perhaps even speak its language fluently, may indeed be a man, but he is certainly not a qualified citizen, and has no moral right to a voice in government. Mr. Lincoln, in spite of his greatness, made the signal mistake of giving the vote to the ignorant freedmen of the South. Subsequent statesmen, less great, have made an equal or even larger mistake in extending it to still less desirable aliens. Universal suffrage is a characteristic example of the democratic failure in discrimination. Desiring all men to be equal, the democratic spirit asserts that they *are* equal, and *if* equal, are entitled to identical privileges. Universal suffrage may properly be the goal of every civilized and progressive state, but it is a political and social crime to bestow the suffrage before it is honestly won. An electorate not properly qualified is an ever-present public danger. An ignorant democracy soon ceases to be a democracy, soon finds it inconvenient to represent and include the whole, and becomes that obnoxious form of tyranny, a dictatorship of the proletariat.

But passing over these grave objections to the democratic insistence upon equality, and accepting for the moment the accomplished fact of universal suffrage, we moderns stand face to face with a new danger, or perhaps an old danger now immensely augmented, which is a direct and inevitable outcome of the method of the whole when carried politically to the extreme. I mean the substitution of impulsive mob rule for a more judicial and temperate representative government. It is entirely possible, even in the complete democracy resulting from an unrestrained suffrage to have such a government, but it presupposes an intelligent electorate which recognizes that government is both an art and a science, and requires for its proper administration a preparation quite as thorough and complete as is required by law or medicine or theology. In this view of things, government, to be successful, requires expert service, is overwhelmingly a matter for experts, and may not be left to the casual whims of the man in the street. But the democratic doctrine of equality, with its method of the whole, has recently shown a disposition, in the referendum and recall, and still more radical measures of popular appeal, to withdraw the government function from the hands of its own chosen representatives and experts, and to place it, in spite of its delicacy and complexity, directly in the hands of the mob. It is not a method which promises wise counsels. This same disposition to ignore the chosen representatives of government, and to appeal over their heads directly to the people is discernible in certain popular leaders in both America and England. It is a tendency much to be regretted, and is largely responsible for the growing disregard of law and order, and the too great readiness of both individuals and groups to take the law into their own hands.

I have spoken at such length about democracy because I have wanted to make it abundantly clear that there is no possible antithesis between aristocracy and democracy since they do not belong in the same category. Aristocracy is a flaming ideal, a defensible goal, a devout rule of life; while democracy has nothing to offer in the way of ends, and in the way of means it offers a method which, in spite of a certain bigness, is quite as likely to land one in a morass as on the mountain.

The third antagonism to the aristocratic spirit is the least creditable of all since it shows humanity at something like its worst. It is the antagonism of resentment. There are few indeed who have not noticed this resentment—the sneering, ill-tempered resentment which a self-conscious, uncomfortable inferiority feels in the presence of every superiority. Many men and women, in all walks of life, have the intelligence to recognize

the beauty of righteousness, but have not the character
to make that beauty their own. They are the people
"who see the right and yet the wrong pursue." In the
last analysis, of course, they do not really see the right
—they only half see it—for no mortal, I honestly believe, can have the full vision of righteousness and not
ever afterwards be constrained to follow it. He may
go haltingly; he may stumble and fall; he may be blinded
and seduced by false lights and siren voices, but always
in his heart of hearts, the great loyalty persists, and
here or elsewhere, he will arrive. The aristocrat is not
disposed of by calling him, however derisively, a very
superior person, for that is precisely what he sets out
to be, under the belief that a world of very superior persons is much more worth while than a world of rowdies
and toughs. If he is sometimes irritating, it must be
remembered that any self-complacency represents a
failure to carry out his own ideal, and is not a part of
the ideal itself. No one is more conscious of failure
than the aristocrat himself—he is his own most severe
critic—but he has the courage to risk this failure, for
he knows that we only learn to walk by falling down.
And often he is constrained to say with Rabbi Ben Ezra,
"What I would be, and am not, comforts me."

The strength of this third antagonism must not be
underestimated. Like the conscience, the aristocratic
spirit calls much in question, and does it so silently,
so persistently, so accusingly that meaner spirits chafe
under the condemnation, and feel a resentment which
rapidly mounts to the pitch of antagonism. The defen-
sive attitude which we all put up when we are tempted
to do a second-rate thing and to brave it out is an all
too common illustration. *Qui s'excuse s'accuse.*

As I said in the beginning, the aristocratic spirit is
the one thing in these very troubled times which would

bring tranquillity and an almost passionate return to the beautiful arts of peace. It would do this great thing because it is not an empty phrase, but a flaming ideal, a devout rule of life, a religion, and as such is the inevitable producer of results. The aristocrat is a devotee, a seeker after perfection, a knight-errant bent upon a tireless quest. Let us inquire, then, very briefly, how the aristocratic spirit meets some of the hot questions of the hour. We shall find that contrary to popular impression this spirit stands aloof from no human issue, but concerns itself with all, from the smallest to the greatest. On none of these issues does it speak with hesitation or equivocation. There is no empty beating of the air, no phrase making. Its verdicts are simple, direct, understandable; and each verdict may be turned at once into practical action.

Let us begin with the most profound of all human concerns, with religion. The status of religion at the present moment is in dispute. The tragic bereavement brought about by the War, the untimely death of such a goodly number of young men, has turned the attention of millions of persons to spiritual matters and to the consolations offered by religion. Rachel, mourning for her children, yearns to be comforted, and spiritualism has come into its own. Whether this is a passing phase, or the herald of a more genuine religious revival, remains to be seen. But meanwhile it is regrettably true that other multitudes have openly thrown aside the decencies imposed by religion, and that wave after wave of crime sweeps over communities once orderly and law-abiding. One could easily believe, after reading the morning's paper, that the world stands face to face with a recurrent Dark Age brought about, as always, by our many sins. In the midst of all this chaos, on the one side excessively personal demands and on the other contemptuous indifference and denial, the aristocratic spirit stands serene and, in a very deep sense, untroubled. It is itself a religion, but while it joins with all those forms of religion which seek the perfect way, it differs from many of them in seeking it with utter disinterestedness. The aristocrat is content to worship and adore, asking nothing of the gods that they have not already given him in the resplendent moral fabric of the world. He is not concerned with personal salvation any more than he is concerned with the impression which he makes upon other persons. He does not keep one eye upon the goods any more than he does upon his fellows. His one passion is the artist's passion for perfection. So far as his prayer is articulate, he prays with Plato: "O Jove, give us that which is good for us, whether we pray for it or not; and withhold that which is evil, even though we pray for it." The aristocrat has, of course, nothing in common with those commercial schemes of salvation which offer large rewards for the exercise of small virtues. Righteousness is to him an end in itself, its own reward. Like any faithful knight of old, his whole heart is filled with the glorious vision which represents his chosen service. It is so great a thing to stand face to face with God, to live constantly day by day, in the divine presence, that one can be occupied with no thought of the self.

Next in importance to religion, to one's general attitude towards life, stands a man's family. The domestic relations are not only the most beautiful of our human relations, but they are also the most delicate. To be a member of a family group is an immense privilege and it should be handled as an integral part of a man's religion. But it is also a severe test of his breeding and on all sides one sees innumerable shipwrecks, shipwrecks brought about for the most part by the vulgar pressing of personal demands. In the face of these daily assaults, the aristocratic spirit may waver and grow faint, but so long as it persists, no permanent disaster is possible. An aristocrat loves his wife, not for the comfort and pleasure she can give him, but for the glory of her perfection as a woman and a wife and a mother. There is about his love a large element of worship, and worship is always unselfish. And the aristocrat loves his children, not because they add to the sense of reality and the importance of his own life, but for the finer and less personal reason that wholesome, well-bred children are adorable for their own sakes, and worthy of all the love the grown-up world can give them. And the aristocrat loves his other relatives and his neighbors and associates, not for the service they can render him, but simply for their own manifold excellence. In these delicate human relations, as in his more formal religion, he has no thought of reward. But quite inevitably the reward is his. It is the large reward of all disinterestedness—when one asks nothing, one receives everything.

In the domain of politics, the aristocratic spirit occupies a position which is equally characteristic. It is opposed to all forms of mob rule, under whatever name they may be put forward, and to that application of the democratic method of the whole which assumes that every man is qualified to be a legislator, and to solve, off-hand, the delicate and intricate problems of government. On the contrary, the aristocrat is a believer in trained and competent experts, that is to say, in a carefully chosen representative government. He believes in a restricted suffrage, a suffrage limited to qualified voters, to men and women who can pass the test of intelligent and participating citizenship. He does not for one moment believe that every chance adventurer who finds himself in our midst, and who goes through certain slender formalities, or who comes here perhaps with the express purpose of stirring up trouble, should have a hand in our American political life. It is not enough that a man has reached twenty-one years; he must have reached a number of other attributes as well before he may properly be classified as a qualified voter. America, in the view of the aristocrat, belongs to Americans, to the men and women who have made the country what it is, and who desire passionately to make it more admirable, not less admirable. It seems to him a grave political and social crime to hand over such a heritage to any rabble to desecrate and disintegrate, whether it be done in the name of democracy or socialism or communism or syndicalism or organized labor. The aristocrat, in a word, believes in nationalism as against internationalism, in a representative government conducted by the best experts, as against a mob rule conducted, on principle, by the incompetent. As a lover of excellence, he wishes to be represented by men wiser than himself, better trained in law and politics and history, and gifted by Nature with the quality of leadership. It is only through such men that excellence in government can be attained. One does not wish to have one's portrait painted by a sign-painter, or one's life put in danger by a quack, or one's business affairs mismanaged by an ignoramus. I do not see why one should be less wise in one's choice of the instruments of government. The aristocratic scheme, let me repeat, is not, as commonly stated, a government of the many by the few—that is an autocracy—but it is a government of all by representative experts chosen by a qualified electorate. The aristocrat firmly believes that the grave affairs of life should be entrusted to trained experts, and not to novices and experimenters. And government, as the Great War has once more shown, is one of the very gravest of all human affairs.

In education and in industry, the aristocratic spirit has an immense theatre for its application. One might say in a broad way that the quest of excellence is the goal of both the school and the factory. But unfortunately one may not add, save in exceptional cases, that the quest is disinterested. It is the absence of disinterestedness which in both cases vitiates the goal and ends by making it more specious than real. When excellence is sought, not for its own sake, but for the sake of the loaves and fishes, it soon ceases to be sought at all, and a cheaper substitute takes its place, —the appearance of excellence. This is true, even in education. In few secondary schools is knowledge sought for its own fair sake, but in nearly every case from some ulterior motive. Boys go to school for the sports, for the companionship, to make a better living, to get into college. These are worthy ends,—the fault lies wholly in the emphasis. They should be taken casually and ought not to obscure the major end of education,—the unfolding and perfecting of the human spirit. And among collegians, themselves, an impartial observer finds little culture and much insincerity. Even in education, the democratic fallacy of alikeness and equality finds frequent and vociferous expression. But the aristocratic spirit seeks excellence in variety. Instead of asking all children to attend the same school and engage in the same studies, it would encourage a wholesome competition among schools, and would help each child to select the best suited to its own individual needs. In spite of all that has been written about sex, its supreme significance has not, I think, been sufficiently remarked and sufficiently acted upon. And that significance is simply this, that Nature, in providing that each child must have two parents, a father and a mother, bestowed two distinct lines of heredity, and with them the possibility of beneficent variation, and the appearance of a new and more desirable type. Yet education, in spite of this obvious and vital lesson, is forever seeking uniformity and all the drab monotony of democratic sameness. The aristocratic spirit resists this tendency to the death, and seeks, instead, a multiform and varied excellence. The aristocratic world is not one of dead levels, but a world of varied interests and constant promise and unfaltering progress. It is, in a word, the world of evolution.

In his industrial life, the aristocrat may occupy any post from the very lowest to the very highest. But whatever the job, he must do it well and he must love it for its own sake. He may not, then, engage in any work where the conditions make excellence impossible, nor may he take part in meaningless toil. It will be easy to define his position towards organized labor and syndicalism and all similar movements that are ready to do evil in order that good may come of it. These modern forms of Jesuit teaching, that the end justifies the means, are not in harmony with the aristocratic spirit,—the whole event must be excellent, the means, as well as the end. And equally at variance with that spirit is the tendency of organized labor to lessen individual responsibility and initiative, to kill the passionate love of excellence, and to substitute for it the smaller efficiency and lower standards of the average worker. Being disinterested and having something excellent to offer, the aristocratic worker stands on his own feet and does not seek to be bolstered up by union or organization. He realizes that salvation is an individual adventure and not a mass movement. In industry as in government, he asks the largest possible individual freedom and the least amount of prescription. He repudiates with vigor all class consciousness, all class distinctions, all class warfare, as wholly inconsistent with that common effort towards righteousness which he conceives all high-minded persons to have entered upon. Perhaps I sum it all up in saying that the aristocratic worker is an uncompromising individualist, and so opposes the major currents of the hour. It is only in the disinterested quest of excellence that anything notable can be accomplished in industry. The case is precisely similar to the case of religion, of family life, of politics, of education, of art. It is not enough to go through the motions,—the work in hand must engage the individual spirit or it cannot possibly be well done. The fatal defect in the present excessive desire to organize the world is that it does not appeal to this love of excellence, but to a narrow and disabling self-interest. It may seem over-optimistic, but the aristocrat, both from his own personal experience, his own experiments in selfishness, and from the tragic lessons of the Great War, is bound to believe that this specialized self-interest always leads to failure, while disinterestedness is the essential condition of success.

One cannot in a series of brief paragraphs say anything much worth saying upon such tremendous themes as religion, family life, politics, education, industry, but what I have tried to indicate is that the aristocratic spirit, being an habitual attitude of mind, a religion, is competent to meet and solve these typical problems of our modern, complicated daily life, and to do it without hesitation or equivocation. The aristocrat sees life in a definite, clear-cut way; he knows what to do both in the ordinary day's work and in the multiform emergencies of life, and as he is true to form, he does it simply, honestly and well. The immense practical value of such an inclusive formula is that it leads to prompt decision and equally prompt action. It does away with all evasion and subterfuge. When a man speaks the truth, it is easy to speak; when he intends to do right, it is easy to act. *Noblesse oblige.*

I am presenting, I know, an unpopular view of life, since it recognizes human inequality, and is in effect a doctrine of perfection. It will meet with little sympathy from those extreme modernists who scorn our feeble individual effort towards righteousness, and who profess to find in the masses, virtues and qualities not discoverable in the component units. But it is a view which stands the test of application and has stood it for centuries. The aristocratic spirit has led to the achievement of worthy tasks, and consequently to individual satisfaction and happiness. The aristocrat is one of the few men who can stand alone. He does not have to wait for others to act, or for the coming of favorable circumstance. His own task is always at hand, his own quest is always on. It may be tragic, but it is nevertheless true that in the serious affairs of life, a man must be able, thus resolutely, to stand alone, as in the final great adventure of death. Destiny brings curious gifts, but in the face of the most difficult of them, the true aristocrat is unafraid and victorious.

QUALITY

BY JOHN GALSWORTHY

I KNEW him from the days of my extreme youth, because he made my father's boots; inhabiting with his elder brother two little shops let into one, in a small by-street—now no more, but then most fashionably placed in the West End.

That tenement had a certain quiet distinction; there was no sign upon its face that he made for any of the Royal Family—merely his own German name of Gessler Brothers; and in the window a few pairs of boots. I remember that it always troubled me to account for those unvarying boots in the window, for he made only what was ordered, reaching nothing down, and it seemed so inconceivable that what he made could ever have failed to fit. Had he bought them to put there? That, too, seemed inconceivable. He would never have tolerated in his house leather on which he had not worked himself. Besides, they were too beautiful— the pair of pumps, so inexpressibly slim, the patent leathers with cloth tops, making water come into one's mouth, the tall brown riding boots with marvellous sooty glow, as if, though new, they had been worn a hundred years. Those pairs could only have been made by one who saw before him the Soul of Boot—so truly were they prototypes incarnating the very spirit of all foot-gear. These thoughts, of course, came to me later, though even when I was promoted to him, at the age of perhaps fourteen, some inkling haunted me of the dignity of himself and brother. For to make boots—such boots as he made—seemed to me then, and still seems to me, mysterious and wonderful.

I remember well my shy remark, one day, while stretching out to him my youthful foot:

"Isn't it awfully hard to do, Mr. Gessler?"

And his answer, given with a sudden smile from out of the sardonic redness of his beard: "Id is an Ardt!"

Himself, he was a little as if made from leather, with his yellow crinkly face, and crinkly reddish hair and beard, and neat folds slanting down his cheeks to the corners of his mouth, and his guttural and one-toned voice; for leather is a sardonic substance, and stiff and slow of purpose. And that was the character of his face, save that his eyes, which were grey-blue, had in them the simple gravity of one secretly possessed by the Ideal. His elder brother was so very like him—though watery, paler in every way, with a great industry—that sometimes in early days I was not quite sure of him until the interview was over. Then I knew that it was he, if the words, "I will ask my brudder," had not been spoken; and that, if they had, it was his elder brother.

When one grew old and wild and ran up bills, one somehow never ran them up with Gessler Brothers. It would not have seemed becoming to go in there and stretch out one's foot to that blue iron-spectacled glance, owing him for more than—say—two pairs, just the comfortable reassurance that one was still his client.

For it was not possible to go to him very often—his boots lasted terribly, having something beyond the temporary—some, as it were, essence of boot stitched into them.

One went in, not as into most shops, in the mood of: "Please serve me, and let me go!" but restfully, as one enters a church; and, sitting on the single wooden chair, waited—for there was never anybody there. Soon, over the top edge of that sort of well—rather dark, and smelling soothingly of leather—which formed the shop, there would be seen his face, or that of his elder brother, peering down. A guttural sound, and the tip-tap of bast slippers beating the narrow wooden stairs, and he would stand before one without coat, a little bent, in leather apron, with sleeves turned back, blinking—as if awakened from some dream of boots, or like an owl surprised in daylight and annoyed at this interruption.

And I would say: "How do you do, Mr. Gessler? Could you make me a pair of Russia leather boots?"

Without a word he would leave me, retiring whence he came, or into the other portion of the shop, and I could continue to rest in the wooden chair, inhaling the incense of his trade. Soon he would come back, holding in his thin, veined hand a piece of gold-brown leather. With eyes fixed on it, he would remark: "What a beautiful biece!" When I, too, had admired it, he would speak again. "When do you wand dem?" And I would answer: "Oh! As soon as you conveniently can." And he would say: "To-morrow fordnighd?" Or if he were his elder brother: "I will ask my brudder!"

Then I would murmur: "Thank you! Good-morning, Mr. Gessler." "Goot-morning!" he would reply, still looking at the leather in his hand. And as I moved to the door, I would hear the tip-tap of his bast slippers restoring him, up the stairs, to his dream of boots. But if it were some new kind of foot-gear that he had not yet made me, then indeed he would observe ceremony—divesting me of my boot and holding it long in his hand, looking at it with eyes at once critical and loving, as if recalling the glow with which he had created it, and rebuking the way in which one had disorganized this masterpiece. Then, placing my foot on a piece of paper, he would two or three times tickle the outer edges with a pencil and pass his nervous fingers over my toes, feeling himself into the heart of my requirements.

I cannot forget that day on which I had occasion to say to him: "Mr. Gessler, that last pair of town walking-boots creaked, you know."

He looked at me for a time without replying, as if expecting me to withdraw or qualify the statement, then said:

"Id shouldn'd 'ave greaked."

"It did, I'm afraid."

"You goddem wed before dey found demselves?"

"I don't think so."

At that he lowered his eyes, as if hunting for memory of those boots, and I felt sorry I had mentioned this grave thing.

"Zend dem back!" he said; "I will look at dem."

A feeling of compassion for my creaking boots surged up in me, so well could I imagine the sorrowful long curiosity of regard which he would bend on them.

"Zome boods," he said slowly, "are bad from birdt. If I can do noding wid dem, I dake dem off your bill."

Once (once only) I went absent-mindedly into his shop in a pair of boots bought in an emergency at some large firm's. He took my order without showing me any leather, and I could feel his eyes penetrating the inferior integument of my foot. At last he said:

"Dose are nod my boods."

The tone was not one of anger, nor of sorrow, not even of contempt, but there was in it something quiet that froze the blood. He put his hand down and pressed a finger on the place where the left boot, endeavouring to be fashionable, was not quite comfortable.

"Id 'urds you dere," he said. "Dose big virms 'ave no self-respect. Drash!" And then, as if something had given away within him, he spoke long and bitterly. It was the only time I ever heard him discuss the conditions and hardships of his trade.

"Dey get id all," he said, "dey get id by adverdisement, nod by work. Dey dake it away from us, who lofe our boods. Id gomes to this—bresently I haf no work. Every year id gets less—you will see." And looking at his lined face I saw things I had never noticed before, bitter things and bitter struggle—and what a lot of grey hairs there seemed suddenly in his red beard!

As best I could, I explained the circumstances of the purchase of those ill-omened boots. But his face and voice made so deep impression that during the next few minutes I ordered many pairs. Nemesis fell! They lasted more terribly than ever. And I was not able conscientiously to go to him for nearly two years.

When at last I went I was surprised to find that outside one of the two little windows of his shop another name was painted, also that of a bootmaker—making, of course, for the Royal Family. The old familiar boots, no longer in dignified isolation, were huddled in the single window. Inside, the now contracted well of the one little shop was more scented and darker than ever. And it was longer than usual, too, before a face peered down, and the tip-tap of the bast slippers began. At last he stood before me, and, gazing through those rusty iron spectacles, said:

"Mr. ——, isn'd it?"

"Ah! Mr. Gessler," I stammered, "but your boots are really *too* good, you know! See, these are quite decent still!" And I stretched out to him my foot. He looked at it.

"Yes," he said, "beople do nod wand good boods, id seems."

To get away from his reproachful eyes and voice I hastily remarked: "What have you done to your shop?"

He answered quietly: "Id was too exbensif. Do you wand some boods?"

I ordered three pairs, though I had only wanted two, and quickly left. I had, I do not know quite what feeling of being part, in his mind, of a conspiracy against him; or not perhaps so much against him as against his idea of boot. One does not, I suppose, care to feel like that; for it was again many months before my next visit to his shop, paid, I remember, with the feeling: "Oh! well, I can't leave the old boy—so here goes! Perhaps it'll be his elder brother!"

For his elder brother, I knew, had not character enough to reproach me, even dumbly.

And, to my relief, in the shop there did appear to be his elder brother, handling a piece of leather.

"Well, Mr. Gessler," I said, "how are you?"

He came close, and peered at me.

"I am breddy well," he said slowly, "but my elder brudder is dead."

And I saw that it was indeed himself—but how aged and wan! And never before had I heard him mention his brother. Much shocked, I murmured: "Oh! I am sorry!"

"Yes," he answered, "he was a good man, he made a good bood; but he is dead." And he touched the top of his head, where the hair had suddenly gone as thin as it had been on that of his poor brother, to indicate I suppose, the cause of death. "He could nod ge

over losing de oder shop. Do you wand any boods?"
And he held up the leather in his hand: "Id's a beau-
diful biece."

I ordered several pairs. It was very long before
they came—but they were better than ever. One simply could not wear them out. And soon after that I
went abroad.

It was over a year before I was again in London.
And the first shop I went to was my old friend's. I
had left a man of sixty, I came back to one of seventy-
five, pinched and worn and tremulous, who genuinely,
this time, did not at first know me.

"Oh! Mr. Gessler," I said, sick at heart; "how
splendid your boots are! See, I've been wearing this
pair nearly all the time I've been abroad; and they're
not half worn out, are they?"

He looked long at my boots—a pair of Russia
leather, and his face seemed to regain steadiness. Putting his hand on my instep, he said:

"Do dey vid you here? I 'ad drouble wid dat bair,
I remember."

I assured him that they had fitted beautifully.

"Do you wand any boods?" he said. "I can make
dem quickly; id is a slack dime."

I answered: "Please, please! I want boots all
round—every kind!"

"I will make a vresh model. Your food must be
bigger." And with utter slowness, he traced round my
foot, and felt my toes, only once looking up to say:

"Did I dell you my brudder was dead?"

To watch him was painful, so feeble had he grown;
I was glad to get away.

I had given those boots up, when one evening they
came. Opening the parcel, I set the four pairs out
in a row. Then one by one I tried them on. There was

no doubt about it. In shape and fit, in finish and quality of leather, they were the best he had ever made me. And in the mouth of one of the Town walking-boots I found his bill. The amount was the same as usual, but it gave me quite a shock. He had never before sent it in till quarter day. I flew down-stairs, and wrote a cheque, and posted it at once with my own hand.

A week later, passing the little street, I thought I would go in and tell him how splendidly the new boots fitted. But when I came to where his shop had been, his name was gone. Still there, in the window, were the slim pumps, the patent leathers with cloth tops, the sooty riding boots.

I went in, very much disturbed. In the two little shops—again made into one—was a young man with an English face.

"Mr. Gessler in?" I said.

He gave me a strange, ingratiating look.

"No, sir," he said, "no. But we can attend to anything with pleasure. We've taken the shop over. You've seen our name, no doubt, next door. We make for some very good people."

"Yes, yes," I said; "but Mr. Gessler?"

"Oh!" he answered; "dead."

"Dead! But I only received these boots from him last Wednesday week."

"Ah!" he said; "a shockin' go. Poor old man starved 'imself."

"Good God!"

"Slow starvation, the doctor called it! You see he went to work in such a way! Would keep the shop on; wouldn't have a soul touch his boots except himself. When he got an order, it took him such a time. People won't wait. He lost everybody. And there he'd sit, goin' on and on—I will say that for him—not a man in London made a better boot! But look at the competition! He never advertised! Would 'ave the best leather, too, and do it all 'imself. Well, there it is. What could you expect with his ideas?"

"But starvation——!"

"That may be a bit flowery, as the sayin' is—but I know myself he was sittin' over his boots day and night, to the very last. You see I used to watch him. Never gave 'imself time to eat; never had a penny in the house. All went in rent and leather. How he lived so long I don't know. He regular let his fire go out. He was a character. But he made good boots."

"Yes," I said, "he made good boots."

And I turned and went out quickly, for I did not want that youth to know that I could hardly see.

THE WAY OF IMPERFECTION

BY FRANCIS THOMPSON

OVID, with the possible exception of Catullus, is the most modern-minded of Latin poets. It is therefore with delight that we first encounter his dictum, so essentially modern, so opposed to the aesthetic feeling of the ancient world, *decentiorem esse faciem in qua aliquis naevus esset*.* It was a dictum borne out by his own practice, a practice at heart essentially romantic rather than classic; and there can therefore be little wonder that the saying was scouted by his contemporaries as an eccentricity of genius. The dominant cult of classicism was the worship of perfection, and the Goth was its iconoclast. Then at length literature reposed in the beneficent and quickening shadow of imperfection, which gave us for consummate product Shakespeare, in whom greatness and imperfection reached their heights. Since him, however, there has been a gradual decline from imperfection. Milton, at his most typical, was far too perfect; Pope was ruined by his quest for the quality; and if Dryden partially escaped, it was because of the rich faultiness with which Nature had endowed him. The stand made by the poets of the early part of the nineteenth century was only temporarily successful; and now (1889), we suppose, no thoughtful person can contemplate without alarm the hold which the renascent principle has gained over the contemporary mind. Unless some voice be

* That a face is better looking for having some kind of imperfection.

raised in timely protest, we feel that English art (in its widest sense) must soon dwindle to the extinction of unendurable excellence.

Over the whole contemporary mind is the trail of this serpent perfection. It even affects the realm of colour, where it begets cloying, enervating harmonies, destitute of those stimulating contrasts by which the great colourists threw into relief the general agreement of their hues. It leads in poetry to the love of minia-ture finish, and that in turn (because minute finish is most completely attainable in short poems) leads to the tyranny of sonnet, ballad, rondeau, triolet, and their kind. The principle leads again to aestheticism; which is simply the aspiration for a hot-house seclusion of beauty in a world which Nature has tempered by brac-ing gusts of ugliness.

The most nobly conceived character, in assuming vraisemblance, takes up a certain quantity of imperfec-tion; it is its water of crystallization: expel this, and far from securing, as the artist fondly deems, a more perfect crystal, the character falls to powder. We by no means desire those improbable incongruities which, frequent enough in actual life, should in art be confined to comedy. But even incongruities may find their place in serious art, if they be artistic incongrui-ties, not too glaring or suggestive of unlikelihood; in-congruities which are felt by the reader to have a whimsical hidden keeping with the congruities of the character, which enhance the consent of the general qualities by an artistically modulated dissent; which just lend, and no more than lend, the ratifying seal of Nature to the dominating regularities of character-ization.

From the neglect of all this have come the hero and heroine; and among all prevalent types of heroine, the worst is one apparently founded on Pope's famous dictum

Most women have no characters at all—

a dictum which we should denounce with scorn, if so acute an observer as De Quincey did not stagger us by defending it. He defends it to attack Pope. Pope (says De Quincey) did not see that what he advances as a reproach against women constitutes the very beauty of them. It is the absence of any definite character which enables their character to be moulded by others: and it is this soft plasticity which renders them such charming companions as wives. We should be inclined to say that the feminine characteristic which De Quincey considered plasticity was rather elasticity. Now the most elastic substance in Nature is probably ivory. What are the odds, you subtle, paradoxical, delightful ghost of delicate thought, what are the odds on your moulding a billiard ball?

Does anyone believe in Patient Grizzel? Still more, does anyone believe in the Nut-brown Maid? Yet their descendants infest literature, from Spenser to Dickens and Tennyson, from Una to Enid; made tolerable in the poem only by their ideal surroundings. The dream of "a perfect woman nobly planned" underlies the thing; albeit Wordsworth goes on to show that his "perfect woman" had her little failings. Shakespeare was not afraid to touch with such failings his finest heroines; he knew that these defects serve only to enhance the large nobilities of character, as the tender imperfections and wayward wilfulnesses of individual rose-petals enhance the prevalent symmetry of the rose. His most consummate woman, Imogen, possesses her little naturalizing traits. Take the situation where she is confronted with her husband's order for her murder.

What the Patient Grizzel heroine would have done we all know. She would have behaved with unimpeachable resignation, and prepared for death with a pathos ordered according to the best canons of art. What does this glorious Imogen do? Why (and we publicly thank Heaven for it) after the first paroxysm of weeping, which makes the blank verse sob, she bursts into a fit of thoroughly feminine and altogether charming jealousy. A perfect woman, indeed, but she is imperfect! Imogen, however, it may be urged is not a Patient Grizzel. Take, then, Desdemona, who is. That is to say, Desdemona represents the type in nature which Patient Grizzel misrepresents. Mark now the difference in treatment. Shakespeare knew that these gentle, affectionate, yielding, all-submissive and all-suffering, dispositions are founded on weakness and accordingly he gave Desdemona the defects of her qualities. He would have no perfection in his characters. Rather than face the anger of the man whom she so passionately loves, Desdemona will lie—a slight lie, but one to which the ideal distortion of her would never be allowed to yield. Yet the weakness but makes Shakespeare's lady more credible, more piteous, perhaps even more lovable.

From the later developments of contemporary fiction the faultless hero and heroine have, we admit, relievingly disappeared. So much good has been wrought by the craze for "human documents." But alas! the disease expelled, who will expel the medicine? And the hydra perfection merely shoots up a new head. It is now a desire for the perfect reproduction of Nature, uninterfered with by this writer's ideals or sympathies; so that we have novelists who stand coldly aloof from their characters, and exhibit them with passionless countenance. We all admire the representations which result: "How beautifully drawn! how exactly like Nature!" Yes, beautifully drawn, but they do not live. They resemble the mask in Phaedrus—a cunning semblance, *at animam non habet*. This attitude of the novelist is fatal to artistic illusion: his personages do not move us because they do not move him. Partridge believed in the ghost because "the little man on the stage was more frightened than I", and in novel reading we are all Partridges, we only believe in the novelist's creations when he shows us that he believes in them himself. Finally, this pestilence attacks in literature the form no less than the essence, the integuments even more than the vitals. Hence arises the dominant belief that mannerism is vicious; and accordingly critics have erected the ideal of a style stripped of everything special or peculiar, a style which should be to thought what light is to the sun. Now this pure white light of style is as impossible as undesirable; it must be splintered into colour by the refracting media of the individual mind, and humanity will always prefer the colour. Theoretically we ought to have no mannerisms, practically we cannot help having them, and without them style would be flavourless—"faultily faultless, icily regular, splendidly null." Men will not drink distilled water, it is entirely pure and entirely insipid. The object of writing is to communicate individuality, the object of style adequately to embody that individuality, and since in every individuality worth anything there are characteristic peculiarities, these must needs be reproduced in the embodiment. So reproduced we call them mannerisms. They correspond to those little unconscious tricks of voice, manner, gesture, in a friend which are to us the friend himself, and which we would not forgo. It is affected to imitate another's tricks of demeanour: similarly, it is affected to imitate another's mannerisms. We should avoid as far as possible in conversation passing conventionalities of speech, because they are brainless; similarly, we should avoid as far as possible in writing the mannerisms of our age, because they corrupt originality. But in essence, mannerisms —individual mannerisms—are a season of style, and happily unavoidable. It is, for instance, stated in the Encyclopaedia Britannica that De Quincey is not a manneristic writer; and, so put, the assertion has much truth. Yet he is full of mannerisms, mannerisms which every student lovingly knows, and without which the essayist would not be our very own De Quincey.

We say, therefore: Guard against this seductive principle of perfection. Order yourselves to a wise conformity with that Nature who cannot for the life of her create a brain without making one half of it weaker than the other half, or even a fool without a flaw in his folly; who cannot set a nose straight on a man's face, and whose geometrical drawing would be tittered at by half the pupils of South Kensington. Consider who is the standing modern oracle of perfection, and what results from his interpretation of it. "Trifles make perfection, and perfection is no trifle." No; it is half a pound of muscle to the square inch—and that is no trifle. One satisfactory reflection we have in concluding. Wherever else the reader may be grieved by perfection, this article, at least, is sacred from the accursed thing.

Now, how much of all this do we mean? Hearken, O reader, to an apologue.

Once on a time there was a hypochondriac who— though his digestion was excellent—believed that his delicate system required a most winnowed choice of viands. His physician, in order to humour him, prescribed a light and carefully varied diet. But the hypochondriac was not satisfied.

"I want to know, Doctor," he said, "how much of this food really contributes to the building up of my system, and how much is waste material."

"That," observed the sage physician, "I cannot possibly tell you without recondite analysis and nice calculation."

"Then," said the hypochondriac, in a rage, "I will not eat your food. You are an impostor, Sir, and a charlatan, and I believe now your friends who told me that you were a homœopath in disguise."

"My dear Sir," replied the unmoved physician, "if you will eat nothing but what is entire nutriment, you will soon need to consult, not a doctor, but a chameleon. To what purpose are digestive organs, unless to secrete what is nutritious, and excrete what is innutritious!"

And the moral is—no, the reader shall have a pleasure denied to him in his outraged childhood. He that hath understanding, let him understand.

IMPATIENT "CULTURE" AND THE LITERAL MIND

BY FRANK MOORE COLBY

I HAVE been reading a gloomy article in the *Didactic Monthly* by a professor of the social sciences, who is sorry he studied Greek. He loves it, he says, but doubts its "cultural value" or effectiveness in the "battle of life."

"Would I trade my Greek," he exclaims, "considered both culturally and practically, for biology, for zoology, or for geology, let alone a combination (which would be a fairer equivalent) of these or similar other studies? A positive affirmative leaps to the lips."

He finds that his teacher fooled him about the classics, for looking back from his middle age he perceives that Cicero was conceited and Thucydides left clauses hanging in the air in a way that no magazine editor would now tolerate. The teacher never told him this, but now as a "reflective graduate he sees it and feels that he has been duped."

Of course, Greek should be better taught. Excellent Greek scholars, like eminent economists and sociologists, often seem strangely ill-nourished by what they feed on. That, indeed, is a frequent accident in the teaching profession—the teacher himself will often seem much damaged by his subject, no matter what the subject is. Educational writers are always blaming subjects instead of men, looking for some galvanic theme or method which when applied by a man without any gift for teaching to a mind without any capacity for learning will somehow produce intellectual results. It is a purely personal question and has nothing to do with Greek. It is odd that anyone should believe at this late date that any conceivable combination of geology, zoology, biology will save a man from these disasters. They happen daily at all points of the educational compass, in subjects the most modern and "culturally" vivacious, genuine "battle-of-life" subjects—pedagogy, potato philosophies, courses in sanitary plumbing, slum seminars in sociology.

"Gentlemen," says a voice from the past, "to give the full force of the Greek particles, which are really very important—very important—the passage should be rendered thus: 'Immediately as the troops advanced, the sun also was setting.'" It happens to come from the Greek class-room, but there are echoes from the other class-rooms quite as absurd, and, now that I think of it, this dried-up and belated old Grecian, long since dead, this eager and enthusiastic old gentleman whose spectacles leaped from his nose whenever he smelled a second aorist, was somehow more humane and less dispiriting, had made his learning more his own, liked it better, had better manners in imparting it, than the most modern and practical and pedagogically indisputable of them all. Greek did not give him these qualities; nor could the social sciences have taken them away. It merely happened that he was the kind of man in whom dead thoughts, whether in a Greek grammar or a government report, seem to come to life again; whereas there is no subject however "vital" that another sort of person cannot easily put to death. Was there ever a "burning" question that could not be immediately extinguished by almost any one at an alumni dinner or in a magazine?

To be sure the present state of my wits is far from

satisfactory and there may have been some magical combination, say, of botany, mechanical drawing, and palæontology, some grouping of studies, so divinely planned, so "culturally" potent, that taken instead of Greek would have raised in me an intellect of unusual size and agility, a comfort to myself, an object of astonishment to visitors, but then again, who knows? Perhaps there was no charm in any part of the curriculum that could have wrought it; perhaps nature had something to say about it. In any event, is it right that a man on considering his head in the forties should blame Greek and an old gentleman twenty years ago for the state of it—write to the *Didactic Monthly* about it, complain that it would have been a better head if other people had not put the wrong things in it or packed it so carelessly that some of the things slipped out, or that it went by mistake to a Greek professor when it should have gone to some geologist? Maybe the face of Heaven was set against that head from the start. Certainly it makes a difference to whom it belongs.

It is one of the pleasures of growing old and getting farther away from educators that we care more for the kind of head and less for the kind of facts that rain upon it, distrust all pedantic educational higgling over the "cultural" value of this or that, doubt the divine efficacy of any subject as a cure for the personal vacuities, doubt, when learned Greek meets scientific Trojan, which of the twain would be the worse to live with. And if a man has to go to middle age to find out that Cicero was somewhat conceited, Isocrates a trifle pompous, Quintilian rather inclined to platitude, it may have been merely a private affair, a secret between him and nature, involving no teacher or system whatever. For certain incipient activities may be expected even of the young. Was the young man waiting for artificial respiration? If Xenophon was merely a noun of the third declension who remarked to some people in the dative plural that either *thalassa* or *thalatta* was correct, if Tacitus was only a careless Roman who often dropped his verbs, obliging some anxious commentator to pick them up in footnotes uttering the startled cry of *scilicet*—even a change of subject might have done no good, for the young mind apparently had not yet emerged.

However, the literal-minded are they that inherit the earth, and if Greek literature or any other literature had really waked up this man's fancy, there is no knowing into what unsocial, unprofitable dream-corner he might have drifted, while progress buzzed past and problems whistled over him and education went fizzling by. He might have been a nympholept, for aught he knows, instead of a useful college professor, and spent days in mooning when he should have been up and doing, getting on in the world, educating, leading people from one place to some other place, no matter whence, no matter whither, but leading them. For it is a forlorn and pitiable thing in a democracy to go anywhere without taking other people—even through a book. Of what use is a citizen whose pleasures are private? We may thank our stars that we are born without imagination in these days or, if we start with a little of it can easily kill it after childhood. It would be, I think, an isolating faculty in this democracy, unsocial, perhaps unpatriotic, a traitor to the sovereignty of the present moment, blind at a bargain, useless in reform, a heretic of social values, a sceptic of the scale of immediate importance.

An imaginative man might never read a newspaper. He could so easily invent more exciting news and more amusing editors. Imagining success, he might not want it. Imagining people, he might not care to meet them. Why should an imaginative man read a president's message or an opposition editor's remarks thereon, or hear the talk of a club member about either? Would not these novel and valuable forms of entertainment be staled in advance to that accursed and proleptic dreamer? He might soon be prefiguring next week's gossip and not reading it, guessing at his compatriots instead of taking them by the hand, guessing himself so vividly in and out of public places that he would not wish to go. Many affairs of vast present importance would not be nearly so entrancing as a good quiet guess about them to an imaginative man. This is not the time and place for any praise of imaginative pleasures. They unfit a man for the travelled routes and main chances of this democracy. They encourage personal divergencies. They lead to conduct unbecoming in a social unit. They are neither civic nor aggressive, but split a man from his race, mass, class or group, by giving him secret diversions and absentminded activities for which not a penny will be paid. They spoil him for an active part in any branch of that great society for the promotion of human homogeneity which under one name or another has been doing great work these many years in all parts of the country toward the obliteration of personal distinctions.

Hence it is better to read books as unimaginatively and impersonally as possible, thinking only of "results," of what may be turned to account, easily communicated, reduced to summaries, talked about, lectured on. Never a private taste without some form of public demonstration, if you wish to "get on in the world." And that is the safest way to write books, also, for an imaginative book is bound to seem a queer one. Readers desire that to which they are accustomed. They are accustomed to memory in a novelist, also to great mimetic skill and industry, but they are not accustomed to imagination. Accordingly they flee in large numbers from such a book, asking what it is "all about." That is one of the strange things about the literal mind. Why does it ask this question of books alone? It does not in the least know what the world is "driving at," but does not on that account run away from the world. It marries, eats, is fond of its children, votes, goes to church, reads the newspapers, slaughters wild fowl, catches needless fish, talks endlessly, plays complicated and unnecessary games, propels unpleasant-smelling engines at enormous speed along the road —all without looking for a reason or being able to find one if it did. It is at any moment of the day an automaton of custom, irrational, antecedently improbable, no more able to give an account of itself than a bit of paper swimming in the wind—but put a fantastic book before it and off goes the creature indignantly grumbling about the lack of an explanation. As if the wildest thing ever written were half so queer, inscrutable, fantastic or *a priori* incredible as the commonest man that ever ran away from it.

We see more nowadays of this queer rage that follows literary incomprehension because there are so many more people who are trying to read and write. When an amusing and fantastic little narrative was printed in England some years ago, I recall many stout Britishers who stamped on it with their hobnailed shoes, merely because it contained no large round meanings like the *London Times* or Mr. Crockett. There is in these matters a sort of loquacity of negation as if every one who could not feel were bound to be a propagandist of apathy. The literary commentator seems strangely jealous of the things undreamt of in his philosophy. He is eager to vindicate his vacuum and the sequel to his "I don't feel it" is "Neither do you," usually with a show of ill-temper.

The theory of it is that all heads are of the same thickness and that the man who finds any meaning where you do not is probably an impostor. The excuse for it is the frequency of fraud, especially in literary cults. Cults as a rule are as soulless as corporations. One feels, for instance, toward certain uncritical lovers of Mr. Henry James as Emerson did toward noisy nature-lovers. "When a man tells you he has the love of nature in his heart," said he, "you may be sure he hasn't any." No one should be blamed for being suspicious of the literary cult. And it is as short-lived as it is deceitful; for it has been observed of its members, as of the blue-bottle fly, that they buzz the loudest just before they drop. Excesses of this sort have of late years been invariably followed by periods of severe repression—of silence almost proportionate to the degree of garrulity when the talking fit was on. The hush that settled upon *Trilby* and *Robert Elsmere* endures to this day. The reader of *The Man with the Hoe,* if there be one, is as the owl in the desert; and upon the lips of the Omarian the spider builds its web. Men still find pleasure in the writings of Stevenson, but where are the Stevensonians? Where are the Smithites, Brownists and Robinsonians of yesteryear? Let a subject once fall to the cult, let the lavish tongues of small expounders have their way, and the waters soon close over it.

But apart from this well-founded suspicion of the cult, there is no doubt that contact with the things that they do not understand is to many minds acutely dis-

agreeable. All the greater dramas contain highly valued passages which are not only wearisome to many
in the audience but actually offensive to them. A dog
not only prefers a customary and unpleasant smell; he
hates a good one. A perfume pricks his nose,—gives a
wrench to his dog nature, perhaps tends to "undermine
those moral principles" without which dog "society
cannot exist," as the early critics used to say of Ibsen.
Hatred of the unfamiliar is surely as common a rule
as *Omne ignotum pro magnifico.*

But the great triumphs of the literal mind occur in
the field of literary criticism, as when experts take the
measure of the poets or tabulate their parts of speech.
Consider, for example, the polemics of literary meas-
urement to be found in almost any literary magazine.
I never know which side to take in these discussions
as to what constitutes true poetry or as to the relative
measurements of bards. This is due, I fear, to gross
inaccuracy. Parnassus has never been for me ringed
with lines showing altitude above prose-level, like the
mountains in the school geographies, nor have I been
able to grade geniuses as accurately as I could wish.
Ranging one bard along with another, old or new, great
or small, I am apt to miscalculate by many centimetres.
I am not even sure of myself in applying the John-
sonian parallel to present poets of a certain degree.
I might say, for example, that, if of Bilder's Muse
the stream pressure is higher, that of Barman is broader
in the beam—but I should do so with little confidence
that it would survive the tests of later investigators.

Hence my pleasure (a little mixed with envy) in
many magazine discussions grading authors, according
to sweetness, girth, weight, height, depth, speed and
durability, with never a moment's doubt. Perhaps a
compatriot of Emerson declares he is entitled to the

first rank anywhere, and from this position shall never be dislodged, and a London reviewer says he cannot allow it because Emerson was lacking in *Je-ne-sais-quoi*-ness, and lived too long at Concord, Massachusetts, and much as he hates to disquiet America, he must rate Emerson two points lower. Or it may be that a visiting American Professor in the course of his Cambridge lecture does not rate the versatility of Dryden so high as it is rated by some Oxford don, who has scheduled the qualities of all the poets and marked them on the scale of ten, and the don turns quickly to his tables and finds that many of the Professor's tastes are inexcusably erroneous, wrong by Troy weight, wrong by avoirdupois, and that they are not always expressed in donnish language, several phrases being merely suggestive and three prepositions misplaced. So on this firm basis he proves the lecturer illiterate and shallow-pated, and then with wider sweep (for he happens to be writing in the London *Bombardinian,* whose policy it is to insult America as no grand division of the earth's surface has ever been insulted before) he dismisses all American scholarship as quite worthless and American.

Or, again, it may be that Mr. Barker (one of those rare expository poets, who after the printing of a poem can live handsomely for several years on the income of their explanations), appears once more in a magazine, and the question immediately arises, Is it a deathless song? And one maintains that Mr. Barker is the true bobolink singing with his breast against a thorn, and another disproves it by citing two or three mixed metaphors or lines that he cannot understand.

"The great white peak of my soul has spoken
"To the depths of my being below."

"How can a peak speak?" says the foe of Barker, but a man from the poets' ranks fells him with the Bible. "Why hop ye so, ye high hills?" says the Bible, and how can a "high hill hop?" And on they go, each deciding the thing absolutely and trying to bind the rest, and Mr. Barker waits cheerfully, knowing that his time will surely come, and meanwhile plans lecture tours along all the principal trade routes of the country. I may not address myself to these grave issues in the clarion tones that they deserve, but I appreciate the spirit of such discussions and like to see them going on.

Or suppose the great question of "English style" reappears in the magazines. A sentinel of "Culture" has been found asleep; a professor of English literature in a book on rhetoric for the young has himself been quite inelegant. Thrice has he ended a sentence with the careless words "and so on," and on one page he has referred coarsely to "the business in hand" and on another he has said he "pitched upon a word,"— as if a gentleman would ever pitch anything; it is the act of a drunkard or a ship. And thereupon some one all aglow with true refinement asks what our native language will become if men in such high station fall into blunders gross as these. And the blunders are then pilloried in italics or marched to jail behind exclamation points, looking very guilty indeed, and the newspapers copy, and editorial writers, straining to sudden dignity of phrase, comment on it with a splendid scorn. Finally, if the weather is warm, "Typicus" and "Philologus" write letters ending either with *"Quis custodes custodiet"* or with *"Verbum sap,"* and others follow, and all concerned are soon debating whether you can be a perfect gentleman and end a sentence with a preposition. It is a scene of great and cheerful activity, and no man with his heart in the right place will begrudge the participants any of their joy.

Yet it puzzles us simpler folk, who did not know that even the best of grammar could really save an "English style." For it is astonishing how vicious an "English style" may be without getting into the grammatical police court. And the man who writes about it at the greatest length on this occasion seems not to have attained it, though he breaks no laws. The sentences are willing to parse for him, but that is all. They deny all complicity with his mind, all ease, intimacy and sense of form; call up no image and suggest no thought; do nothing, in short, that might distinguish him from the Comptroller of the Mint, the Board of Education, a Consular Report, or the Turveydrop on the morning newspaper who took his treatise as a text for a lecture on literary deportment. Of course this is no fault of his, but in the capricious region of "English style" the personally blameless seem often to be the deepest damned. We forgive some men sooner for breaking the silence; and there is something about these staunch upholders of the law that drives all uncouth persons, like myself, to mad excesses. We rush into some lonely shed and split infinitives.

And of what use is it to attack one Dr. Drybosh, as a daily paper did, because he wrote six hundred pages on Tennyson's diction and arranged the poet's idioms in classes and convicted his co-ordinate clauses of illicit intercourse? Dr. Drybosh is a mere pupil of the Drier Criticism, of which sad science masters are to be found everywhere, not only in college chairs of literature, but in newspapers, magazines, reading circles and women's clubs. Few people read a poet nowadays. They take a course in him. Some one arranges him first into an early, a middle and a later period. Somebody builds an approach to his "works" and somebody else a trestle over them. A Dr. Dowden may perhaps be found who will show how the buoyant tone of the poet's youth was tempered by the reflective note of his middle age. Then there is his relation to his time and to other times and the pedigree of his main idea and whether poetry had ever broken out in the family before, and, if so, why, and his likeness to somebody and unlikeness to somebody else, and the list of his ingredients, and how long they had to be stirred, and when they actually "came to a boil," and what his place was in literature.

True, Drybosh is a type much loved by college presidents, and rewarded usually with a Ph. D. (no mere ornamental appendage, but the indispensable prehensile tail for academic climbing), and often promoted to a special literary chair for dehumanising the humanities. But to be a Drier Critic, whether of the college chair or not, that is the best way to begin, and the Drier Criticism is at this day inexpugnable. For by means of it a man who has no heart for his subject may still draw from it his daily bread. Commensalism is by no means limited to bivalves, but runs all through the Drier Criticism. Shakespeare to his commentators is as the oyster to the oyster crab. The very definition of commensalism reminds one of the latest essay on Browning or Walt Whitman; and why rebuke the manners of invertebrates, whether literary or marine? In all these matters one should strive for a more than human, an almost zoological, charity, and the hope that even a Ph. D. may have its use in nature.

Hundreds of naturally book-shy people, disliking the essentials of literature, are kept busy in its neighbourhood by just such tinker-work in its non-essentials; or they may at least be made to tarry near by papers on the "human side" of him, how the great man looked, wherewithal he was clothed, whence his thoughts came, and what he ate. I have before me a "Chat with an Author," profusely illustrated, and taking up the best part of a page of a newspaper. In the upper left-hand corner is the author's full face. At a distance of two inches to the right is his profile, the intervening space being filled by a picture of a rose from the author's garden. In the lower left-hand corner is the author's front door. In the middle is a larger picture of the author, this time including his legs and the library table. In the right-hand corner is the library table again, but this time without the author, and below the library table may be seen an elm-tree belonging to the author. These are not the mementoes of the dead. The author is still living. The "chat" itself abounds in the same reverent miscellany. The author declares his preference for high ideals as opposed to low ones, and the interviewer jots it down. He breathes, and the interviewer notes it. A similar "chat" follows with another author, also "in the public eye," who supplies three portraits and maintains with equal firmness that high ideals ought to be raised and their seeds freely distributed. And so it goes. Scores of these literary interviews were appearing at that time, some papers making them a regular feature of Sunday or Saturday supplements. They were studies in effaced personality. Not a tumultuous or self-willed person at any time, the American author on these occasions faded completely away. He seemed a jelly-fish floating on the current of universal assent and owing his success, one would say from his remarks, not to any efforts of his own but to the country's willingness. It may have been the fault of the interviewer that he could detect in these authors only the qualities that are common to the race, and record only those sentiments which it would be a sin for mankind not to share. But I remember that one of them was made to say:

"The atmosphere in which ideals are found must be preserved to insure their accuracy, and atmosphere is the divine promise of ideals that the true artist finds wrapped around an otherwise sordid fact."

And the other interviews abounded in just such comatose passages. Perhaps it was due to the benumbing effect of publicity. Just as many animals will not touch their food in the presence of man, so there may be authors who will not use their minds if they think anybody is watching them. Excited by the camera, and unmanned by the sense of impending advertisement, they are on these occasions not themselves, often utterly swooning away into the general morality. Later, perhaps, they find they have been saying that the world on the whole is growing better every day, or if it is not it ought to be, and that they do their best literary work between meals and with an earnest purpose, and that this is a great country, and culture clubs are dotting the prairies, and the atmosphere is full of ideals, plenty for everybody, so give the baby one. Which involuntary remarks, subjoining a scene of pillage, wherein their profiles, full faces and frock coats alternate with chairs, desks, tables, detached doors, bulrushes, twigs and other objects torn from the premises, constitute what is known as a literary "chat" published for the benefit of persons who might have taken grave offence at anything more intimately literary.

Apparently one of the chief objects of writing about books today is to entice these alien and reluctant souls into their vicinity and to comfort the aching hearts of "Culture"-seekers with the sense that "Culture" has been attained. Readers are seized in the midst of their reading with a mad Chautalkative philanthropy, and disdaining their own digestions, tell us what to read. I am constantly receiving advice as to my book consumption from people who look starved. "Culture" is always preoccupied with my conversion. There are writers for the London *Bombardinian* who have never read a line except for the discipline of me. In my own country there is the literature of the helping hand, more active than the Salvation Army. Unselfish men running back and forth all their lives between their books and me; devoted women telling me how to approach poets who are by no means fugitive; engines of literary "uplift," ably manned or womaned, from heavy hoisting, academic derrick to smoothest of ladies' escalators; societies formed to make me feel as if I had read what I have not; roadhouses on the way to every well-known author for the pilgrims who never arrive. In England the duty which the man who has read something owes to the man who has not is tinged, to be sure, with a certain sternness. The Briton with a bit of literary knowledge in him makes it a class distinction, accentuating the ignominy of the man who has it not, pointing more unmercifully than we do to the horrid gap between them—but always for that vulgar person's good. With us there are more who lend a hand or smooth the pillows. But common to this abounding helpfulness is the tendency to begin too soon. Too soon does the thought of others extrude all other thoughts. Too early and devotedly do readers plunge into the care of all minds but their own. The self-indulgent partaker is rare; the toil-spent, literal-minded, ill-nourished, eleemosynary book-executive or taste-commissioner is almost the rule.

I forbear to add any reflections of my own to the

vast body of expository or satiric comment on this familiar democratic tendency, but I do protest against the view that even the most solemn of these missionaries are people who take themselves in the least seriously. There is no point in the common gibe about taking one's self too seriously. These people are swept away from themselves on waves of premature benevolence. In a humanitarian era they are clean gone into other-mindedness, having no private tastes, only ministerial inclinations, no personal pleasures, only social subsidiary utilities. These are not the cares of your self-serious person. The more seriously he took himself, the more lightly would he be apt to take the duties of this literary motherhood. He would leave us to make our way as best we might into Meredith or toward Dante or under Shakespeare or around Browning. No signposts from him, or guide-books, path-finders, step-ladders, "aspects," "appreciations," central thoughts, dominant notes, real messages, helps to, peeps at, or glimpses of; in short, none of the apparatus of literary approach, and none of the devices for getting done with authors. For what should he care—that seriously-selfish man—about our propinquities and juxtapositions, our first views and early totterings? *Sauve qui peut* would be his feeling in these matters, coupled with no especial unwillingness to see us hanged.

A foolish phrase, that of taking one's self too seriously, and doubly so when applied to writers, accusing them, as it does, of quite incredible excesses—thinking too long, feeling too keenly, enjoying too heartily, living too much. And, as is well known, true literature is compact of very lordly egotisms, the work of men preoccupied with self-delight. Never a philosopher without his own first egotistic certainties, or a poet who was not the first adorer of his dreams, or a humorist whose own earliest and private laughter was not the nearest to his heart. Never a good fisher of men in these waters who had not first landed himself, taken himself so very seriously that we cannot mistake him for anybody else, maintained his egotism in a master-piece—that most unblushing, self-interested device ever yet achieved for the preservation of personal identity.

ON KNOWING THE DIFFERENCE

BY ROBERT LYND

IT WAS only the other day that I came upon a full-grown man reading with something like rapture a little book—*Ships and Seafaring Shown to Children*. His rapture was modified, however, by the bitter reflection that he had already passed so great a part of his life without knowing the difference between a ship and a barque; and, as for sloops, yawls, cutters, ketches, and brigantines, they were simply the Russian alphabet to him. I sympathise with his regret. It was a noble day in one's childhood when one had learned the names of sailing-vessels, and, walking to the point of the harbour beyond the bathing-boxes, could correct the ignorance of a friend: "That's not a ship. That's a brig." To the boy from an inland town every vessel that sails is a ship. He feels he is being shown a new and bewildering world when he is told that the only ship that has the right to be called a ship is a vessel with three masts (at least), all of them square-rigged. When once he has learned his lesson, he finds an unaccustomed delight in wandering along the dirtiest coal-quay, and recognising the barques by the fact that only two of their three masts are square-rigged, and the brigs by the fact that they are square-rigged throughout—a sort of two-masted ships. Vessels have suddenly become as real to him in their differences as the different sorts of common birds. As for his feelings on the day on which he can tell for certain the upper fore topsail from the upper fore top-gallant sail, and either of these from the fore skysail, the crossjack, or the mizzen-royal, they are those of a man who has mastered a language and discovers himself, to his surprise, talking it fluently. The world of shipping has become articulate poetry to him instead of a monotonous abracadabra.

It is as though we can know nothing of a thing until we know its name. Can we be said to know what a pigeon is unless we know that it is a pigeon? We may have seen it again and again, with its bottle-shoulders and shining neck, sitting on the edge of a chimney-pot, and noted it as a bird with a full bosom and swift wings. But if we are not able to name it except vaguely as a "bird," we seem to be separated from it by an immense distance of ignorance. Learn that it is a pigeon, however, and immediately it rushes towards us across the distance, like something seen through a telescope. No doubt to the pigeon-fancier this would seem but the first lisping of knowledge, and he would not think much of our acquaintance with pigeons if we could not tell a carrier from a pouter. That is the charm of knowledge—it is merely a door into another sort of ignorance. There are always new differences to be discovered, new names to be learned, new individualities to be known, new classifications to be made. The world is so full of a number of things that no man with a grain of either poetry or the scientific spirit in him has any right to be bored, though he lived for a thousand years. Terror or tragedy may overwhelm him, but boredom never. The infinity of things forbids it. I once heard of a tipsy young artist who, on his way home on a beautiful night, had his attention called by a maudlin friend to the stars, where they twinkled like a million larks. He raised his eyes to the heavens, then shook his head. "There are too many of them,"

232 ROBERT LYND

he complained wearily. It should be remembered, however, that he was drunk, and that he did not know astronomy. There could be too many stars only if they were all turned out on the same pattern, and made the same pattern on the sky. Fortunately, the universe is the creation not of a manufacturer but of an artist.

There is scarcely a subject that does not contain sufficient Asias of differences to keep an explorer happy for a lifetime. It would be easy to do nothing but chase butterflies all one's days. It is said that thirteen thousand species of butterflies have been already discovered, and it is suggested that there may be nearly twice as many that have so far escaped the naturalists. After so monstrous a figure, we are not surprised to learn that there are sixty-eight species of butterflies in Great Britain and Ireland. We should be astonished, however, had we not already expended our astonishment on the large number. How many of us are there who could name even half-a-dozen varieties? We all know the tortoiseshell and the white and the blue—the little blue butterflies that flutter over the gold and red of the cornfields. But the average man does not even know by name such varieties as the Camberwell Beauty, the Dingy Skipper, the Pearl-bordered Fritillary, and the White-letter Hairstreak. As for the moth, are there not as many sorts of moths as there are words in a dictionary? Many men give all the pleasant hours of their lives to learning how to know the difference between one of them and another. One used to see these moth-hunters on windless nights in a Hampstead lane pursuing their quarry fantastically with nets in the light of the lamps. In pursuing moths, they pursue knowledge. This, they feel, is life at its most exciting, its most intense. They regard a man who does not know and is not interested in the difference be-

tween one moth and another as a man not yet thoroughly awakened from his pre-natal sleep. And, indeed, one could not conceive a more appalling sort of
blank idiocy than the condition of a man who could not
tell one thing from another in any department of life
whatever. We would rather change lives with such a
man. This luxury of variety was not meant to be ig-
nored. We throw ourselves into it with exhilaration
as a swimmer plunges into the sea. There are few
forms of happiness I know which are more enviable
than that of those who have eyes for birds and flowers.
How they rejoice on learning that, according to one
theory, there are a hundred and three different species
of brambles to be found in these islands! They would
not have them fewer by a single one. It is extraor-
dinarily pleasant even for one who is mainly ignorant
of the flowers and their families to come on two or
three varieties of one flower in the course of a country
walk. As a boy, he is excited by the difference between
the pinheaded and the thrum-headed primrose. As he
grows older, he scans the roadside for little peeping
things that to a lazy eye seem as like each other as two
peas—the dove's foot geranium, the round-leaved geranium and the lesser wild geranium. "As like each
other as two peas," we have said; but *are* two peas like
each other? Who knows whether the peas have not
the same difference of feature among themselves that
Englishmen have? Half the similarities we notice are
only the results of our ignorance and idleness. The
townsman passing a field of sheep finds it difficult to
believe that the shepherd can distinguish between one
and another of them with as much certainty as if they
were his children. And do not most of us think of foreigners as beings who are all turned out as if on a pattern, like sheep? The further removed the foreigners

are from us in race, the more they seem to us to be like each other. When we speak of negroes, we think of millions of people most of whom look exactly alike. We feel much the same about Chinamen and even Turks. Probably to a Chinaman all English children look exactly alike, and it may be that all Europeans seem to him to be as indistinguishable as sticks of barley-sugar. How many people think of Jews in this way! I have heard an Englishman expressing his wonder that Jewish parents should be able to pick out their own children in a crowd of Jewish boys and girls.

Thus our first generalisations spring from ignorance rather than from knowledge. They are true, so long as we know that they are not entirely true. As soon as we begin to accept them as absolute truths, they become lies. One of the perils of a great war is that it revives the passionate faith of the common man in generalisations. He begins to think that all Germans are much the same, or that all Americans are much the same, or that all Conscientious Objectors are much the same. In each case he imagines a lay figure rather than a human being. He may hate his lay figure or he may like it; but, if he is in search of truth, he had better throw the thing out of the window and try to think about a human being instead. I do not wish to deny the importance of generalisations. It is not possible to think or even to act without them. The generalisation that is founded on a knowledge of and a delight in the variety of things is the end of all science and poetry. Keats said that he sought the principle of beauty in all things, and poems are in a sense simply beautiful generalisations. They subject the unclassified and chaotic facts of life to the order of beauty. The mystic, meditating on the One and the Many, is also in pursuit of a generalisation—the perfect generalisation of the universe. And what is science but the attempt to arrange in a series of generalisations the facts of what we are vain enough to call the known world? To know the resemblances of things is even more important than to know the difference of things. Indeed, if we are not interested in the former, our pleasure in the latter is a mere scrap-book pleasure. If we are not interested in the latter, on the other hand, our sense of the former is apt to degenerate into guesswork and assertion and empty phrases. Shakespeare is greater than all the other poets because he, more than anybody else, knew how very like human beings are to each other and because he, more than anybody else, knew how very unlike human beings are to each other. He was master of the particular as well as of the universal. How much poorer the world would have been if he had not been so in regard not only to human beings but to the very flowers—if he had not been able to tell the difference between fennel and fumitory, between the violet and the gillyflower!

THE TYRANNY OF MERE THINGS

BY L. P. JACKS

"Thou marshall'st me the way that I was going;
And such an instrument I was to use."—Macbeth.

WE OFTEN learn, when it is too late, that the existence
of an instrument for performing an action is the cause
of that action being performed. If there are daggers,
the likelihood is that sooner or later there will be stab-
bing; if armaments, wars; if tools, trade; if rhetoric,
argument. Many a murderer would have remained
innocent had he not possessed a knife or a gun; many
a man would have written sonnets or painted pictures
had his father not been the owner of a mill; many an
unprofitable controversy would have been avoided had
not a weapon been provided by a tempting phrase, or
well-turned period, suddenly occurring to one or other
of the disputants.

These statements when applied to the actions of individuals are commonplace to the point of truism. But
they acquire a new interest when applied on the large
scale to the lives of nations and to the great movements
of history.

This extension of scope is what I propose in the
present essay. I shall endeavour to draw attention to
the enormous influence exercised over the form and
direction of modern civilisation by the power which
resides in machinery of all kinds. I shall suggest that
this power, intended originally for the service of man,
has become in several respects his master. The theme,
of course, is not new. But it seems to me that current

events give it a new importance and a commanding interest.

In their origin tools and machines represent the effort of man to facilitate the satisfaction of his natural wants. These natural wants are the necessity which is mother to invention.

But every such tool or machine, when invented, gives rise to a further necessity, economic in nature, which the inventor perhaps did not foresee, and which in course of time tends to overshadow and obscure the original wants served by the contrivance. This is the necessity of keeping the machine in continuous working. Once constructed it must be "kept going"; otherwise the owner of it will suffer loss. Thus we could hardly contend that the conscious motive of the Lancashire cotton trade, or of the Yorkshire wool trade, is the desire to clothe the naked. No doubt the naked are clothed by these industries; but the "spring of action" is primarily economic. It lies in the necessity of carrying on the business, keeping the vast machinery in commission, and the multitudes of employes in work. The manufacturer or the workman may gladly assent, when reminded, that his labour meets the primary want of man for clothes or food, and he may receive a moral stimulus or consolation from the reminder. But this thought is not in the forefront of his mind as he sits in his office or stands at his loom. His motive is "business." He is there to make profits or to earn his living, which he can only do by using the machinery to the uttermost. If this is allowed to fall idle he will become bankrupt or starve.

The more complex and costly the machinery becomes, the more will this secondary motive tend to push the primary into the background, until at last the original purpose passes out of immediate consciousness. The time comes when thousands of millions of capital are invested in "plant," and nations are employed in the task of keeping it in commission. At all costs it must be kept going or the nation will perish economically. Thus if decay threatens an industry, like the making of cloth, the question before our legislators and the public is not primarily as to the effect on the nakedness of mankind, but as to the effect on the manufacturers and workmen employed in the industry, and through them on the industrial organisation at large. In this way industrial civilisation comes at last to mean that the need of using the machinery which man has created takes the first place in thought: while the needs the machinery was originally created to serve take the second. The means become the end.

Our attention is constantly being called by social reformers to certain tyrannies, and vested interests of an obnoxious kind, in our present system of industry. I do not here deny that these things exist and call for remedy. But I suggest that behind the tyrannies indicated there stands a major tyranny of which all parties to the system are the victims in differing degrees. This is the tyranny of the enormous accumulations of complicated mechanical contrivances which, in their organised totality, compel the human race to keep them going or run the risk of perishing. Man by "his wisdom and his brightness" has created this monster, and the monster has rewarded his creator by laying down the terms on which he is to live. He may continue to live only so long as he feeds the fires he has lit and turns the wheels he has invented. To this he must devote the major part of his energies, his intelligence and his soul—or perish. The relation of his vital to his economic interests has thus been reversed. Whereas at the first the economic served the vital, it is now the vital that serves the economic. The machine—meaning by this the whole mechanical complex of civilisation—rules the man.

To be sure, the machine rewards its servants; but it rewards them on its own terms. It confers prosperity on communities which serve it diligently; but has not our very notion of what prosperity is been imposed upon us by the necessity of satisfying the economic rather than the human conditions of our life? Here we have, I venture to think, the deeper explanation of the "social unrest" of which we have heard so much. Fundamentally, it is not a rebellion of class against class, but of the human soul in all classes against the limitations set to its life by economic mechanism. Never will man feel himself really prosperous so long as his well-being is defined by these limits. Never will he be satisfied by a reward which is measured in purely economic terms, no matter what the amount nor how distributed. This was the burden of Ruskin, and for sixty years the course of social history has been confirming it in every particular.

And yet it does not appear to have been sufficiently weighed by social reformers. With them the question is—Who shall possess the machine, the State or the individual? But a closer scrutiny of social conditions suggests that this question might with advantage be reversed. Whichever of the two—State or individual—wins the coveted position, that position, unless accompanied by far more radical changes, would not be one of mastery but one of servitude. What is called State-ownership of machinery is really machinery-ownership of the State. It would not free man from economic servitude, but merely readjust its terms, making no great difference to the fundamental conditions under which human life is being lived. Those conditions would still be, as now, that man, in his societies, must accommodate his vital interests to the supreme necessity of keeping the machine in commission, and must seek no "ends" which are incompatible with this. Such an outcome is not the "freedom" which our dreams demand for the soul.

To understand these conditions in the sphere of our industrial life requires an effort of the imagination greater, perhaps, than some of us are willing to put forth, and greater than many would deem permissible. When, however, we turn from industrial to military organisation, the tyranny of the machine is set forth in characters which admit of no mistake.

A glance at the present state of Europe reveals the extraordinary spectacle of great and intelligent nations whose warlike policies are largely dictated by their armaments. For there is no more certain truth than this: that if you create a vast fighting machine it will sooner or later compel you to fight, whether you want to fight or no. That peace can be maintained indefinitely while millions of men are training themselves for war with every conceivable kind of mechanical device, is one of those childish suppositions which only infatuated minds could entertain. These vast machines, whether armies or engines of war, are made to be used; and though the day when they will be used may be long deferred by a process of spectacular playing at war, the impulse to use them for their intended purpose will ultimately brush this aside as insufficient, and will prevail against every consideration of reason, humanity, and common sense. The military machine will overpower the minds which have called it into being. It may not allow them even to choose the time when war is to begin. The time comes inevitably when the mechanism has reached a certain degree of perfection.

This creates its own occasion by the fact that the power is now at the maximum, the ammunition at hand, the bearings oiled, the guns loaded and the matches lit. Nations make war when armies are ready to begin.

Armaments possess what I have no hesitation in calling a will of their own—a will to be used as armaments. Make them big enough and costly enough, and they will assuredly get out of hand and control the governments by which they are nominally controlled. Some of them, perhaps, were created originally for the purpose of keeping the peace, under the leading of that most fallacious of maxims—*si vis pacem para bellum*. But "bellum" is what the armament is fitted for making; and "bellum" is what the armament will one day make. Europe, confronted with a vision of its embattled armies and fleets, might well say to the vast assemblage, as Macbeth said to the air-drawn dagger:

> "Thou marshall'st me the way that I was going;
> And such an instrument I was to use."

Such, then, are two striking forms in which the tyranny of the machine makes itself felt in modern life. I have now to suggest that they are symptoms of a deeper tyranny whose seat is in the ideal world. The conditions we have noted are like an immense mirror which reveals to the modern man the workings of his own mind and shows him what spirit he is of.

Throughout the whole of its history the human mind has been engaged in fabricating conceptions, or, as some prefer to say, in giving birth to ideas. "Force," "matter," "law," "knowledge," "happiness," "virtue," "society," "government," "popular rights," "order," "progress," "evolution," are examples of these ideas. In their simpler form they are the "tools" of thought; in the more complicated they may be compared to "machines"; in the most complicated—that is, when combined into systems of science—they resemble the economic mechanism of an industrial society, or even a great military organisation.

The origin of these spiritual tools is of like nature with the origin of spades, steel saws, spinning-jennies, aeroplanes, and Krupp guns. Necessity is the mother of their invention. They are means to the satisfaction of some want, need, or desire. "Conceptions" are not copies or photographic reproductions of anything external to themselves. Their nature is explained by their function, which is to economise, facilitate, extend, and expedite the work of the spirit, thereby attaining a larger, richer, speedier satisfaction of the wants they are intended to serve. Ideas and systems of thought are, strictly speaking, "inventions." Man wants to fly, and contrives an aeroplane. He wants to explain the universe, and constructs a metaphysical system. The metaphysic no less than the aeroplane has a purpose in view and is to be understood accordingly. Both things bespeak the nature of man as a tool-making animal. Of the ideal tools so invented some have, as it were, a stationary use; for example, the geometrical ideas, which are like optical instruments, enabling us to penetrate the secrets of space. Others suggest locomotion, like the idea of evolution, which seems to carry the mind at enormous speed over vast ranges of time.

The ideal tools are interdependent in their working. Like the mechanical industries of a nation, they are associated into groups; and they grow more numerous and more complex as the needs of the mind increase. The sciences are intellectual "industries"; they satisfy wants which multiply like the population of the earth. To meet the growing demand these wants create ther-

must be closer organisation of the working parts of mental industry—knowledge must become more systematic. Moreover, since many of the ideas are not complete in themselves, but only "components" of much larger conceptual systems, a special science, which is itself another system of conceptions, must come into being, to adapt the parts to one another and define the formulæ which are to regulate their common action. This science is logic. Thus the work of ideal invention grows by what it feeds on: one notion calls for another; each depends more intimately on the rest; until at the end of long ages the world of knowledge becomes like the Black Country in a time of roaring trade—the smoke belching from the chimneys, the furnaces in full blast, the air quivering to the grind and rattle of engines, while millions of men and women hurry hither and thither or stand at their posts, stoking, hammering, filing, oiling, receiving their wages and computing their gains.

But the parallel does not end at this point.

As the power and complexity of the intellectual machine develop, it tends to absorb more and more of the attention and energies of thought. The process is here repeated which we have already noted in the economic sphere. Over against the vital necessities which the work of thought has, in the first place, to satisfy, there grow up necessities of a second order, which in course of time usurp the place of their primaries. Little by little the essential needs of man as a living soul become obscured by the overwhelming presence of the logical apparatus originally created to satisfy those needs. An enormous vested interest grows up round the mere mechanism of thought. At all costs the furnaces must be kept in blast; at all costs the machinery must continue to work; at all costs the logical armament—I use the term advisedly—must not be balked of its office. Hence, in close analogy to economic civilisation, there arises the scientific type of culture, under which the human spirit is still free to live and move, but only within the limits prescribed by the paramount need of giving employment to the mechanism of thought. This becomes at length the supreme authority of life and the dictator of philosophy. The cult of mechanism has established itself in the innermost chambers of the spirit.

Deeply characteristic of this cult is the inability of its followers to perceive the limitations it imposes upon them. Our devotion—for we are all devotees—is blind. That our life should be susceptible of any other form or direction save that which the prevalent dictatorship allows seems to us an unthinkable absurdity, and the mere suggestion of such a thing is denounced as the surrender of the reason. It is only at times of shock and upheaval like the present, when the foundations of life are being laid bare, that we are able to discern within ourselves a deeper rationality, whose freedom we have *already* surrendered, against its nature, to an immensely potent but inferior principle.

Thus, in the first place, our very notions of Truth are formed under the necessity of satisfying the requirements of the cult. Truth must be something of which the logical apparatus can make use. Therefore, whatever fits in with the mechanism, whatever enlarges the scope of the working, whatever contributes to the smoothness of the running, whatever augments the final product of argument—is Truth. Whatever fails to fulfill these conditions is Error.

Our notion of the Good is formed in like manner. The test of the Good is its tendency to give employment to ratiocination. The good of man becomes more and more closely identified with logical success. That man is most virtuous or happy whose life exhibits the character of a logically working "whole." That society is nearest the Kingdom of God in which the relationships of man with man approximate most nearly to the ideal logical structure. Whatever else the Good may be, it must always be that which provides the good man with the opportunity of explaining his goodness. Anything else is unthinkable.

A like conformity to the prevalent cult is to be observed in the realms of Art and Religion. In both these realms "criticism" is the ruling power; "criticism" being only another name for the spirit which has yielded its activities, for the time being, to the demands of the machine. In a critical age we are apt to test the worth of all things, even of Art and Religion, by the quality of the grist which they bring to the argumentative mill: the real interest at stake being not that of Art or Religion but that of criticism itself. In addition to their original function, which is to delight or inspire, Art and Religion have now won a secondary function, which is to provide subjects for discussion, to feed the critical powers. This in itself is no evil; the mischief begins at the next stage. For as criticism increases in range, complexity, and skill, this secondary function, as before, absorbs to itself the energies intended for the primary. Creativeness wanes, argument waxes: the Poet retires to the shadows, the Professor of Poetry steps into the light; the text is lost in the commentary; prayer sinks to the position of an incident in public worship, the sermon becomes the centre of attraction and the essential thing. Hence the forms of religion most honoured in a critical age are apt to be, not those which touch the human heart most deeply, but those which give argument the widest scope, discussion the most numerous topics, and rhet-

oric the most tempting themes. We may often watch
our minds or the minds of our neighbours picking their
way, like wary travellers, among the green pastures
where these opportunities abound. Art, also, may be
seen at such times to be following a theory. Several
recent developments in the arts, such as Impressionism and Futurism, show unmistakable signs of having
originated in an argument. Only a soulless dialectic
could produce the confusion they exhibit. We may
well doubt whether the great artists of earlier ages—
Phidias, Tintoretto—knew precisely what they were
doing. But our Impressionists and Futurists know—
though perhaps we who watch them do not. Like the
Germans in their quest for world-dominion, they are
under the orders of a theory. First, they give you a
lecture on their art; then they show you a specimen
of it. Once more, policy conforms to armaments.

We may say, in general, that every object of thought
and every motion of the spirit is transformed by the
prevalent cult into a "problem." First the thing must
be identified with the problem of the thing; then, and
then only, can the iron teeth of ratiocination get to
work upon its substance. Thus at the present time we
have the problem of Truth, the problem of Good, the
problem of Life, the problem of Art, the problem of
Religion, the problem of Society, the problem of the
Universe—the problem of everything. It is to be
observed that though the dominant power has forced all
these things to assume the problematic form, it has not,
so far, provided satisfactory answers. But if on observing this a thinker should suggest, as some have
done, that the answer to the problem of Life, for example, lies in the discovery that Life is something
greater than a problem, he will immediately find himself in conflict with the vested interests of mechanical

culture, and his reputation, in consequence, will run no inconsiderable risk. Claiming liberty for his thinking, he is treated as the enemy of thought.

These tendencies having acquired a certain strength give rise to a corresponding system of intellectual discipline, which embraces every form of education and has for its object the cultivation of the tendency into a fixed habit of mind.

Of which system the first thing to be said is that it affords little scope for genuine freedom of thought.

In an age when everybody is supposed to think for himself, this, I am well aware, may seem an absurd statement. And so, indeed, it would be were the presence of freedom to be attested by the amount of thinking which is permitted. But the true test lies in the quality of our thinking and not in the amount. The whole world may roar with thought, and this may yet remain essentially servile. So long as thought merely copies an existing pattern it is not free, no matter how much of it there may be. There is only one sure mark by which the presence of liberty in the life of the spirit may be detected—and that is creation, or, if you will, originality. A very little of this is worth more as a witness to liberty than any assignable amount of standardised thinking.

Freedom of thought implies, among other things, that the teacher—of anything from the "three R's" to theology—provokes the originality of his pupil, treats the pupil not as a recipient but as a reacting agent, accepts him as the predominant partner in the work of education, and aims at a result which shall contain a large contribution from the free activity of his mind. Under genuine freedom nothing can be further from the aim of the teacher than to impress upon the minds of others a slavish copy of the doctrine taught, even though this should happen to be the doctrine of freedom itself. On the contrary, he invites reaction to the uttermost, and is not the least cast down if the pupil adds so much of his own to the thought which is being given him that the two together issue in a third thought widely different from that which started the process. If the teacher be a true liberal he will be careful not to make positive instruction (especially moral instruction) so large in amount as to overwhelm, nor so insistent in form as to cramp, the energies of the receiving mind; and will gladly reduce his own share in the joint operation, or soften its emphasis, or even remain altogether silent for long intervals, in order that larger room may be provided for the answering contribution of his partner. "He must increase, but I must decrease," will be his motto.

Freedom of thought, therefore, does not mean merely that every individual is licensed to address his opinions to the world in unlimited monologue. It should rather be compared to a conversation between men of good manners, in which the object of each speaker is not to impress his own mind on the rest, but rather to elicit from the joint contributions of the whole company some higher wisdom than he, or any other individual present, can severally claim to possess.

But in a critical age, when the logical apparatus has got the upper hand of the spirit it was intended to serve, freedom of thought takes the more restricted form. Freedom of criticism is indeed permitted; but inasmuch as thought has been standardised in accordance with the requirements of the machine, criticism, though enormous in amount, will tend to be uniformly mechanical in quality. The supreme interests at stake being those of the system of intellectual discipline now in vogue, no reaction will be encouraged, or perhaps allowed, which places these in peril. That is a most serious limitation. It means that you may argue as you will, provided you raise no voice of rebellion against the system which lays down the rule of the argument.

Our culture has, on the whole, submitted to these conditions without protest. I do not say that it leaves room for no originality. But most of the originality there is moves within the limits prescribed, and has in consequence a purely argumentative character. The amount of intellectual activity is enormous; but of creativeness, which is the mark of freedom, there is remarkably little.

Of further symptoms, confirmatory of this diagnosis, I will mention only one, and that without elaboration. This is the exaggerated estimate we are in the habit of placing on the value of mere moral exhortation. By far the greater part of the moral exhortation now being offered so plentifully is, I fear, futile. Either it produces no reaction at all or the reaction it does produce is one of moral indifference, which is worse than none. And this futility, I believe, if traced to its source, would be found to originate in the twofold illusion that morality is a standardised product, and that the soul of man has no answering function save the passive acceptance of morals in the form turned out by ratiocination. The Great Preacher was free from this pedantry. He presented morality as concrete and living, leaving it to tell its own story and evoke its own reactions. "Without a parable spake he not unto them, according as it is written: I will declare things hidden from the foundation of the world."

THE PLACE OF SCIENCE IN
A LIBERAL EDUCATION

BY BERTRAND RUSSELL

SCIENCE, to the ordinary reader of newspapers, is represented by a varying selection of sensational triumphs, such as wireless telegraphy and aeroplanes, radio-activity and the marvels of modern alchemy. It is not of this aspect of science that I wish to speak. Science, in this respect, consists of detached up-to-date fragments, interesting only until they are replaced by something newer and more up-to-date, displaying nothing of the systems of patiently constructed knowledge out of which, almost as a casual incident, have come the practically useful results which interest the man in the street. The increased command over the forces of nature which is derived from science is undoubtedly an amply sufficient reason for encouraging scientific research, but this reason has been so often urged and is so easily appreciated that other reasons, to my mind quite as important, are apt to be overlooked. It is with these other reasons, especially with the intrinsic value of a scientific habit of mind in forming our outlook on the world, that I shall be concerned in what follows.

The instance of wireless telegraphy will serve to illustrate the difference between the two points of view. Almost all the serious intellectual labour required for the possibility of this invention is due to three men—Faraday, Maxwell, and Hertz. In alternating layers of experiment and theory these three men built up the modern theory of electromagnetism, and demonstrated the identity of light with electromagnetic waves. The system which they discovered is one of profound intellectual interest, bringing together and unifying an endless variety of apparently detached phenomena, and displaying a cumulative mental power which cannot but afford delight to every generous spirit. The mechanical details which remained to be adjusted in order to utilize their discoveries for a practical system of telegraphy demanded, no doubt, very considerable ingenuity, but had not that broad sweep and that universality which could give them intrinsic interest as an object of disinterested contemplation.

From the point of view of training the mind, of giving that well-informed, impersonal outlook which constitutes culture in the good sense of this much-misused word, it seems to be generally held indisputable that a literary education is superior to one based on science. Even the warmest advocates of science are apt to rest their claims on the contention that culture ought to be sacrificed to utility. Those men of science who respect culture, when they associate with men learned in the classics, are apt to admit, not merely politely, but sincerely, a certain inferiority on their side, compensated doubtless by the services which science renders to humanity, but none the less real. And so long as this attitude exists among men of science, it tends to verify itself: the intrinsically valuable aspects of science tend to be sacrificed to the merely useful, and little attempt is made to preserve that leisurely, systematic survey by which the finer quality of mind is formed and nourished.

But even if there be, in present fact, any such inferiority as is supposed in the educational value of science, this is, I believe, not the fault of science itself, but the fault of the spirit in which science is taught. If its full possibilities were realized by those who teach it, I believe that its capacity of producing those habits of mind which constitute the highest mental excellence would be at least as great as that of literature, and more particularly of Greek and Latin literature. In saying this I have no wish whatever to disparage a classical education. I have not myself enjoyed its benefits, and my knowledge of Greek and Latin authors is derived almost wholly from translations. But I am firmly persuaded that the Greeks fully deserve all the admiration that is bestowed upon them, and that it is a very great and serious loss to be unacquainted with their writings. It is not by attacking them, but by drawing attention to neglected excellences in science, that I wish to conduct my argument.

One defect, however, does seem inherent in a purely classical education—namely, a too exclusive emphasis on the past. By the study of what is absolutely ended and can never be renewed, a habit of criticism towards the present and the future is engendered. The qualities in which the present excels are qualities to which the study of the past does not direct attention, and to which, therefore, the student of Greek civilisation may easily become blind. In what is new and growing there is apt to be something crude, insolent, even a little vulgar, which is shocking to the man of sensitive taste; quivering from the rough contact, he retires to the trim gardens of a polished past, forgetting that they were reclaimed from the wilderness by men as rough and earth-soiled as those from whom he shrinks in his own day. The habit of being unable to recognize merit until it is dead is too apt to be the result of a purely bookish life, and a culture based wholly on the past will seldom be able to pierce through every-day surroundings to the essential splendour of contemporary things, or to the hope of still greater splendour in the future.

> "My eyes saw not the men of old;
> And now their age away has rolled
> I weep—to think I shall not see
> The heroes of posterity."

So says the Chinese poet; but such impartiality is rare in the more pugnacious atmosphere of the West, where the champions of past and future fight a never-ending battle, instead of combining to seek out the merits of both.

This consideration, which militates not only against the exclusive study of the classics, but against every form of culture which has become static, traditional, and academic, leads inevitably to the fundamental question: What is the true end of education? But before attempting to answer this question it will be well to define the sense in which we are to use the word "education." For this purpose I shall distinguish the sense in which I mean to use it from two others, both perfectly legitimate, the one broader and the other narrower than the sense in which I mean to use the word.

In the broader sense, education will include not only what we learn through instruction, but all that we learn through personal experience—the formation of character through the education of life. Of this aspect of education, vitally important as it is, I will say nothing, since its consideration would introduce topics quite foreign to the question with which we are concerned.

In the narrower sense, education may be confined to instruction, the imparting of definite information on various subjects, because such information, in and for itself, is useful in daily life. Elementary education —reading, writing and arithmetic—is almost wholly of this kind. But instruction, necessary as it is, does not *per se* constitute education in the sense in which I wish to consider it.

Education, in the sense in which I mean it, may be defined as *the formation, by means of instruction, of certain mental habits and a certain outlook on life and the world.* It remains to ask ourselves, what mental habits, and what sort of outlook, can be hoped for as the result of instruction? When we have answered this question we can attempt to decide what science has to contribute to the formation of the habits and outlook which we desire.

Our whole life is built about a certain number—not a very small number—of primary instincts and impulses. Only what is in some way connected with these instincts and impulses appears to us desirable or important; there is no faculty, whether "reason" or "virtue" or whatever it may be called, that can take our active life and our hopes and fears outside the region controlled by these first movers of all desire. Each of them is like a queen-bee, aided by a hive of workers gathering honey; but when the queen is gone the workers languish and die, and the cells remain empty of their expected sweetness. So with each primary impulse in civilised man: it is surrounded and protected by a busy swarm of attendant derivative desires, which store up in its service whatever honey the surrounding world affords. But if the queen-impulse dies, the death-dealing influence, though retarded a little by habit, spreads slowly through all the subsidiary impulses, and a whole tract of life becomes inexplicably colourless. What was formerly full of zest, and so obviously worth doing that it raised no questions, has now grown dreary and purposeless: with a sense of disillusion we inquire the meaning of life, and decide, perhaps, that all is vanity. The search for an outside meaning that can *compel* an inner response must always be disappointed: all "meaning" must be at bottom related to our primary desires, and when they are extinct no miracle can restore to the world the value which they reflected upon it.

The purpose of education, therefore, cannot be to create any primary impulse which is lacking in the uneducated; the purpose can only be to enlarge the scope of those that human nature provides, by increasing the number and variety of attendant thoughts, and by showing where the most permanent satisfaction is to be found. Under the impulse of a Calvinistic horror of the "natural man," this obvious truth has been too often misconceived in the training of the young; "nature" has been falsely regarded as excluding all that is best in what is natural, and the endeavour to teach virtue has led to the production of stunted and contorted hypocrites instead of full-grown human beings. From such mistakes in education a better psychology or a kinder heart is beginning to preserve the present generation; we need, therefore, waste no more words on the theory that the purpose of education is to thwart or eradicate nature.

But although nature must supply the initial force of desire, nature is not, in the civilised man, the spasmodic, fragmentary, and yet violent set of impulses that it is in the savage. Each impulse has its constitutional ministry of thought and knowledge and reflection, through which possible conflicts of impulses are foreseen, and temporary impulses are controlled by the unifying impulse which may be called wisdom. In this way education destroys the crudity of instinct, and increases through knowledge the wealth and variety of the individual's contacts with the outside world, making

him no longer an isolated fighting unit, but a citizen
of the universe, embracing distant countries, remote
regions of space, and vast stretches of past and future
within the circle of his interests. It is this simul-
taneous softening in the insistence of desire and en-
largement of its scope that is the chief moral end of
education.

Closely connected with this moral end is the more
purely intellectual aim of education, the endeavour to
make us see and imagine the world in an objective
manner, as far as possible as it is in itself, and not
merely through the distorting medium of personal desire. The complete attainment of such an objective
view is no doubt an ideal, indefinitely approachable, but
not actually and fully realisable. Education, considered as a process of forming our mental habits and
our outlook on the world, is to be judged successful in
proportion as its outcome approximates to this ideal;
in proportion, that is to say, as it gives us a true view
of our place in society, of the relation of the whole
human society to its non-human environment, and of
the nature of the non-human world as it is in itself
apart from our desires and interests. If this standard
is admitted, we can return to the consideration of
science, inquiring how far science contributes to such
an aim, and whether it is in any respect superior to
its rivals in educational practice.

II

Two opposite and at first sight conflicting merits belong to science as against literature and art. The one,
which is not inherently necessary, but is certainly true
at the present day, is hopefulness as to the future of
human achievement, and in particular as to the useful

work that may be accomplished by any intelligent student. This merit and the cheerful outlook which it engenders prevent what might otherwise be the depressing effect of another aspect of science, to my mind also a merit, and perhaps its greatest merit—I mean the irrelevance of human passions and of the whole subjective apparatus where scientific truth is concerned. Each of these reasons for preferring the study of science requires some amplification. Let us begin with the first.

In the study of literature or art our attention is perpetually riveted upon the past: the men of Greece or of the Renaissance did better than any men do now; the triumphs of former ages, so far from facilitating fresh triumphs in our own age, actually increase the difficulty of fresh triumphs by rendering originality harder of attainment; not only is artistic achievement not cumulative, but it seems even to depend upon a certain freshness and *naïveté* of impulse and vision which civilisation tends to destroy. Hence comes, to those who have been nourished on the literary and artistic productions of former ages, a certain peevishness and undue fastidiousness towards the present, from which there seems no escape except into the deliberate vandalism which ignores tradition and in the search after originality achieves only the eccentric. But in such vandalism there is none of the simplicity and spontaneity out of which great art springs: theory is still the canker in its core, and insincerity destroys the advantages of a merely pretended ignorance.

The despair thus arising from an education which suggests no pre-eminent mental activity except that of artistic creation is wholly absent from an education which gives the knowledge of scientific method. The discovery of scientific method, except in pure mathematics, is a thing of yesterday; speaking broadly, we may say that it dates from Galileo. Yet already it has transformed the world, and its success proceeds with ever-accelerating velocity. In science men have discovered an activity of the very highest value in which they are no longer, as in art, dependent for progress upon the appearance of continually greater genius, for in science the successors stand upon the shoulders of their predecessors; where one man of supreme genius has invented a method, a thousand lesser men can apply it. No transcendent ability is required in order to make useful discoveries in science; the edifice of science needs its masons, bricklayers, and common labourers as well as its foremen, master-builders, and architects. In art nothing worth doing can be done without genius; in science even a very moderate capacity can contribute to a supreme achievement.

In science the man of real genius is the man who invents a new method. The notable discoveries are often made by his successors, who can apply the method with fresh vigor, unimpaired by the previous labour of perfecting it; but the mental calibre of the thought required for their work, however brilliant, is not so great as that required by the first inventor of the method. There are in science immense numbers of different methods, appropriate to different classes of problems; but over and above them all, there is something not easily definable, which may be called *the* method of science. It was formerly customary to identify this with the inductive method, and to associate it with the name of Bacon. But the true inductive method was not discovered by Bacon, and the true method of science is something which includes deduction as much as induction, logic and mathematics as much as botany and geology. I shall not attempt the difficult task of stating what the scientific method is, but I will try to indicate the temper of mind out of which the scientific method grows, which is the second of the two merits that were mentioned above as belonging to a scientific education.

The kernel of the scientific outlook is a thing so simple, so obvious, so seemingly trivial, that the mention of it may almost excite derision. The kernel of the scientific outlook is the refusal to regard our own desires, tastes, and interests as affording a key to the understanding of the world. Stated thus baldly, this may seem no more than a trite truism. But to remember it consistently in matters arousing our passionate partisanship is by no means easy, especially where the available evidence is uncertain and inconclusive. A few illustrations will make this clear.

Aristotle, I understand, considered that the stars must move in circles because the circle is the most perfect curve. In the absence of evidence to the contrary, he allowed himself to decide a question of fact by an appeal to aesthetico-moral considerations. In such a case it is at once obvious to us that this appeal was unjustifiable. We know now how to ascertain as a fact the way in which the heavenly bodies move, and we know that they do not move in circles, or even in accurate ellipses, or in any other kind of simply describable curve. This may be painful to a certain hankering after simplicity of pattern in the universe, but we know that in astronomy such feelings are irrelevant. Easy as this knowledge seems now, we owe it to the courage and insight of the first inventors of scientific methods, and more especially to Galileo.

We may take as another illustration Malthus's doctrine of population. This illustration is all the better for the fact that his actual doctrine is now known to be largely erroneous. It is not his conclusions that are valuable, but the temper and method of his inquiry. As everyone knows, it was to him that Darwin owed an essential part of his theory of natural selection, and this was only possible because Malthus's outlook was truly scientific. His great merit lies in considering man not as the object of praise or blame, but as a part of nature, a thing with a certain characteristic behaviour from which certain consequences must follow. If the behaviour is not quite what Malthus supposed, if the consequences are not quite what he inferred, that may falsify his conclusions, but does not impair the value of his method. The objections which were made when his doctrine was new—that it was horrible and depressing, that the people ought not to act as he said they did, and so on—were all such as implied an unscientific attitude of mind; as against all of them, his calm determination to treat man as a natural phenomenon marks an important advance over the reformers of the eighteenth century and the Revolution.

Under the influence of Darwinism the scientific attitude towards man has now become fairly common, and is to some people quite natural, though to most it is still a difficult and artificial intellectual contortion. There is, however, one study which is as yet almost wholly untouched by the scientific spirit—I mean the study of philosophy. Philosophers and the public imagine that the scientific spirit must pervade pages that bristle with allusions to ions, germ-plasms, and the eye of shell-fish. But as the devil can quote Scripture, so the philosopher can quote science. The scientific spirit is not an affair of quotation, of externally acquired information, any more than manners are an affair of the etiquette-book. The scientific attitude of mind involves a sweeping away of all other desires in the interests of the desire to know—it involves suppression of hopes and fears, loves and hates, and the whole subjective emotional life, until we become subdued to the material, able to see it frankly, without preconceptions, without bias, without any wish except to see it as it is, and without any belief that what it is must be determined by some relation, positive or negative, to what we should like it to be, or to what we can easily imagine it to be.

Now in philosophy this attitude of mind has not as yet been achieved. A certain self-absorption, not personal, but human, has marked almost all attempts to conceive the universe as a whole. Mind, or some aspect of it—thought or will or sentence—has been regarded as the pattern after which the universe is to be conceived, for no better reason, at bottom, than that such a universe would not seem strange, and would give us the cosy feeling that every place is like home. To conceive the universe as essentially progressive or essentially deteriorating, for example, is to give to our hopes and fears a cosmic importance which *may,* of course, be justified, but which we have as yet no reason to suppose justified. Until we have learnt to think of it in ethically neutral terms, we have not arrived at a scientific attitude in philosophy; and until we have arrived at such an attitude, it is hardly to be hoped that philosophy will achieve any solid results.

I have spoken so far largely of the negative aspect of the scientific spirit, but it is from the positive aspect that its value is derived. The instinct of constructiveness, which is one of the chief incentives to artistic creation, can find in scientific systems a satisfaction more massive than in any epic poem. Disinterested curiosity, which is the source of almost all intellectual effort, finds with astonished delight that science can unveil secrets which might well have seemed for ever undiscoverable. The desire for a larger life and wider interests, for an escape from private circumstances, and even from the whole recurring human cycle of birth and death, is fulfilled by the impersonal cosmic outlook of science as by nothing else. To all these must be added, as contributing to the happiness of the man of science, the admiration of splendid achievement, and the consciousness of inestimable utility to the human race. A life devoted to science is therefore a happy life, and its happiness is derived from the very best sources that are open to dwellers on this troubled and passionate planet.

BACK TO NATURE

BY HENRY S. CANBY

No ONE tendency in life as we live it in America to-day is more characteristic than the impulse, as recurrent as summer, to take to the woods. Sometimes it disguises itself under the name of science; sometimes it is mingled with hunting and the desire to kill; often it is sentimentalized and leads strings of gaping "students" bird-hunting through the wood lot; and again it perilously resembles a desire to get back from civilization and go "on the loose." Say your worst of it, still the fact remains that more Americans go back to nature for one reason or another annually than any civilized men before them. And more Americans, I fancy, are studying nature in clubs or public schools —or, in summer camps and the Boy Scouts, imitating nature's creatures, the Indian and the pioneer—than even statistics could make believable.

What is the cause? In life, it is perhaps some survival of the pioneering instinct, spending itself upon fishing, or bird-hunting, or trail hiking, much as the fight instinct leads us to football, or the hunt instinct sends every dog sniffing at dawn through the streets of his town. Not every one is thus atavistic, if this be atavism; not every American is sensitive to spruce spires, or the hermit thrush's chant, or white water in a forest gorge, or the meadow lark across the frosted fields. Naturally. The surprising fact is that in a bourgeois civilisation like ours, so many are affected.

And yet what a criterion nature love or nature indifference is. It seems that if I can try a man by a silent minute in the pines, the view of a jay pirating through the bushes, spring odors, or December flush on evening snow, I can classify him by his reactions. Just where I do not know; for certainly I do not put him beyond the pale if his response is not as mine. And yet he will differ, I feel sure, in more significant matters. He is not altogether of my world. Nor does he enter into this essay. There are enough without him, and of every class. In the West, the very day laborer pitches his camp in the mountains for his two weeks' holiday. In the East and Middle West, every pond with a fringe of hemlocks, or hill view by a trolley line, or strip of ocean beach, has its cluster of bungalows where the proletariat perform their *villeggiatura* as the Italian aristocracy did in the days of the Renaissance. Patently the impulse exists, and counts for something here in America.

It counts for something, too, in American literature. Since our writing ceased being colonial English and began to reflect a race in the making, the note of woods-longing has been so insistent that one wonders whether here is not to be found at last the characteristic "trait" that we have all been patriotically seeking.

I do not limit myself in this statement to the professed "nature writers" of whom we have bred far more than any other race with which I am familiar. In the list—which I shall not attempt—of the greatest American writers, one cannot fail to include Emerson, Hawthorne, Thoreau, Cooper, Lowell, and Whitman. And every one of these men was vitally concerned with nature, and some were obsessed by it. Lowell was a scholar and man of the world, urban therefore; but his poetry is more enriched by its homely New England background than by its European polish. Cooper's ladies and gentlemen are puppets merely, his plots melodrama; it is the woods he knew, and the creatures of the woods, Deerslayer and Chingachgook, that preserve his books. Whitman made little distinction between nature and human nature, perhaps too little. But read "Out of the Cradle Endlessly Rocking" or "The Song of the Redwood-Tree," and see how keen and how vital was his instinct for native soil. As for Hawthorne, you could make a text-book on nature study from his "Note-Books." He was an imaginative moralist first of all; but he worked out his visions in terms of New England woods and hills. So did Emerson. The day was "not wholly profane" for him when he had "given heed to some natural object." Thoreau needs no proving. He is at the forefront of all field and forest lovers in all languages and times.

These are the greater names. The lesser are as leaves in the forest: Audubon, Burroughs, Muir, Clarence King, Lanier, Robert Frost, and many more—the stream broadening and shallowing through literary scientists and earnest forest lovers to romantic "nature fakers," literary sportsmen, amiable students, and tens of thousands of teachers inculcating this American tendency in another generation. The phenomenon asks for an explanation. It is more than a category of American literature that I am presenting, it is an American trait.

The explanation I wish to proffer in this essay may sound fantastical; most explanations that explain anything usually do—at first. I believe that this vast rush of nature into American literature is more than a mere reflection of a liking for the woods. It represents a search for a tradition, and its capture.

Good books, like well-built houses, must have tradition behind them. The Homers and Shakespeares and

Goethes spring from rich soil left by dead centuries; they are like native trees that grow so well nowhere else. The little writers—hacks who sentimentalize to the latest order, and display their plot novelties like bargains on an advertising page—are just as traditional. The only difference is that their tradition goes back to books instead of life. Middle-sized authors —the very good and the probably enduring—are successful largely because they have gripped a tradition and followed it through to contemporary life. This is what Thackeray did in "Vanity Fair," Howells in "The Rise of Silas Lapham," and Mrs. Wharton in "The House of Mirth." But the back-to-nature books —both the sound ones and those shameless exposures of the private emotions of ground hogs and turtles that call themselves nature books—are the most traditional of all. For they plunge directly into what might be called the adventures of the American sub-consciousness.

It is the sub-consciousness that carries tradition into literature. That curious reservoir where forgotten experiences lie waiting in every man's mind, as vivid as on the day of first impression, is the chief concern of psychologists nowadays. But it has never yet had due recognition from literary criticism. If the sub-consciousness is well stocked, a man writes truly, his imagination is vibrant with human experience, he sets his own humble observation against a background of all he has learned and known and forgotten of civilization. If it is under-populated, if he has done little, felt little, known little of the traditional experiences of the intellect, he writes thinly. He can report what he sees but it is hard for him to create. It was Chaucer's rich sub-consciousness that turned his simple little story of Chauntecleer into a comment upon humanity. Other men had told that story—and made it scarcely more than trivial. It is the promptings of forgotten memories in the sub-consciousness that give to a simple statement the force of old, unhappy things, that keep thoughts true to experience, and test fancy by life. The sub-consciousness is the governor of the waking brain. Tradition—which is just man's memory of man—flows through it like an underground river from which rise the springs of every-day thinking. If there is anything remarkable about a book, look to the sub-consciousness of the writer and study the racial tradition that it bears.

Now, I am far from proposing to analyze the American sub-consciousness. No man can define it. But of this much I am certain. The American habit of going "back to nature" means that in our sub-consciousness nature is peculiarly active. We react to nature as does no other race. We are the descendants of pioneers —all of us. And if we have not inherited a memory of pioneering experiences, at least we possess inherited tendencies and desires. The impulse that drove Boone westward may nowadays do no more than send some young Boone canoeing on Temagami, or push him up Marcy or Shasta to inexplicable happiness on the top. But the drive is there. And furthermore, nature is still strange in America. Even now the wilderness is far from no American city. Birds, plants, trees, even animals have not, as in Europe, been absorbed into the common knowledge of the race. There are discoveries everywhere for those who can make them. Nature, indeed, is vivid in a surprising number of American brain cells, marking them with a deep and endurable impress. And our flood of nature books has served to increase her power.

It was never so with the European traditions that we brought to America with us. That is why no one reads early American books. They are pallid, ill-nourished, because their traditions are pallid. They draw upon the least active portion of the American sub-consciousness, and reflect memories not of experience, contact, live thought, but of books. Even Washington Irving, our first great author, is not free from this indictment. If, responding to some obscure drift of his race towards humor and the short story, he had not ripened his Augustan inheritance upon an American hillside, he, too, would by now seem juiceless, withered, like a thousand cuttings from English stock planted in forgotten pages of his period. It was not until the end of our colonial age and the rise of democracy towards Jackson's day, that the rupture with our English background became sufficiently complete to make us fortify pale memories of home by a search for fresher, more vigorous tradition.

We have been searching ever since, and many eminent critics think that we have still failed to establish American literature upon American soil. The old traditions, of course, were essential. Not even the most self-sufficient American hopes to establish a brand-new culture. The problem has been to domesticate Europe, not to get rid of her. But the old stock needed a graft, just as an old fruit tree needs a graft. It requires a new tradition. We found a tradition in New England; and then New England was given over to the alien and her traditions became local or historical merely. We found another in border life; and then the Wild West reached the Pacific and vanished. Time and again we have been flung back upon our English sources, and forced to imitate a literature sprung from a riper soul. Of course, this criticism, as it stands, is too sweeping. It neglects Mark Twain and the tradition of the American boy; it neglects Walt Whitman and the literature of free and turbulent democracy; it neglects Longfellow and Poe and that romantic tradition of love and beauty common to all Western races. But, at least, it makes one understand why the American writer has passionately sought anything that would put an American quality into his transplanted style.

He has been very successful in local color. But then local color is local. It is a minor art. In the field of human nature he has fought a doubtful battle. An occasional novel has broken through into regions where it is possible to be utterly American even while writing English. Poems too have followed. But here lie our great failures. I do not speak of the "great American novel," yet to come. I refer to the absence of a school of American fiction, or poetry, or drama, that has linked itself to any tradition broader than the romance of the colonies, New England of the 'forties, or the East Side of New York. The men who most often write for all America are mediocre. They strike no deeper than a week-old interest in current activity. They aim to hit the minute because they are shrewd enough to see that for "all America" there is very little continuity just now between one minute and the next. The America they write for is contemptuous of tradition, although worshipping convention, which is the tradition of the ignorant. The men who write for a fit audience though few are too often local or archaic, narrow or European, by necessity if not by choice.

And ever since we began to incur the condescension of foreigners by trying to be American, we have been conscious of this weak-rootedness in our literature and trying to remedy it. This is why our flood of nature books for a century is so significant. They may seem peculiar instruments for probing tradition—particularly the sentimental ones. The critic has not yet admitted some of the heartiest among them—Audubon's sketches of pioneer life, for example—into literature at all. And yet, unless I am mightily mistaken, they are signs of convalescence as clearly as they are symptoms of our disease. These United States, of course, are infinitely more important than the plot of mother earth upon which they have been erected. The intellectual background that we have inherited from Europe is more significant than the moving spirit of woods and soil and waters here. The graft, in truth, is less valuable than the tree upon which it is grafted. Yet it determines the fruit. So with the books of our nature lovers. They represent a passionate attempt to acclimatize the breed. Thoreau has been one of our most original writers. He and his multitudinous followers, wise and foolish, have helped establish us on our new soil.

I may seem to exaggerate the services of a group of writers who, after all, can show but one great name, Thoreau's. I do not think so, for if the heart of the nature lover is sometimes more active than his head, the earth intimacies he gives us are vital to literature in a very practical sense. Thanks to the modern science of geography, we are beginning to understand the profound and powerful influence of physical environment upon men. The geographer can tell you why Charleston was aristocratic, why New York is hurried and nervous, why Chicago is self-confident. He can guess at least why in old communities, like Hardy's Wessex or the North of France, the inhabitants of villages not ten miles apart will differ in temperament and often in temper, hill town varying from lowland village beneath it sometimes more than Kansas City from Minneapolis. He knows that the old elemental forces—wind, water, fire, and earth—still mold men's thoughts and lives a hundred times more than they guess, even when pavements, electric lights, tight roofs, and artificial heat seem to make nature only a name. He knows that the sights and sounds and smells about us, clouds, songs, and wind murmurings, rain-washed earth, the fruit trees blossoming, enter into our sub-consciousness with a power but seldom appraised. Prison life, factory service long continued, a clerk's stool, a housewife's day-long duties— these things stunt and transform the human animal as nothing else, because of all experiences they most restrict, most impoverish the natural environment. And it is the especial function of nature books to make vivid and warm and sympathetic our background of nature. They make conscious our sub-conscious dependence upon earth that bore us. They do not merely inform (there the scientist may transcend them), they enrich the subtle relationship between us and our environment. Move a civilization and its literature from one hemisphere to another, and their adapting, adjusting services become most valuable. Men like Thoreau are worth more than we have ever guessed.

No one has ever written more honest books than Thoreau's "Walden," his "Autumn," "Summer," and the rest. There is not one literary flourish in the whole of them, although they are done with consummate literary care; nothing but honest, if not always accurate, observation of the world of hill-slopes, waves, flowers, birds, and beasts, and honest, shrewd philosophizing as to what it all meant for him, an American. Here is a man content to take a walk, fill his mind with observation, and then come home to think. Repeat the walk, repeat or vary the observation, change or expand the thought, and you have Thoreau. No wonder he brought his first edition home, not seriously depleted, and made his library of it! Thoreau needs excerpting to be popular. Most nature books do. But not to be valuable!

For see what this queer genius was doing. Lovingly, laboriously, and sometimes a little tediously, he was studying his environment. For some generations his ancestors had lived on a new soil, too busy in squeezing life from it to be practically aware of its differences. They and the rest had altered Massachusetts. Massachusetts had altered them. Why? To what? The answer is not yet ready. But here is one descendant who will know at least what Massachusetts is—wave, wind, soil, and the life therein and thereon. He begins humbly with the little things; but humanly, not as the out-and-out scientist goes to work, to classify or to study the narrower laws of organic development; or romantically as the sentimentalist, who intones his "Ah!" at the sight of dying leaves or the cocoon becoming a moth. It is all human, and yet all intensely practical with Thoreau. He envies the Indian not because he is "wild," or "free," or any such nonsense, but for his instinctive adaptations to his background,—because nature has become traditional, stimulative with him. And simply, almost naïvely, he sets down what he has discovered. The land I live in is like this or that; such and such life lives in it; and this is what it all means for me, the transplanted European, for us, Americans, who have souls to shape and characters to mold in a new environment, under influences subtler than we guess. "I make it my business to extract from Nature whatever nutriment she can furnish me, though at the risk of endless iteration. I milk the sky and the earth." And again: "Surely it is a defect in our Bible that it is not truly ours, but a Hebrew Bible. The most pertinent illustrations for us are to be drawn not from Egypt or Babylonia, but from New England. Natural objects and phenomena are the original symbols or types which express our thoughts and feelings. Yet American scholars, having little or no root in the soil, commonly strive with all their might to confine themselves to the imported symbols alone. All the true growth and experience, the living speech, they would fain reject as 'Americanisms.' It is the old error which the church, the state, the school, ever commit, choosing darkness rather than light, holding fast to the old and to tradition. When I really know that our river pursues a serpentine course to the Merrimac, shall I continue to describe it by referring to some other river no older than itself, which is like it, and call it a meander? It is no more meandering than the Meander is musketaquiding."

This for Thoreau was going back to nature. Our historians of literature who cite him as an example of how to be American without being strenuous, as an instance of leisure nobly earned, are quite wrong. If any man has striven to make us at home in America, it is Thoreau. He gave his life to it; and in some measure it is thanks to him that with most Americans you reach intimacy most quickly by talking about "the woods."

Thoreau gave to this American tendency the touch of genius and the depth of real thought. After his day the "back-to-nature" idea became more popular and perhaps more picturesque. Our literature becomes more and more aware of an American background. Bobolinks and thrushes take the place of skylarks; sumach and cedar begin to be as familiar as heather and gorse; forests, prairies, a clear, high sky, a snowy winter, a summer of thunderstorms, drive out the misty England which, since the days of Cynewulf, our ancestors had seen in the mind's eye while they were writing. Nature literature becomes a category. Men make their reputations by means of it.

No one has yet catalogued—so far as I am aware—
the vast collection of back-to-nature books that followed
Thoreau. No one has ever seriously criticized it, except
Mr. Roosevelt, who with characteristic vigor of phrase,
stamped "nature-faking" on its worser half. But every
one reads in it. Indeed, the popularity of such writing
has been so great as to make us distrust its serious literary value. And yet, viewed internationally, there are
few achievements in American literature so original. I
will not say that John Muir and John Burroughs, upon
whom Thoreau's mantle fell, have written great books.
Probably not. Certainly it is too soon to say. But
when you have gathered the names of Gilbert White, Jef-
feries, Fabre, Maeterlinck, and in slightly different
genres, Izaak Walton, Hudson, and Kipling from various
literatures you will find few others abroad to list with
ours. Nor do our men owe one jot or tittle of their
inspiration to individuals on the other side of the water.

Locally, too, these books are more noteworthy than
may at first appear. They are curiously passionate, and
passion in American literature since the Civil War is
rare. I do not mean sentiment, or romance, or eroticism.
I mean such passion as Wordsworth felt for his lakes,
Byron (even when most Byronic) for the ocean, the
author of "The Song of Roland" for his Franks. Muir
loved the Yosemite as a man might love a woman. Every
word he wrote of the Sierras is touched with intensity.
Hear him after a day on Alaskan peaks. "Dancing down
the mountain to camp, my mind glowing like the sun-
beaten glaciers, I found the Indians seated around a good
fire, entirely happy now that the farthest point of the
journey was safely reached and the long, dark storm
was cleared away. How hopefully, peacefully bright that
night were the stars in the frosty sky, and how impres-

sive was the thunder of icebergs, rolling, swelling, rever-
berating through the solemn stillness! I was too happy
to sleep."

Such passion, and often such style, is to be found in
all these books when they are good books. Compare a
paragraph or two of the early Burroughs on his birch-
clad lake country, or Thoreau upon Concord pines, with
the "natural history paragraph" that English magazines used to publish, and you will feel it. Compare any
of the lesser nature books of the mid-nineteenth century
—Clarence King's "Mountaineering in the Sierras," for
example—with the current novel writing of the period
and you will feel the greater sincerity. A passion for
nature! Except the New England passion for ideals,
Whitman's passion for democracy, and Poe's lonely devotion to beauty, I sometimes think that this is the only
great passion that has found its way into American literature.

Hence the "nature fakers." The passion of one generation becomes the sentiment of the next. And sentiment is easily capitalized. The individual can be stirred
by nature as she is. A hermit thrush singing in moonlight above a Catskill clove will move him. But the
populace will require something more sensational. To
the sparkling water of truth must be added the syrup of
sentiment and the cream of romance. Mr. Kipling, following ancient traditions of the Orient, gave personalities to his animals so that stories might be made from
them. Mr. Long, Mr. Roberts, Mr. London, Mr. Thomp-
son-Seton, and the rest, have told stories about animals
so that the American interest in nature might be ex-
ploited. The difference is essential. If the "Jungle
Books" teach anything it is the moral ideals of the British
Empire. But our nature romancers—a fairer term than

"fakers," since they do not willingly "fake"—teach the background and tradition of our soil. In the process they inject sentiment, giving us the noble desperation of the stag, the startling wolf-longings of the dog, and the picturesque outlawry of the ground hog,—and get a hundred readers where Thoreau got one.

This is the same indictment as that so often brought against the stock American novel, that it prefers the gloss of easy sentiment to the rough, true fact, that it does not grapple direct with things as they are in America, but looks at them through optimist's glasses that obscure and soften the scene. Nevertheless, I very much prefer the sentimentalized animal story to the sentimentalized man story. The first, as narrative, may be romantic bosh, but it does give one a loving, faithful study of background that is worth the price that it costs in illusion. It reaches my emotions, as a novelist who splashed his sentiment with equal profusion never could. My share of the race mind is willing even to be tricked into sympathy with its environment. I would rather believe that the sparrow on my telephone wire is swearing at the robin on my lawn than never to notice either of them!

How curiously complete and effective is the service of these nature books, when all is considered. There is no better instance, I imagine, of how literature and life act and react upon one another. The plain American takes to the woods because he wants to, he does not know why. The writing American puts the woods into his books, also because he wants to, although I suspect that sometimes he knows very well why. Nevertheless, the same general tendency, the same impulse, lie behind both. But reading nature books makes us crave more nature, and every gratification of curiosity marks itself upon the subconsciousness. Thus the clear, vigorous tradition of the soil passes through us to our books, and from our books to us. It is the soundest, the sweetest, if not the greatest and deepest inspiration of American literature. In the confusion that attends the meeting here of all the races it is something to cling to; it is our own.

THE HORIZON

BY ALICE MEYNELL

To MOUNT a hill is to lift with you something lighter and brighter than yourself or than any meaner burden. You lift the world, you raise the horizon; you give a signal for the distance to stand up. It is like the scene in the Vatican when a Cardinal, with his dramatic Italian hands, bids the kneeling groups to arise. He does more than bid them. He lifts them, he gathers them up, far and near, with the upward gesture of both arms; he takes them to their feet with the compulsion of his expressive force. Or it is as when a conductor takes his players to successive heights of music. You summon the sea, you bring the mountains, the distances unfold unlooked-for wings and take an even flight. You are but a man lifting his weight upon the upward road, but as you climb the circle of the world goes up to face you.

Not here or there, but with a definite continuity, the unseen unfolds. This distant hill outsoars that less distant, but all are on the wing, and the plain raises its verge. All things follow and wait upon your eyes. You lift these up, not by the raising of your eyelids, but by the pilgrimage of your body. "Lift thine eyes to the mountains." It is then that other mountains lift themselves to your human eyes.

It is the law whereby the eye and the horizon answer one another that makes the way up a hill so full of universal movement. All the landscape is on pilgrimage. The town gathers itself closer, and its inner harbours literally come to light; the headlands repeat them-

selves; little cups within the treeless hills open and
show their farms. In the sea are many regions. A
breeze is at play for a mile or two, and the surface is
turned. There are roads and curves in the blue and
in the white. Not a step of your journey up the height
that has not its replies in the steady motion of land and
sea. Things rise together like a flock of many-feathered
birds.

But it is the horizon, more than all else, you have
come in search of; that is your chief companion on your
way. It is to uplift the horizon to the equality of your
sight that you go high. You give it a distance worthy
of the skies. There is no distance, except the distance
in the sky, to be seen from the level earth; but from the
height is to be seen the distance of this world. The line
is sent back into the remoteness of light, the verge is
removed beyond verge, into a distance that is enormous
and minute.

So delicate and so slender is the distant horizon that
nothing less near than Queen Mab and her chariot can
equal its fineness. Here on the edges of the eyelids,
or there on the edges of the world—we know no other
place for things so exquisitely made, so thin, so small and
tender. The touches of her passing, as close as dreams,
or the utmost vanishing of the forest or the ocean in
the white light between the earth and the air; nothing
else is quite so intimate and fine. The extremities of a
mountain view have just such tiny touches as the closeness of closing eyes shut in.

On the horizon is the sweetest light. Elsewhere colour
mars the simplicity of light; but there colour is effaced,
not as men efface it, by a blur or darkness, but by mere
light. The bluest sky disappears on that shining edge;
there is not substance enough for colour. The rim of the
hill, of the woodland, of the meadowland, of the sea—

let it only be far enough—has the same absorption of colour; and even the dark things drawn upon the bright edges of the sky are lucid, the light is among them, and they are mingled with it. The horizon has its own way of making bright the pencilled figures of forests, which are black but luminous.

On the horizon, moreover, closes the long perspective of the sky. There you perceive that an ordinary sky of clouds—not a thunder sky—is not a wall but the under-side of a floor. You see the clouds that repeat each other grow smaller by distance; and you find a new unity in the sky and earth that gather alike the great lines of their designs to the same distant close. There is no longer an alien sky, tossed up in unintelligible heights.

Of all the things that London has foregone, the most to be regretted is the horizon. Not the bark of the trees in its right colour; not the spirit of the growing grass, which has in some way escaped from the parks; not the smell of the earth unmingled with the odour of soot; but rather the mere horizon. No doubt the sun makes a beautiful thing of the London smoke at times, and in some places of the sky; but not there, not where the soft sharp distance ought to shine. To be dull there is to put all relations and comparisons in the wrong, and to make the sky lawless.

The horizon dark with storm is another thing. The weather darkens the line and defines it, or mingles it with the raining cloud; or softly dims it, or blackens it against a gleam of narrow sunshine in the sky. The stormy horizon will take wing, and the sunny. Go high enough, and you can raise the light from beyond the shower, and the shadow from behind the ray. Only the shapeless and lifeless smoke disobeys and defeats the summons of the eyes.

Up at the top of the seaward hill your first thought is one of some compassion for sailors, inasmuch as they see but little of their sea. A child on a mere Channel cliff looks upon spaces and sizes that they cannot see in the Pacific, on the ocean side of the world. Never in the solitude of the blue water, never between the Cape of Good Hope and Cape Horn, never between the Islands and the West, has the seaman seen anything but a little circle of sea. The Ancient Mariner, when he was alone, did but drift through a thousand narrow solitudes. The sailor has nothing but his mast, indeed. And but for his mast he would be isolated in as small a world as that of a traveller through the plains.

A close circlet of waves is the sailor's famous offing. His offing hardly deserves the name of horizon. To hear him you might think something of his offing, but you do not so when you sit down in the centre of it.

As the upspringing of all things at your going up the heights, so steady, so swift, is the subsidence at your descent. The further sea lies away, hill folds down behind hill. The whole upstanding world, with its looks serene and alert, its distant replies, its signals of many miles, its signs and communications of light, gathers down and pauses. This flock of birds which is the mobile landscape wheels and goes to earth. The cardinal weighs down the audience with his downward hands. Farewell to the most delicate horizon.

SHADOWS

BY ALICE MEYNELL

ANOTHER good reason why we ought to leave blank,
unvexed and unencumbered with paper patterns the
ceiling and walls of a simple house is that the plain surface may be visited by the unique designs of shadows.
The opportunity is so fine a thing that it ought oftener
to be offered to the light and to yonder handful of long
sedges and rushes in a vase. Their slender gray design
of shadows upon white walls is better than tedious,
trivial, or anxious devices from the shop.

The shadow has all intricacies of perspective simply
translated into line and intersecting curve, and pictorially
presented to the eyes, not to the mind. The shadow
knows nothing except its flat designs, having no third
dimension. It is single; it draws a decoration that was
never seen before, and will never be seen again, and that
untouched, varies with the journey of the sun, shifts the
inter-relation of a score of delicate lines at the mere
passing of time, though all the room be motionless. Why
will design insist upon its importunate immortality?
Wiser is the drama, and wiser the dance, that do not
pause upon an attitude. But these walk with passion
or pleasure, while the shadow walks with the earth. It
alters as the hours wheel.

Moreover, while the habit of your sunward thoughts
is still flowing southward, after the winter and the
spring, it surprises you in the sudden gleam of a north-
western sun. It decks a new wall; it is shed by a late
sunset through a window unvisited for a year past; it

betrays the flitting of the sun into unwonted skies—a sun that takes the mid-summer world in the rear, and shows his head at a sally-porte, and is about to alight on an unused horizon. So does the gray dawning, with which you have allowed the sun and your pot of rushes to adorn your room, play the stealthy game of the year.

You need not stint yourself of shadows, for an occasion. It needs but four candles to make a hanging Oriental bell play the most buoyant jugglery overhead. Two lamps make of one palm-branch a symmetrical counterchange of shadows, and here two palm-branches close with one another in shadow, their arches flowing together, and their paler grays darkening. It is hard to believe that there are many to prefer a "repeating pattern."

It must be granted to them that a gray day robs of their decoration the walls that should be sprinkled with shadows. Let, then, a plaque or a picture be kept for hanging on shadowless days. To dress a room once for all, and to give it no more heed, is to neglect the units of the days.

Shadows within doors are yet only messages from that world of shadows which is the landscape of sunshine. Facing a May sun you see little except an infinite number of shadows. Atoms of shadow—be the day bright enough —compose the very air through which you see the light. The trees show you a shadow for every leaf, and the poplars are sprinkled upon the shining sky with little shadows that look translucent. The liveliness of every shadow is that some light is reflected into it; shade and shine have been entangled as though by some wild wind through their million molecules.

By these shadows of mere mid-air the coolness and the dark of night are interlocked with the unclouded sun.

Turn sunward from the north, and shadows come into life, the action, and the transparence of their day.

To eyes tired and retired all day within lowered blinds, the light looks still and changeless. So many squares of sunshine abide for so many hours, and when the sun has circled away, they pass and are extinguished. Him who lies alone there the outer world touches less by this long sunshine than by the haste and passage of a shadow. Although there may be no tree to stand between his window and the south, and although no noon-day wind may blow a branch of roses across the blind, shadows and their life will be carried across by a brilliant bird.

To the sick man a cloud-shadow is nothing but an eclipse; he cannot see its shape, its colour, its approach, or its flight. It does but darken his window as it darkens the day, and is gone again; he does not see it pluck and snatch the sun. But the flying bird shows him wings. What flash of light could be more bright for him than such a flash of darkness?

It is the pulse of life, where all change had seemed to be charmed. If he had seen the bird itself he would have seen less—the bird's shadow was a message from the sun.

There are two separated flights for the fancy to follow, the flight of the bird in the air, and the flight of its shadow on earth. This goes across the window blind, across the wood, where it is astray for a while in the shades; it dips into the valley, growing vaguer and larger, runs, quicker than the wind, uphill, smaller and darker on the soft and dry grass, and rushes to meet its bird when the bird swoops to a branch and clings.

In the great bird country of the north-eastern littoral of England, about Holy Island and the basaltic rocks, the shadows of the high birds are the movement and the pulse of the solitude. Where there are no woods to make a shade, the sun suffers the brilliant eclipse of flocks or pearl-white sea birds, or of the solitary creature driving on the wind. Theirs is always a surprise of flight. The clouds go one way, but the birds go all ways: in from the sea or out, across the sands, inland to high northern fields, where the crops are late by a month. They fly so high that though they have the shadow of the sun under their wings, they have the light of the earth there also. The waves and the coast shine up to them, and they fly between lights.

Black flocks and white, they gather their delicate shadows up, "swift as dreams," at the end of their flight into the clefts, platforms, and ledges of harbourless rocks, dominating the North Sea. They subside by degrees, with lessening and shortening volleys of the wings and cries, until there comes the general shadow of night wherewith the shadows close, complete.

The evening is the shadow of another flight. All the birds have traced wild and innumerable paths across the mid-Way earth; their shadows have fled all day faster than her streams, and have overtaken all the movement of her wingless creatures. But now, at nightfall, it is the flight of the very earth that carries her clasped shadow from the sun.

CLOUDS

BY ALICE MEYNELL

DURING a part of the year London does not see the
clouds. Not to see the clear sky might seem her chief
loss, but that is shared by the rest of England, and is,
besides, but a slight privation. Not to see the clear sky
is, elsewhere, to see the cloud. But not so in London.
You may go for a week or two at a time, even though
you hold your head up as you walk, and even though
you have windows that really open, and yet you shall see
no whole cloud, or but a single edge, the fragment of a
form.

Guillotine windows never wholly open, but are filled
with a doubled glass toward the sky when you open them
towards the street. They are, therefore, a sure sign that
for all the years when no other windows were used in
London, nobody cared very much for the sky, or even
knew so much as whether there was a sky.

But a privation of cloud is indeed a graver loss than
the world knows. Terrestrial scenery is much, but it is
not all. Men go in search of it; but the celestial scenery
journeys to them; it goes its way round the world. It
has no nation, it costs no weariness, it knows no bonds.
The terrestrial scenery—the tourist's—is a prisoner
compared with this. The tourist's scenery moves indeed,
but only like Wordsworth's maiden, with earth's diurnal
course; it is made as fast as its own graves. And for
its changes it depends upon the mobility of the skies.
The mere green flushing of its own sap makes only the
least of its varieties; for the greater it must wait upon

the visits of the light. Spring and autumn are inconsiderable events in a landscape compared with the shadows of a cloud.

The cloud controls the light, and the mountains on earth appear or fade according to its passage; they wear so simply, from head to foot, the luminous gray or the emphatic purple, as the cloud permits, that their own local colour and their own local season are lost and cease, effaced before the all-important mood of the cloud. The sea has no mood except that of the sky and of its winds. It is the cloud that, holding the sun's rays in a sheaf as a giant holds a handful of spears, strikes the horizon, touches the extreme edge with a delicate revelation of light or suddenly puts it out and makes the foreground shine.

Everyone knows the manifest work of the cloud when it descends and partakes in the landscape obviously, lies half-way across the mountain slope, stoops to rain heavily upon the lake, and blots out part of the view by the rough method of standing in front of it. But its greatest things are done from its own place, aloft. Thence does it distribute the sun.

Thence does it lock away between the hills and valleys more mysteries than a poet conceals, but, like him, not by interception. Thence it writes out and cancels all the tracery of Monte Rosa, or lets the pencils of the sun renew them. Thence, hiding nothing, and yet making dark, it sheds deep colour upon the forest land of Sussex, so that, seen from the hills, all the country is divided between grave blue and graver sunlight.

But the cloud is never so victorious as when it towers above some little landscape of rather paltry interest—a conventional river heavy with water, gardens with their little evergreens, walks, and shrubberies; and thick trees, impervious to the light, touched, as the novelists always have it, with "autumn tints." High over these rises, in the enormous scale of the scenery of clouds, what no man expected—an heroic sky. Few of the things that were ever done upon earth are great enough to be done under such a heaven. It was surely designed for other days; it is for an epic world. Your eyes sweep a thousand miles of cloud. What are the distances of earth to these, and what are the distances of the clear and cloudless sky? The very horizons of the landscape are near, for the round world dips so soon; and the distances of the mere clear sky are unmeasured—you rest upon nothing until you come to a star, and the star itself is immeasurable.

The cloud, moreover, controls the sun, not merely by keeping the custody of his rays, but by becoming the counsellor of his temper. The cloud veils an angry sun, or, more terribly, lets fly an angry ray, suddenly bright upon tree and tower, with iron-gray storm for a background. Or when anger had but threatened the cloud reveals him, gentle beyond hope. It is in the confidence of the winds, and wears their colours. There is a heavenly game, on south-west wind days, when the clouds are bowled by a breeze from behind the evening. They are round and brilliant, and come leading up from the horizon for hours. This is a frolic and haphazard sky.

All unlike this is the sky that has a centre, and stands composed about it. As the clouds marshalled the earthly mountains, so the clouds in turn are now ranged. The tops of all the celestial Andes aloft are swept at once by a single ray, warmed with a single colour. Promontory after league-long promontory of a stiller Mediterranean in the sky is called out of mist and gray by the same finger. The cloudland is very great, but a sunbeam makes all its nations and continents sudden with light.

The cloud has a name suggesting darkness; nevertheless, it is not merely the guardian of the sun's rays and their director. It is the sun's treasurer; it holds the light that the world has lost. We talk of sunshine and moon-shine, but not of cloud-shine, which is yet one of the illuminations of our skies. A shining cloud is one of the most majestic of all secondary lights. If the reflecting moon is the bride, this is "the friend of the bridegroom."

SKYLARKS

BY GEORGE SANTAYANA

THERE is a poet in every nice Englishman; there is a little fund of free vitality deep down in him which the exigencies of his life do not tap and which no art at his command can render articulate. He is able to draw upon it, and to drink in the refreshment and joy of inner freedom, only in silent or religious moments. He feels he is never so much himself as when he has shed for the time being all his ordinary preoccupations. That is why his religion is so thin or (as he might say) so pure: it has no relevance to any particular passions or events; a featureless background, distant and restful, like a pale clear sky. That is why he loves nature, and country life, and hates towns and vulgar people; those he likes he conceives emasculated, sentimentalized, and robed in white. The silent poet within him is only a lyric poet. When he returns from those draughts of rare and abstract happiness, he would find it hard to reconcile himself to the world, or to himself, did he not view both through a veil of convention and make-believe; he could not be honest about himself and retain his self-respect; he could not be clear about other people and remain kind. Yet to be kind to all, and true to his inner man, is his profound desire; because even if life, in its unvarnished truth, is a gross medley and a cruel business, it is redeemed for him, nevertheless, by the perfect beauty of soul that here and there may shine through it. Hamlet is the classic version of this imprisoned spirit; the skylark seems a symbol of what it would be in its freedom.

Poor larks! Is the proportion of dull matter in their bodies, I wonder, really less than in ours? Must they not find food and rear their young? Must they not in their measure work, watch, and tremble? Cold, hunger, and disease probably beset them more often and more bitterly than they do most of us. But we think of them selfishly, as of actors on the stage, only in the character they wear when they attract our attention. As we walk through the fields we stop to watch and to listen to them performing in the sky, and never think of their home troubles; which they, too, seem for the moment to have eluded; at least they have energy and time enough left over from those troubles for all this luxury of song. It is this glorious if temporary emancipation, this absolute defiant emphasis laid with so much sweetness on the inner life that the poet in every nice Englishman loves in the lark; it seems to reveal a brother-spirit more fortunate than oneself, almost a master and a guide.

Larks made even Shelley envious, although no man ever had less reason to envy them for their gift, either in its rapture or in its abstraction. Even the outer circumstances of Shelley's life were very favourable to inspiration and left him free to warble as much and as ardently as he chose; but perhaps he was somewhat deceived by the pathos of distance and fancied that in Nephelococcygia * bad birds and wicked traditions were less tyrannous than in parliamentary England. He seems to have thought that human nature was not really made for puddings and port wine and hunting and elections, nor even for rollicking at universities and reading Greek, but only for innocent lyrical ecstasies and fiery convictions that nevertheless should somehow not render people covetous

* Cloud-cuckoo-land.

or jealous or cruelly disposed, nor constrain them to prevent any one from doing anything that any one might
choose to do. Perhaps in truth the cloisters of Oxford
and the streets of London are quite as propitious to the
flights of which human nature is really capable as English fields are to the flights of larks; there is food in
them for thought. But Shelley was impatient of human
nature; he was horrified to find that society is a web of
merciless ambitions and jealousies, mitigated by a quite
subsidiary kindness; he forgot that human life is pre-
carious and that its only weapon against circumstances,
and against rival men, is intelligent action, intelligent
war. The case is not otherwise with larks, on the fundamental earthly side of their existence; yet because their
flight is bodily, because it is a festive outpouring of animal vitality, not of art or reflection, it suggests to us a
total freedom of the inner man, a freedom which is impossible.

In the flight of larks, however, by a rare favour of
fortune, all seems to be spontaneity, courage, and trust,
even within this material sphere; nothing seems to be
adjustment or observation. Their life in the air is a sort
of intoxication of innocence and happiness in the blind
pulses of existence. They are voices of the morning,
young hearts seeking experience and not remembering it;
when they seem to sob they are only catching their
breath. They spring from the ground as impetuously
as a rocket or the jet of a fountain, that bursts into a
shower of sparks or of dew-drops; they circle as they
rise, soaring through veil after veil of luminous air, or
dropping from level to level. Their song is like the
gurgling of little rills of water, perpetual through its
delicate variations, and throbbing with a changed volume
at every change in the breeze. Their rapture seems to
us seraphic, not merely because it descends to us invisibly

from a luminous height, straining our eyes and necks—
in itself a cheap sublimity—but rather because the lark
sings so absolutely for the mad sake of singing. He is
evidently making high holiday, spending his whole
strength on something ultimate and utterly useless, a
momentary entrancing pleasure which (being useless and
ultimate) is very like an act of worship or of sacrifice.
Sheer life in him has become pure. That is what we
envy; that is what causes us, as we listen, to draw a
deeper breath, and perhaps something like tears to come
to our eyes. He seems so triumphantly to attain what all
our labors end by missing, yet what alone would justify
them: happiness, selflessness, a moment of life lived in
the spirit. And we may be tempted to say to ourselves:
Ah, if I could only forget, if I could cease to look before
and after, if the pale cast of thought did not make a
slave of me, as well as a coward!

Vital raptures such as the lark's are indeed not unknown even to man, and the suggestion of them powerfully allures the Englishman, being as he is a youth
morally, still impelled to sport, still confident of carrying
his whole self forward into some sort of heaven, whether
in love, in politics, or in religion, without resigning to
nature the things that are nature's nor hiding in God the
things that are God's. Alas, a sad lesson awaits him, if
he ever grows old enough to learn it. Vital raptures,
unless long training or a miracle of adaptation has antecedently harmonized them with the whole orchestration
of nature, necessarily come to a bad end. Dancing and
singing and love and sport and religious enthusiasm are
mighty ferments: happy he who vents them in their season. But if ever they are turned into duties, pumped up
by force, or made the basis of anything serious, like
morals or science, they become vicious. The wild breath
of inspiration is gone which hurried them across the soul

like a bright cloud. Inspiration, as we may read in Plato between the lines, inspiration is animal. It comes from the depths, from that hearth of Hestia, the Earth-Mother, which conservative pagans could not help venerating as divine. Only art and reason, however, are divine in a moral sense, not because they are less natural than inspiration (for the Earth-Mother with her seeds and vapours is the root of everything) but because they mount toward the ultimate heaven of order, beauty, intellectual light, and the achievement of eternal dignities. In that dimension of being even featherless bipeds can soar and sing with a good grace. But space is not their element; airmen, now that we have them, are only a new sort of sailor. They fly for the sake of danger and of high wages; it is a boyish art, with its romantic glamour soon tarnished, and only a material reward left for all its skill and hardships. The only sublimity possible to man is intellectual; when he would be sublime in any other dimension he is merely fatuous and bombastic. By intelligence, so far as he possesses it, a man sees things as they are, transcends his senses and his passions, uproots himself from his casual station in space and time, sees all things future as if they were past, and all things past as for ever present, at once condemns and forgives himself, renounces the world and loves it. Having this inner avenue open to divinity, he would be a fool to emulate the larks in their kind of ecstasy.

His wings are his intelligence; not that they bring ultimate success to his animal will, which must end in failure, but that they lift his failure itself into an atmosphere of laughter and light, where is his proper happiness. He cannot take his fine flight, like the lark, in the morning, in mad youth, in some irresponsible burst of vitality, because life is impatient to begin: that sort of thing is the fluttering of a caged bird, a rebellion against circumstance and against commonness which is a sign of spirit, but not spirit in its self-possession, not happiness nor a school of happiness. The thought which crowns life at its summit can accompany it throughout its course, and can reconcile us to its issue. Intelligence is Homeric in its pervasive light. It traces all the business of nature, eluding but not disturbing it, rendering it in fact more amiable than it is, and rescuing it from vanity.

Sense is like a lively child always at our elbow, saying, Look, look, what is that? Will is like an orator, indignantly demanding something different. History and fiction and religion are like poets, continually recomposing the facts into some tragic unity which is not in them. All these forms of mind are spiritual, and therefore materially superfluous and free; but their spirit is pious, it is attentive to its sources, and therefore seems to be care-laden and not so gloriously emancipated as the music of larks, or even of human musicians; yet thought is pure music in its essence, and only in its subject-matter retrospective and troubled about the facts. It must indeed be troubled about them, because in man spirit is not a mere truant, as it seems to be in the lark, but is a faithful chronicler of labour and wisdom. Man is hard-pressed; long truancies would be fatal to him. He is tempted to indulge in them—witness his languages and pyramids and mythologies; yet his margin of safety is comparatively narrow, and he cannot afford to spend such relatively prodigious amounts of energy in mere play as the lark does with a light heart and in the grand manner. There are words to man's music; he gives names to things; he tries to catch the rhythm of his own story, or to imagine it richer and more sublime than it is. His festivals are heavy with pathos; they mark the events on which his existence turns—harvests, funerals, redemptions, wooings, and wars. When he disregards all these tiresome things, he becomes a fop or a fanatic. There is no worthy transport for him except sane philosophy—a commentary, not a dream. His intelligence is most intense and triumphant when there is least waste in his life; for if hard thinking sometimes makes the head ache, it is because it comes hard, not because it is thinking; our fuddled brain grates and repeats itself in that it *can't* think. But if your business is in order, it requires no further pains to understand it. Intelligence is the flower of war and the flower of love. Both, in the end, are comprehension. How miraculously in our happy moments we understand, how far we jump, what masses of facts we dominate at a glance! There is no labour then, no friction or groping, no anxious jostling against what we do not know, but only joy in this intricate outspread humorous world, intoxication as ethereal as the lark's, but more descriptive. If his song is raised above the world for a moment by its wantonness and idle rapture, ours is raised above it essentially by its scope. To look before and after is human; it would not be sincere nor manly in us not to take thought for the morrow and not to pine for what is not. We must start on that basis, with our human vitality (which is art) substituted for the vegetative prayerfulness of the lily, and our human scope (which is knowledge of the world) substituted for the outpourings of larks.

On this other plane we could easily be as happy as the larks, if we were as liberal. Men when they are civilized and at ease are liberal enough in their sports, and willing to *desipere in loco,* like kittens, but it is strange how barbarous and illiberal, at least in modern times, they have remained about thought. They wish to harness thought like a waterfall, or like the blind

Samson, to work for them night and day, in the tread-
mill of their interests or of their orthodoxy. Fie upon
their stupidity and upon their slavishness! They do not
see that when nature, with much travail, brings something living to birth, inevitable thought is there already,
and gratis, and cannot possibly be there before. The
seething of the brain is indeed as pragmatic as the habit
of singing and flying, which in its inception doubtless
helped the larks to survive, as even the whiteness of the
lily may have done through the ministry of insects which
it attracted; but even material organs are bound to
utility by a very loose tie. Nature does not shake off
her baroque ornaments and her vices until they prove
fatal, and she never thinks of the most obvious invention or pressing reform, until some complication brings
her, she knows not how, to try the experiment. Nature,
having no ulterior purpose, has no need of parsimony or
haste or simplicity. Much less need she be niggardly
of spirit, which lays no tax upon her, and consumes no
energy, but laughs aloud, a marvel and a mystery to her,
in her very heart. All animal functions, whether helpful or wasteful, have this fourth dimension in the realm
of spirit—the joy, or the pain, or the beauty that may
be found in them. Spirit loads with a lyric intensity
the flying moment in which it lives. It actually paints
the lily and casts a perfume on the violet; it turns into
vivid presences a thousand forms which, until its flame
lighted them up, were merged in the passive order and
truth of things, like the charms of Lucy by the springs
of Dove, before Wordsworth discovered them. The
smile of nature is not ponderable; and the changing
harmonies of nature, out of which spirit springs, are
like the conjunctions or eclipses of planets, facts obvious enough to sense in their specious simplicity, yet

materially only momentary positions of transit for wayfarers bound each on his own errand. The songs of larks are like shooting stars that drop downwards and vanish; human intelligence is a part of the steadier music of the spheres.

AT HEAVEN'S GATE

BY GEORGE SANTAYANA

SKYLARKS, if they exist elsewhere, must be homesick for England. They need these kindly mists to hide and to sustain them. Their flexible throats would soon be parched, far from these vaporous meadows and hedgerows rich in berries and loam. How should they live in arid tablelands, or at merciless altitudes, where there is nothing but scorching heat or a freezing blizzard? What space could they find for solitude and freedom in the tangle of tropical forests, amongst the monkeys and parrots? What reserve, what tenderness, what inward springs of happiness could they treasure amid those gross harlot-like flowers? No, they are the hermits of this mild atmosphere, fled to its wilderness of gentle light. Well may they leave it to the eagles to rush against the naked sun, as if its round eye challenged them to single combat: not theirs the stupid ferocity of passion against fact, anger against light, swiftness against poise, beak and talons against intangible fire. Larks may not be very clever, but they are not so foolish as to be proud, or to scream hoarsely against the nature of things. Having wings and voluble throats they play with them for pure pleasure; they are little artists and little gentlemen; they disdain to employ their faculties for their mere utility, or only in order to pounce down to the earth whenever they spy a dainty morsel, or to return to sulk shivering on some solitary crag, their voracity but half appeased, like eagles dreaming of their next victim. Of course, even the most playful songster must eat, and sky-

larks no doubt keep an eye open for worms, and their
nest calls them back to terrene affections; but they are
as forgetful of earth as they can be, and insatiable craving does not stamp itself on their bent necks, as if they
were vultures, nor strain their feathers of iron. No more
are they inspired by sentimental pangs and love-sick like
the nightingale; they do not hide in the labyrinthine
shade of ilex or cypress, from there to wail in the melancholy moonlight, as it were a seductive serenade addressed to mortal lovers. No, the trilling of larks is
not for mankind. Like English poets they sing to themselves of nature, inarticulately happy in a bath of light
and freedom, sporting for the sake of sport, turning what
doubts they may have into sweetness, not asking to see
or to know anything ulterior. They must needs drink
the dew amongst these English fields, peeping into the
dark little hearts and flushed petals of these daisies, like
the heart and cheeks of an English child, or into these
buttercups, yellow like his Saxon hair. They could
hardly have built their nests far from this maze of little
streams, or from these narrow dykes and ditches, arched
with the scented tracery of limes and willows. They
needed this long, dull, chilly winter in which to gather
their unsuspected fund of yearning and readiness for
joy; so that when high summer comes at last they may
mount with virgin confidence and ardour through these
sunlit spaces, to pour their souls out at heaven's gate.

At heaven's gate, but not in heaven. The sky, as these
larks rise higher and higher, grows colder and thinner;
if they could rise high enough, it would be a black void.
All this fluid and dazzling atmosphere is but the drapery
of earth; this cerulean vault is only a film round the
oceans. As these choristers pass beyond the nether veils
of air, the sun becomes fierce and comfortless; they
freeze and are dazzled; they must hurry home again to

earth if they would live. They must put fuel in their little engines: after all it was flesh and blood in them that were praising the Lord. And accordingly, down they drop to their nests and peck about, anxious and silent; but their song never comes down. Up there they leave it, in the glittering desert it once ravished, in what we call the past. They bore their glad offering to the gate and returned empty; but the gladness of it, which in their palpitation and hurry they only half guessed, passed in and is part of heaven. In the home of all good, from which their frail souls fetched it for a moment, it is still audible for any ear that ever again can attune itself to that measure. All that was loved or beautiful at any time, or that shall be so hereafter, all that never was but that ought to have been, lives in that paradise, in the brilliant treasure-house of the gods.

How many an English spirit, too modest to be heard here, has now committed its secret to that same heaven! Caught by the impulse of the hour, they rose like larks in the morning, cheerily, rashly, to meet the unforeseen, fatal, congenial adventure, the goal not seen, the air not measured, but the firm heart steady through the fog or blinding fire, making the best of what came, trembling but ready for what might come, with a simple courage which was half joy in living and half willingness to die. Their first flight was often their last. What fell to earth was only a poor dead body, one of a million; what remained above perhaps nothing to speak of, some boyish sally or wistful fancy, less than the song of a lark for God to treasure up in his omniscience and eternity. Yet these common brave fools knew as well as the lark the thing that they could do, and did it; and of other gifts and other adventures they were not envious. Boys and free men are always a little inclined to flout what is not the goal of their present desires, or is beyond their present scope; spontaneity in them has its ebb-flow in mockery. Their tight little selves are too vigorous and too clearly determined to brood much upon distant things; but they are true to their own nature, they know and love the sources of their own strength. Like the larks, those English boys had drunk here the quintessence of many a sunlit morning; they had rambled through these same fields, fringed with hedges and peeping copse and downs purple with heather; these paths and streams had enticed them often; they had been vaguely happy in these quiet, habitable places. It was enough for them to live, as for nature to revolve; and fate, in draining in one draught the modest cup of their spirit, spared them the weary dilution and waste of it in the world. The length of things is vanity, only the height is joy.

Of myself also I would keep nothing but what God may keep of me—some lovely essence, mine for a moment in that I beheld it, some object of devout love enshrined where all other hearts that have a like intelligence of love in their day may worship it; but my loves themselves and my reasonings are but a flutter of feathers weaker than a lark's, a prattle idler than his warblings, happy enough if they too may fly with him and die with him at the gate of heaven.

HOLIDAYS

BY C. E. MONTAGUE

CHILDREN are often too tired to sleep, and the worst thing about overwork is the way it may make you unfit for a holiday. You may be left able only to stand still and blink, like used-up horses when put out to grass, while the man who has worked in reason, and worried no more than he should, is off for the day or the month, to plunge into some kind of work not his own, just for the fun of the thing.

For all the best sport is the doing, for once, of somebody else's work. The wise cashier puts in a spell of steady exertion as a gardener. Statesmen, prelates and judges of appeal come as near as they can to fulfilling the functions of good professional golfers, fishermen or chauffeurs. The master minds who run our railways for us may seem to flee the very sight of a permanent way; but they don ruck-sacks for ten-hour tramps over rock, peat and bracken, such as the lighter kind of porters used to take for their living in the days before steam. The new-made husband and head of a house, released from his desk in a public office, will labor absorbedly from morning until dewy eve to put the attic in order or get the whole of the tool-shed painted while yet it is light, proud and happy as Pepys when after a day of such application he put the glorious result down in his diary, adding—lest pride should grow sinful—"Pray God my mind run not too much upon it."

Is it, then, mere change of work that makes the best holiday? Scarcely. The master cotton-spinner would

303

not find it sport to spend his August in ruling a dye-
works. There is no rush of Civil Service clerks for a
month's diversion, each year, among the ledgers of joint-
stock banks in the City. A doubtful legend, as we all
know, reports that if ever one of the old London drivers
of horsed 'buses had a holiday—and even this is uncertain—he spent it in driving his wife and himself out into
the country in a small trap. Suppose it was true. Yet
even then, mark you, a small trap of the period had only
one horse. And that leads to the point. What most
charms us as play is not merely some other kind of
work than our own. It is some kind more elementary.

Not that we want to bestow on this holiday work anything less than the whole of our energy. On our Bank
Holidays do not we bend up every corporal agent to
the sport? We sweat in the eye of Phœbus: we take it
out of ourselves, yea, all of it. Just what we want, in
our hearts, is to put forth our powers for once in a
while, upon some occupation in which our endeavor shall
go, or at least seem to go, a mighty long way, and not go
it in some direction which we have never intended. Most
of our working time is spent in making for some distant
objective—fame, or the good of our kind, or a golden
wall or spire, or some other estimable thing. But the
line of approach to these goals is not very clear, and
there is always the plaguey chance that, if ever we get
there, the gold may turn out to be gilt. If we be
parsons, Heaven knows when we shall have the parish
reasonably sober. If we be doctors, perhaps casting out
one bacterial devil by letting another loose at it, how
can we feel secure against making some deadly slip in
the dark, like the man who let the first rabbit loose in
Australia? In any kind of responsible work, be it only
the work of rearing a family decently well, the way is
dark and we are far from home. That is the real curse

of Adam; not the work in itself but the worry and doubt
of ever getting it done; perhaps the doubt, also, whether,
after all, it ought to be done, or done at the Price. All
your working year you chase some phantom moment at
which you might fairly say "Now I am there." Then
Easter comes; you sail your own boat through a night
of dirty weather from the Mersey to the Isle of Man;
and, as you lower sail in Douglas harbour, you *are* there;
no phantom this time; the curse of Adam is taken clean
off you, at any rate for that morning. Or those seeds
that you sowed in the back garden on that thrilling Saturday evening amaze and exalt you by coming up, and
you learn in your proper person what the joys of discovery and creation are; you have, so far, succeeded in
life and done what it piqued you to do in this world. All
play, of course, and the victory tiny. Still, on its own
scale and for its miniature lifetime, the little model is
perfect; the humble muddler has come nearer than anything else is likely to bring him to feeling what the big
triumphs of human power must taste like.

II

Man's job on the earth seems to be always becoming
more intricate and advanced. Quite early he has to
plunge on and on into deepening forests of complexity
as his youth penetrates with uncertain feet the central
wilds and dark places of algebra-books. The toughness
of our task, as compared with that of a hen, is said to
be roughly indicated by the contrast between the preparation required for each; the hen is fairly ripe for its
labour the day it is born; a man is by no means always
efficient after he has afforded employment to a cohort of
nurses, governesses, schoolmasters, tutors and professors

for more than a score of years. And so, as we proceed with this obscure and intractable undertaking, we dearly like, on our days off, to turn back and do over again, for the fun and easiness of the thing, what we or others really had to do, for dear life, in the infancy of the race.

When Easter releases the child, in any provincial suburb, from his inveterate bondage to grammar and sums, you will see him refreshing himself with sportive revivals of one of the earliest anxieties of man. Foraging round like a magpie or rook, he collects old bits of cast-away tarpaulin and sacking, dusters, old petticoats, broken broom-sticks and fragments of corrugated iron. Assembling these building materials on some practicable patch of waste grass, preferably in the neighborhood of water, he raises for himself a simple dwelling. The blessing of a small fire crowns these provisions for domestic felicity, and marvellous numbers of small persons may be seen sitting round these rude hearths, conversing with the gravity of Sioux chieftains or, at a menace of rain, packing themselves into incredibly small cubic spaces of wigwam.

Houses, of course, have been somewhat scarce in late years. Parents, no doubt, have shaken their heads over the dearth, and this may have reinforced in their young the primitive human craving to start by getting a roof over one's head. The war, too, with all its talk of tent and hut, dug-out and bivouac, may have fortified the old impulse. Still, it is there, always and anyhow. It is the holiday impulse of self-rescue from that strange and desolating blindness which comes of knowing things too well and taking them as matters of course. Most of us have long become so used to the idea of living in a house that the idea has lost its old fascination. Of course we do value a house, in a way. That is, we are sorely put out if we cannot obtain one. And, having obtained it, we feel deeply wronged if we have forgotten the latch-key some night and cannot get in. But sheer delight in the very notion of a house, the chuckling, thigh-slapping triumph of early man when first he built one—this has died down in us, just as has the grinning and capering glee of the same pioneer when he got the first fire to kindle.

In the orally transmitted Scriptures of some of the Australian blacks the Creator, Pund-jel, was so well pleased when he had fashioned the first man out of clay and bark that he danced for joy around this admirable piece of handiwork. Even the more staid Jehovah of our own Book of Genesis went on from finding his earlier products "good" to find the whole week's work "very good," the exultant complacency of the artist increasing, as it always does, *pari passu* with the activity of his invention. Man has been proceeding, ever since, with the work that was thus started. A house, a bed, a wheel, a boat, a plough—rapturously must his mind have capered, like Pund-jel's, round each of these happy masterpieces, when it was new. So, too, would it caper now, but for some pestilent bar that familiarity interposes between us and the deft miracles of gumption that make us able to sit and look out, dry and warm, half an inch from a tempest of snow, and lie ensconced in tiny cubes of snug stillness hoisted up as high as the top of a tree amidst the raving and whining of violent winter winds.

In poets, perhaps, and in a few other people doubly charged with relish for all the contents of existence, some traces of that jubilation persist. Any child who is happily placed and wisely reared has his chance of reviving it for himself. There come to him exultant ecstasies of climbing in trees with the zest of the first

tree-dweller in his ancient pedigree; he huddles in holes
that he has digged for himself with all the gusto and
pride of a pioneer caveman; then from the joys of the
domestic cave he passes on to the sweets of the original
ramshackle tent, symbol of the opening of the nomad
stage in the life of his kind. Packed as miraculously
tight into his own small life as a hyacinth, flower and
leaves and all, is compressed in the bulb, there unfolds
itself for his diversion a stirring recapitulation of the
adventurous life of mankind on the earth: he re-lives
with relish the whole career of his race; he has been
with other ape-like figures in the upper boughs of trees
and has shivered with delicious apprehension in caverns
of the earth, undergoing a sort of painless return of the
terrors of naked savages crouched in imperfect cover,
with roaring beasts ranging the forests without. No
wonder the little ragged boys are happy and grave as
they sit in pow-wow at the door of a tabernacle composed
of two aged sacks, or lean upon their one-foot-high
stockade of bits of turf and scan the enigmatic horizon.

III

All fortunate holiday travel, like all good recovery
after illness, is a renewal of youth. All the rest of the
year your youth is running down within you. The salt
of living—not of success and arrival but of mere living,
the conscious adventure—is losing its savor; insensibly
the days are coming near "when thou shalt say, I have
no pleasure in them." We may be toiling or fussing
away in the van of some sort of big human march. And
quite right too of course; marches have to go on; there
is no dropping out of the column; on active service you
cannot resign. And yet it may grow hard to keep your

zest for the simpler, ruder, basic good things of existence while fingering some of its latest subtleties. What
fun the alphabet was, once! But you almost forget, in
your present wrestlings with words of six syllables. The
rooms where you work are so well heated, without any
effort of yours, that willy-nilly you come to forget what
the joy of repelling cold is; you may have to sit for so
much of the day that the rapture of rest after real fa-
tigue of the body becomes merely words, a thing in a
book, not an object of sense; streets and trains and
cars are rendered, by some impersonal forces unknown,
so utterly safe that safety becomes a mere matter of
course, with no power to rouse or astonish; meals appear
with an unfailing air of automatism, so that the start
of delight with which, in another state of yourself, you
look upon a laid dinner-table, with all its centuries of ac-
cumulation of 'cute dodges for refining the use of pas-
ture, does not visit you now; even that divine and yet
most human contrivance, a bed, the ultimate product
of tens of thousands of years of man's nightly consideration of means for being still snugger next night, may
lose its power of making you chuckle as you plunge in
between the sheets.

But then come holidays. They soon put things to
rights. In his story of Marius, Walter Pater describes
his hero's recovery of a lost interest in common things
—household customs, the daily meals, just the eating of
ordinary food at appointed and recurrent times: Marius
awoke to regained enjoyment of "that poetic and, as it
were, moral significance which surely belongs to all the
means of daily life, could we but break through the veil
of our familiarity with things by no means vulgar in
themselves." Some such retransfiguration of things that
had sunk into triteness blesses the fortunate holiday-

maker. The sandwiches eaten with grimy fingers at the
top of the Napes on Great Gable attain a strange quality
of pleasantness; the meal, like every meal that has not
somehow gone wrong, achieves a touch of sacramental
significance; and the subsequent smoke is the true pipe
of peace once more, redolent of spiritual harmonies and
romantic dreams. Bodily safety, a treasure charmless to
the mind in ordinary life, regains the piquant value of
a thing that will not just come of itself; it has to be
wooed; the winning of it depends on the right exertion
of some faculty not too perplexing to be joyous—the
yachtsman's handling of his craft, the climber's hold on
rock, the swimmer's sureness of himself across half a
mile of deep water. Best of all when the security of
every one in a party depends upon the alertness and
fitness of each of the others. Then you revivify all
human comradeship too; it comes back cleared of the
blur that may have dulled your sense of it at home,
where human interdependence may be so intricate and so
incessant and often so muddled up with annoying circumstances that it seems more tiresome than real, like
a virtue vulgarized by the stale eulogistic phrasing of
rhetoricians.

In such a sport as mountaineering, vicissitudes of heat
and cold are again, for a few make-believe hours, the
hazards that they must have been to the houseless man
of the prime; sunset and dawn are recharged with the
freshness and wonder that they might have had on the
morning and evening of the first day. Rightly to perceive a thing, in all the fullness of its qualities, is really
to create it. So, on perfect holidays, you re-create your
world and sign on again as a pleased and enthusiastic
member of the great air-ship's company. The word
recreation seems to tell you as much, and I suppose the
old poets hinted it too in their tale of Antæus, whose

strength would all come back with a rush whenever he got a good kiss of his mother the earth.

IV

Something in modern ways of work seems to make some little nip of artificial excitement, of one sort or another, an object of sharper desire than it was. Labor in great mills and workshops and large counting-houses is probably healthier now, for the body, than ever before. Yet there seems to have been some loss for the mind and the spirits. Perhaps it comes of a cause that cannot be helped any more than an army can help the defects of a long march. The cause, I suppose, is the inevitable minute subdivision of labor. To put it roughly, the old-time workman made a thing; the modern workman only gives a passing touch to a thing while it is being made. Forty years ago a small Thames boat-builder, working alone in his shed, would make a whole boat, of a very beautiful build, by himself, from its keel to the last lick of its varnish. He got his share—and you could see him get it if you were friends with him—of that joy and excitement of creation in which healthy children at play are at one with inventors and discoverers. The passing of the greater part of that happy excitement away from so many modern modes of manufacture has been a real Fall of Man. It has gone some way to make work what it is said to have been to Adam after his misfortune—a thing to be got through and borne with, because you cannot go on living upon any other terms.

The thing has gone so far that at any trade-union meeting to-day you would not expect to hear a word implying that the work its members do is anything but a mere cause of weariness, only made endurable by pay;

this although all work which has not somehow gone wrong is like the work of a normal artist—a thing for which the artist means to get properly paid if he can, but also a thing which he would go on doing anyhow, whether any one paid him or not. You will see men fairly rushing away from the factory gate to get a little excitement out of a bet or a League match. Many of them, and some of the best, may be unconsciously looking for something to put in the place of that satisfying stir of heart and mind which visits every good craftsman during his exhilarating struggle with a testing piece of work. *Their* work has failed to yield it. They hunt for substitutes for the lost joys of their trade, and of all substitutes an active holiday is the best. The finer or longer holiday a man or woman can get whose work is eternal picking-up of pins or dipping of match-heads in phosphorus, the greater their chance of remaining decently human. Some inarticulate sense of this may be showing itself in the almost frenzied grasp which new millions are making now at every possible holiday—not in laziness but in a sane instinctive effort to keep the salt of their existence from losing its savor.

v

One special kind of holiday deserves a note to itself. The military experience of the nation went to show that one of the best days of a leave, during the war, was the day before you went. And then it sometimes happened, for reasons of State, that you did not go, after all. Still, you had had your hour. *Pro tem.*, at any rate, you had divinely lived. To put it at the lowest, you had, like the three famous sportsmen of song, powler't up and down a bit and had a rattling day with the home railway time-tables, tasting, as you looked up train by train, the delights of passing the hedged closes of tasseled hops in Kent or the blue bloom of the moors about your home in Yorkshire. Well, if that was better than nothing, why not go in for such fragments of joy, on a system?

The plan is to say to yourself in a firm tone that on such or such a date you are going to some longed-for place; then to make all the fond mental preparations of good travellers, tracking every mile on the map, forming conjectural visions of what you would see from this point and from that; and then, at the last moment, not to go at all, being quite unable to afford it, as you had always known. One solid merit in this sort of travel is that the fares cannot be raised against you, as has so often and so lamentably been done to the impoverishment or immobilisation of those who travel in the flesh. Another advantage is that it overcomes the difficulty which so many of us find in leaving our work for more than a month, perhaps even a fortnight, at a time. From the journey over the Andes, for instance, from the Argentine to the Chilean coast, most of us are inexorably barred by iron laws of time, space, and finance. Yet it is evidently a delectable passage; and by a proper use of South American time-tables you can adjust consummately the timing of your transit across the spacious place of origin of bully beef to the iced spike of Aconcagua or the snowy dome of Chimborazo; freely you choose the hour at which it will give you the most exquisite vibrations to stare for the first time at the Pacific; sagaciously you distribute your time between the Arctic, the sub-Arctic, the temperate, the sub-tropical and the tropical zones of the rapid western slope, right down from the high ice to the palms and the warm surf. Much valuable time, again, may doubtless be saved, when visiting New Zealand and crossing her Alps from the side tangled with almost tropical jungle, if you have disengaged yourself in time from the conventional impression that your mere bodily presence is required. And yet, yet—I fear I am a carnal man; the homeliest meal of new places seen with the vulgar bodily eye—a mere dish of herbs—allures me more than the lordliest of Barmecide banquets, even the stalled oxen of fancy. And yet, again, there may be something in it if all actual travel, the positive transport of the rejoicing tenement of clay, be wholly precluded. It may be better to have counted visionary chickens, and not hatched them out, than never to have counted chickens at all. And perhaps it is what we may all have to come to, in time, however stoutly we have preferred the heard melody, while we could get to it, to any unheard superior.

AT THE THRESHOLD
OF PERFECTION

BY JOSEPH EDGAR CHAMBERLIN

THERE is a place I have lately visited where I have
found myself, in the supreme August days, nearer to
the Eternal Secret than anywhere else,—nearer than in
the unprofaned forest, nearer than on the stainless shore
of the ocean, where poets and philosophers often wait
in the hope of taking that secret by surprise. The poet,
indeed, might turn away from the place with a shudder.
It is a great tract of burned woodland,—a long reach
of hill and dale where, before the leaves came last spring,
a terrible fire raged, which left scarcely a living thing in
its path. Far and near one sees blackened trunks, or
the branches of pines standing against the sky like dark
antlers. The ledges of rock have dark cindery spaces.
My first impulse was to run away from so much desolation. I remained, and found more of divinity here
than I could have guessed; two great gods, indeed,
walked side by side in beautiful agreement,—the divinities of Destruction and of Creation: the force which
tears down, and the force which builds up. Now, in
August, at this real flood-tide of the year, this great
burned tract is not merely a scene of death, but also
one of exuberant and all-conquering life.

From every stump of a burned tree scores of young
shoots have sprung, all crowding their juicy boughs and
great young leaves up into the air with tremendous haste
and vigor. From the powdery earth, enriched by the
ashes of the holocaust, young poplar-trees and birches

and many other growths have pushed up independently from seeds or roots, and are thriving as one never heard of trees thriving before. The young oaks and hickories are growing so fast that their topmost leaves have had no time to get their green pigment,—of which, indeed, there seems not enough to go around in such a mob of furiously growing things,—and so they are of all colors, hit or miss, red, brown, purple, and sometimes almost blue. But the older, lower leaves have come in for their share of greenness, and wear their proper hues, with even a little added intensity thrown in for good measure. Here and there among the young thickets a splendid red lily lingers, beyond its season, as if reluctant to leave such a scene of natural riot; and the rosy plumes of the fireweed nod in frequent clumps. But there is no need of flowers for color; the young leaves of the oak and hickory give that in abundance.

It is not alone the presence of these two divinities of Death and Life, with Death thus ministering to a new and more splendid Life, that suggests the eternal balance of things,—the divine Equilibrium which the philosopher dreams in his moments of highest insight. All other things in Nature, even her peculiar August silences, tell of that. This is the month when all life reaches its maximum, its summit, and when as yet the decline of autumn has not begun. The very landscape trembles in an ecstasy of accomplishment,—an exquisite conscious-ness of perfection. Nature breathes her love upon the earth in ardent heat. The birds are silent, as if awed beyond utterance; a little while ago a vireo tried to set up his monotonous work-a-day song, as if knowing that his is as little irreverential as any song could be, but it fluttered away and died. Only the unabashed cicada translates the heat and the tremor of earth and air into a long ecstatic thrill. This is the time when the poet or the philosopher, if he be of those who have been admitted to the secret of Nature, may hear her very heart-beat,—not in fancy at all, but in sober truth.

Though the burned woodland is a rare place in which to meet something of these mysteries which many yearn to know, and only a few will ever understand, and no one will ever impart by words to any other, it is not the only place where one may in August meet them face to face. There is a special quality about the flowers of the month. The clethra, which abounds along the lake-side, and reigns over all the scents of August, has not the over-sweet *growing* perfume of the azalea, which blooms in spring, nor the tender, modest, retiring fragrance of the violets; it is a pervasive odor, that goes a long way on the breeze with woody ripeness, and is spicy and satisfying but never coarse. The goldenrod, so very long and so wonderfully deliberate in perfecting its flowers,—we have seen them forming for months,—is perfect now, and will be as long in letting go its gold as it has been in gaining it. The button-push holds its white globules in the air, each one a perfect little planet, a symbol of pure completeness; and the cardinal-flower flames out along the brooks as if to show that, if August can produce perfect whiteness and pure gold, it has also the reddest blood of all the months in its veins.

Animal life is very quiet now. If the birds still make love, they do not chatter about it. The squirrels have some running about to do, but they do it silently. All manner of queer insect life is exuberant and interesting. On a clethra branch I came yesterday upon a curious white spider, with two faint little yellow-brown bars on its back; as soon as it saw that a dangerous being had plucked its branch, the little creature, eruditely aware of the principle of protective resemblances, ran swiftly and placed itself on the white blossom, where it assuredly would not have been perceived at all if it had not already been seen on a green leaf. All the little toads have come out of the water and have stationed themselves on the hottest, sunniest banks they can find, whence they scatter in a sort of living shower if you disturb them. The milk-adder unwinds his spotted length in the flickering shade of a sassafras bush,—a beautiful creature, whose like you will not encounter in every summer day's journey.

Every night now, August reveals her celestial perfections in the supremest beauty. The waxing moon, Saturn, the white Vega, Arcturus, rule the evening; the great planets reserve their splendor for a more auroral hour, when Jupiter and Venus appear in their magnificence. In the south the Scorpion trails his length across the skies, just a little of him lost in the haze of the horizon; but the bow of the Archer is bent upon him. The young moon goes down and down, reddening as she sinks to the horizon; her path slowly fades out from the bosom of the lake even before she has reached the earth's rim. The other night, on my bed in a cottage in the depths of the woods, I heard some hounds baying, as they hunted on their own account. Their voices rose and fell, receded, once more approached, fell away again, bringing back to my soul the wild, perfect music of wolves on elemental western plains; for a moment I felt an instinct to go out and join them in their mad hunt through the forest. I know that this moment's strange alliance with the animal world has its part in the perfectness of the season, for it is born out of the depths of the beautiful old wildness that lies latent in all our natures, and splendidly gives the lie to the artifices and hypocrisies of civilization.

The August night passes in happy waking that one would not exchange for sleep. With the rising of the sun, its coolness, the one premonition of autumn and of dying, takes to flight, and the living heat comes on apace. A few birds sing faintly in the cool of the dawn; but presently the hawk, screaming high above the clearing, has uttered the real keynote of the August day. It is not a time of gentle, modest melodies, nor of soft venturing life, but of high tones, and of all things strong, complete, full-grown, and bold.

AN AUTUMN HOUSE

BY EDWARD THOMAS

ON THAT October day, nothing was visible at first save yellow flowers, and sometimes a bee's quiet shadow crossing the petals: a sombre river, noiselessly sauntering seaward, dropped with a murmur, far away among leaves, into a pool. That sound alone made tremble the glassy dome of silence that extended miles and miles. All things were light-powdered with gold, by a lustre that seemed to have been sifted through gauze. The hazy sky, striving to be blue, was reflected as purple in the waters. There, too, sunken and motionless, lay amber willow leaves; some floated down. Between the sailing leaves, against the false sky, hung the willow shadows, —shadows of willows overhead, with waving foliage, like the train of a bird of paradise. One standing on a bridge was seized by a Hylean shock, and wondered as he saw his face, death-pale, among the ghostly leaves below. Everywhere, the languid perfumes of corruption. Brown leaves laid their fingers on the cheek as they fell; and here and there the hoary reverse of a willow leaf gleamed at the crannied foot of the trees.

One lonely poplar, in a space of refulgent lawn, was shedding its leaves as if it scattered largess among a crowd. Nothing that it gave it lost; for each leaf lay sparkling upon the turf, casting a splendor upward. A maiden unwreathing her bridal garlands would cast them off with a grace as pensive as when the poplar shed its leaf.

We could not walk as slowly as the river flowed; yet

that seemed the true pace to move in life, and so reach the great sea. Hand in hand with the river wound the path, and that way lay our journey.

In one place slender coils of honeysuckle tried to veil the naked cottage stone, or in another the subtle handiwork of centuries had covered the walls with lichen. And it was in the years when Nature said

"Incipient magni procedere menses,"

when a day meant twenty miles of sunlit forest, field, and water,

"Oh! moments as big as years,"

years of sane pleasure, glorified in later reveries of remembrance. . . . Near a reedy, cooty backwater of that river ended our walk.

The day had been an august and pompous festival. On that day, burning like an angry flame until noon, and afterwards sinking peacefully into the soundless deeps of vesperal tranquillity as the light grew old, life seemed in retrospect like the well-told story of a rounded, melodious existence, such as one could wish for one's self. How mild, dimly golden, the comfortable dawn! Then the canvas of a boat creeping like a spider down the glassy river pouted feebly. The slumberous afternoon sent the willow shadows to sleep and the aspens to feverish repose, in a landscape without horizon. Evening chilled the fiery cloud, and a gray and level barrier, like the jetsam of a vast upheaval, but still and silent, lay alone across the west. Thereafter a light wind knitted the willow branches against a silver sky with a crescent moon. Against that sky, also, we could not but scan the fixed grasses bowing on the wall top. For a little while, troubled tenderly by autumnal maladies of soul, it was sweet and suitable to follow the path towards our place of rest,—a gray, immemorial house with innumerable windows.

The house, in that wizard light "sent from beyond the sky"—for the moon cast no beams through her prison of oak forest—seemed to be one not made with hands. Was it empty? The shutters of the plain, square windows remained unwhitened, flapped ajar. Up to the door ran a yellow path, levelled by moss, where a blackbird left a worm half swallowed, as he watched our coming. A large red rose, divided and split by birds, petal by petal, lay as beautiful as blood, upon the ground. This path and another carved the lawn into three triangles; and in each an elm rose up, laying forth foliage against the house in November even.

The leaves that had dropped earlier lay, crisp and curled, in little ripples upon the grass. There is a perfect moment for coming upon autumn leaves, as for gathering fruit. The full, flawless color, the false, hectic well-being of decay, and the elasticity, are attained at the same time in certain flavored leaves; and dying is but a refinement of life.

In one corner of the garden stood a yew tree and its shadow; and the shadow was more real than the tree,—the shadow inlaid in the sparkling verdure like ebony. In the branches the wind made a low note of incantation, especially if a weird moon of blood hung giddily over it in tossing cloud. To noonday the ebony shadow was as lightning to night. Towards this tree the many front windows guided the sight; and beyond, a deep valley was brimmed with haze that just exposed the tree tops to the play of the sunset's last random fires. To the left, the stubborn leaves of an oak wood soberly burned like rust, among accumulated shadow. To the right, the woods on a higher slope here and there crept out of the haze, like cloud, and received a glory, so that the hill

was by this touch of the heavens exaggerated. And still
the sound of waters falling among trees. Quite another
scene was discovered by an ivy-hidden oriel, lit by ancient light, immortal light travelling freely from the
sunset, and from the unearthly splendor that succeeds.
There the leaves were golden for half a year upon the
untempestuous oaks in that sunken land. The tranquillity, the fairness, the unseasonable hues, were melancholy; that is to say, joy was here under strange skies;
sadness was fading into joy, joy into sadness, especially
when we looked upon this gold, and heard the dark
sayings of the wind in far-off woods, while these were
still. Many a time and oft was the forest to be seen,
when the chillest rain descended, fine and hissing,—seen
standing like enchanted towers, amidst it all, untouched
and aloof, as in a picture. But when the sun had just
disappeared red-hot in the warm, gray, still eventide, and
left in the west a fiery tissue of wasting cloud, when the
gold of the leaves had an April freshness, in a walk
through the sedate old elms there was "a fallacy of high
content."

Several roses nodded against the gray brick, as if all
that olden austerity was expounded by the white blossoms that emerged from it, like water magically struck
from the rock of the wilderness. In the twilight silence
the rose petals descended. So tender was the air, they
lay perfect on the grass, and caught the moonlight.

In ways such as these the mansion spoke. For the
house had a characteristic personality. Strangely out of
keeping with the trees, it grew incorporate with them,
by night. Behold it, as oft we did, early in the morning,
when a fiery day was being born in frost, and neither
wing nor foot was abroad, and it was clothed still in
something of midnight; then its shadows were homes of
awful thoughts; you surmised who dwelt therein. Long

after the sun was gay, the house was sombre, unresponsive to the sky, with a Satanic gloom.

The forest and meadow flowers were rooted airily in the old walls. The wildest and delicatest birds had alighted on the trees.

Things inside the house were contrasted with the lugubrious wall as with things without. The hangings were indeed sad, with a design of pomegranates; but the elaborate silver candelabra dealt wonderfully with every thread of light entering contraband. One braided silver candlestick threw white flame into the polished oaken furniture, and thence by rapid transit to the mirror. An opening door would light the apartment as by lightning. Under the lights at night the shadowy concaves of the candelabra caught streaked reflections from the whorls of silver below. The Holy Grail might have been floating into the room when a white linen cloth was unfolded, dazzling the eyes.

In the upper rooms, the beds (and especially that one which owned the falcon's eye of an oriel)—the beds, with their rounded balmy pillows, and unfathomable eiderdown that cost much curious architecture to shape into a trap for weary limbs, were famous. All the opiate influence of the forest was there. Perhaps the pillow was daily filled with blossoms that whisper softliest of sleep. There were perfumes in the room quite inexplicable. Perhaps they had outlived the flowers that bore them ages back, flowers now passed away from the woods. The walls were faded blue; the bed canopy a combination of three gold and scarlet flags crossed by a device in scarlet and gold, "Blessed is he that sleepeth well, but he that sleeps here is twice blessed."

The whole room was like an apse, with altar, and pure, hieratic ornament. To sleep there was a sacramental thing. Such dreams we had.

Against that window were flowers whose odor the breeze carried to our nostrils when it puffed at dawn. If excuses could be found, it was pleasant to be early abed in summer, for the sake of that melancholy western prospect, when the songs of the lark and the nightingale arose together. We fell suddenly asleep with a faint rush of the scent of juniper in the room, and the light still fingering the eyelashes. Or, if we closed the window, in that chamber—

"That chamber deaf of noise and blind of sight,"

we could hear our own thoughts. Moreover, there was a graceful usage of making music while the owl hooted vespers; for a bed without music is a sty, the host used to say,—as the philosopher called a table without it a manger.

Alongside the bed, and within reach of the laziest hand, ran two shelves of books. One shelf held an old *Montaigne,* the *Lyrical Ballads;* the *Morte d'Arthur;* the *Compleat Angler;* Lord Edward Herbert's *Autobiography;* George Herbert's *Temple,* Browne's *Urn Burial;* Cowper's *Letters.* The other shelf was filled by copies, in a fine feminine hand and charmingly misspelt, of the long-dead hostess's favorites, all bound according to her fancy by herself: Keats' *Odes; Twelfth Night; L'Allegro* and *Il Penseroso;* the *Twenty-first Chapter of St. John,* and the *Twenty-third Psalm;* Virgil's *Eclogues,* Shelley's *Adonais;* part ii. section ii. member 4, of the *Anatomy of Melancholy,* called "Exercise Rectified of Body and Mind"; Lord Clarendon's Eulogy of Falkland, in the *History of the Great Rebellion;* a great part of *The Opium Eater,* and Walter Pater's *Child in the House* and *Leonardo da Vinci* added by a younger but almost equally beautiful hand.

What healing slumbers had here been slept, what

ravelled sleaves of care knit up! Ancient room that
had learned peacefulness in centuries, to them whose
hunger bread made of wheat doth not assuage, to those
that are weary beyond the help of crutches, you, ancient
room in that gray immemorial house, held sweet food
and refuge. To the bereaved one, sleeping here, you
redeemed the step that is soundless forever, the eyes
that are among the moles, the accents that no subtlest
hearing shall ever hear again;—You, ancient bed, full of
the magic mightier than "powerfullest lithomancy," had
blessings greater than St. Hilary's bed, on which dis-
tracted men were laid, with prayer and ceremonial, and
in the morning rose restored. With you, perhaps, was
Sleep herself: Sleep that sits, more august than Solomon
or Minos, in a court of ultimate appeal, whither move
the footsteps of those who have mourned for justice at
human courts, and mourned in vain: Sleep, by whose
equity divine the bruised and dungeoned innocent roams
again emparadised in the fields of home, under the smiles
of familiar skies: Sleep, whose mercy is not bounded,
but

"droppeth as the gentle rain from heaven,"

even upon the beast. Sleep soothes the hand of poverty
with gold, and pleases with the ache of long-stolen coro-
nets the brows of fallen kings. Had Tantalus dropped
his eyelids, sleep had ministered to his lips. The firman
of sleep goes forth: the peasant is enthroned, and accomplished in the superb appurtenances of empire; the
monarch finds himself among the placid fireside blisses
of light at eventide; and those in cities pent sleep be-
guiles with the low summons,

"Ad claras Asiæ volemus urbes."

Because sleep clothes the feet of sorrow with leaden
sandals and fastens eagle's wings upon the heels of joy,
I wonder that some ask at nightfall what the morrow
shall see concluded: I would rather ask what sleep shall
bring forth, and whither I shall travel in my dreams.
It seems indeed to me that to sleep is owed a portion
of the deliberation given to death. If life is an apprenticeship to death, waking may be an education for sleep.
We are not thoughtful enough about sleep; yet it is
more than half of that great portion of life spent really
in solitude. *"Nous sommes tous dans le desert! Personne ne comprend personne."* In the desert what then
shall we do? We truly ought to enter upon sleep as into
a strange fair chapel. Fragrant and melodious ante-
chamber of the unseen, sleep is a novitiate for the beyond. Nevertheless, it is likely that those who compose
themselves carefully for sleep are few as those who die
holily; and most are ignorant of an art of sleeping (as
of dying). The surmises, the ticking of the heart, of an
anxious child,—the awful expectation of Columbus spy-
ing the fringes of a world,—such are my emotions, as I
go to rest. I know not whether before the morrow I
shall not pass by the stars of heaven and behold the
"pale chambers of the west," returning before dawn.
To many something like Jacob's dream often happens.
The angels rising are the souls of the dreamers dignified by the insignia of sleep. Without vanity, I think in
my boyhood, in my sleep, I was often in heaven. Since
then, I have gone dreaming by another path, and heard
the sighs and chatterings of the underworld; have gone
from my pleasant bed to a fearful neighborhood, like the
fifth Emperor Henry, who, for penance, when lights
were out, the watch fast asleep, walked abroad barefoot,
leaving his imperial habiliments, leaving Matilda the
Empress. And when the world is too much with me,

when the past is a reproach harrying me with dreadful faces, the present a fierce mockery, the future an open grave, it is sweet to sleep. I have closed a well-loved book, ere the candle began to fail, that I might sleep, and let the soul take her pleasure in the deeps of eternity. It may be that the light of morning is ever cold, when it breaks in upon my sleep and disarrays the palaces of my dreams.

"Each matin bell . . .
Knells us back to a world of death."

The earth then seems but the fragments of my dream, that was so high.

LAUGHTER

BY MAX BEERBOHM

M. Bergson, in his well-known essay on this theme, says
. . . well, he says many things; but none of these,
though I have just read them, do I clearly remember,
nor am I sure that in the act of reading I understood
any of them. That is the worst of these fashionable
philosophers—or rather, the worst of me. Somehow I
never manage to read them till they are just going out
of fashion, and even then I don't seem able to cope with
them. About ten years ago, when everyone suddenly
talked to me about Pragmatism and William James, I
found myself moved by a dull but irresistible impulse
to try Schopenhauer, of whom years before that, I had
heard that he was the easiest reading in the world, and
the most exciting and amusing. I wrestled with Schopenhauer for a day or so, in vain. Time passed: M. Bergson appeared "and for his hour was lord of the ascend-
ant"; I tardily tackled William James. I bore in mind,
as I approached him, the testimonials that had been
lavished on him by all my friends. I could make nothing of William James. And now, in the fullness of time,
I have been floored by M. Bergson.

It distresses me, this failure to keep up with the leaders of thought as they pass into oblivion. It makes me
wonder whether I am, after all, an absolute fool. Yet
surely I am not that. Tell me of a man or a woman, a
place or an event, real or fictitious; surely you will find
me a fairly intelligent listener. Any such narrative will
present to me some image, and will stir me to not alto-

gether fatuous thoughts. Come to me in some grievous difficulty; I will talk to you like a father, even like a lawyer. I'll be hanged if I haven't a certain mellow wisdom. But if you are by way of weaving theories as to the nature of things in general, and if you want to try those theories on someone who will luminously confirm them or powerfully rend them, I must, with a hangdog air, warn you that I am not your man. I suffer from a strong suspicion that things in general cannot be accounted for through any formula or set of formulae, and that any one philosophy, howsoever new, is no better than another. That is in itself a sort of philosophy, and I suspect it accordingly; but it has for me the merit of being the only one I can make head or tail of. If you try to expound any other philosophic system to me, you will find not merely that I can detect no flaw in it (except the one great flaw just suggested), but also that I haven't, after a minute or two, the vaguest notion of what you are driving at. "Very well," you say, "instead of trying to explain all things all at once, I will explain some little, simple, single thing."

It was for the sake of such shorn lambs as myself, doubtless, that M. Bergson sat down and wrote about— Laughter. But I have profited by his kindness no more than if he had been treating of the cosmos. I cannot tread even a limited space of air. I have a gross satisfaction in the crude fact of being on hard ground again, and I utter a coarse peal of—Laughter.

At least, I say I do so. In point of fact, I have merely smiled. Twenty years ago, ten years ago, I should have laughed, and have professed to you that I had merely smiled. A very young man is not content to be very young, nor even a young man to be young; he wants to share the dignity of his elders. There is no dignity in laughter, there is much of it in smiles. Laughter is but a joyous surrender, smiles give token of mature criticism. It may be that in the early ages of this world there was much more laughter than is to be heard now, and that æons hence laughter will be obsolete, and smiles universal—everyone, always, mildly, slightly, smiling. But it is less useful to speculate as to mankind's past and future than to observe men. And you will have observed with me in the club-room that young men at most times look solemn, whereas old men or men of middle age mostly smile; and also that those young men do often laugh loud and long among themselves, while others —the gayest and best of us in the most favorable circumstances—seldom achieve more than our habitual act of smiling. Does the sound of that laughter jar on us? Do we liken it to the crackling of thorns under a pot? Let us do so. There is no cheerier sound. But let us not assume it to be the laughter of fools because we sit quiet. It is absurd to disapprove of what one envies, or to wish a good thing were no more because it has passed out of our possession.

But (it seems that I must begin every paragraph by questioning the sincerity of what I have just said) has the gift of laughter been withdrawn from me? I protest that I do, still, at the age of forty-seven, laugh often and loud and long. But not, I believe, so long and loud and often as in my less smiling youth. And I am proud, nowadays, of laughing, and grateful to anyone who makes me laugh. That is a bad sign. I no longer take laughter as a matter of course. I realize, even after reading M. Bergson on it, how good a thing it is. I am qualified to praise it.

As to what is most precious among the accessories to the world we live in, different men hold different opinions. There are people whom the sea depresses, whom mountains exhilarate. Personally, I want the sea al-

ways—some not populous edge of it for choice; and with
it sunshine, and wine, and a little music. My friend on
the mountain yonder is of tougher fibre and sterner outlook, disapproves of the sea's laxity and instability, has
no ear for music and no palate for the grape, and regards the sun as a rather enervating institution, like
central heating in a house. What he likes is a grey day
and the wind in his face; crags at a great altitude; and a
flask of whisky. Yet I think that even he, if we were
trying to determine from what inner sources mankind
derives the greatest pleasure in life, would agree with
me that only the emotion of love takes higher rank than
the emotion of laughter. Both these emotions are partly
mental, partly physical. It is said that the mental symptoms of love are wholly physical in origin. They are not
the less ethereal for that. The physical sensations of
laughter, on the other hand, are reached by a process
whose starting-point is in the mind. They are not the
less "gloriously of our clay." There is laughter that
goes so far as to lose all touch with its motive, and to
exist only, grossly, in itself. This is laughter at its best.
A man to whom such laughter has often been granted
may happen to die in a workhouse. No matter. I will
not admit that he has failed in life. Another, who has
never laughed thus, may be buried in Westminster Abbey,
leaving more than a million pounds overhead. What
then? I regard him as a failure.

Nor does it seem to me to matter one jot how such
laughter is achieved. Humor may rollick on high places
of fantasy or in depths of silliness. To many people it
appeals only from those depths. If it appeals to them
irresistibly, they are more enviable than those who are
sensitive only to the finer kind of joke and not so sensitive as to be mastered and dissolved by it. Laughter is
a thing to be rated according to its own intensity.

Many years ago I wrote an essay in which I poured scorn on the fun purveyed by the music halls, and on the great public for which that fun was quite good enough. I take that callow scorn back. I fancy that the fun itself was better than it seemed to me, and might not have displeased me if it had been wafted to me in private, in the presence of a few friends. A public crowd, because of a lack of broad impersonal humanity in me, rather insulates than absorbs me. Amidst the guffaws of a thousand strangers I become unnaturally grave. If these people were the entertainment, and I the audience, I should be sympathetic enough. But to be one of them is a position that drives me spiritually aloof. Also, there is to me something rather dreary in the notion of going anywhere for the specific purpose of being amused. I prefer that laughter shall take me unawares. Only so can it master and dissolve me. And in this respect, at any rate, I am not peculiar. In music halls and such places you may hear loud laughter, but—not see silent laughter, not see strong men weak, helpless, suffering, gradually convalescent, dangerously relapsing. Laughter at its greatest and best is not there.

To such laughter nothing is more propitious than an occasion that demands gravity. To have good reason for not laughing is one of the surest aids. Laughter rejoices in bonds. If music halls were schoolrooms for us, and the comedians were our schoolmasters, how much less talent would be needed for giving us how much more joy! Even in private and accidental intercourse, few are the men whose humor can reduce us, be we never so susceptible, to paroxysms of mirth. I will wager that nine-tenths of the world's best laughter is laughter *at*, not *with*. And it is the people set in authority over us that touch most surely our sense of the ridiculous. Freedom is a good thing, but we lose through it golden moments. The schoolmaster to his pupils, the monarch to his courtiers, the editor to his staff—how priceless they are! Reverence is a good thing, and part of its value is that the more we revere a man, the more sharply are we struck by anything in him (and there is always much) that is incongruous with his greatness. Reverence, like subjection, is a rich source of laughter. And herein lies one of the reasons why as we grow older we laugh less. The men we esteemed so great are gathered to their fathers. Some of our coevals may, for ought we know, be very great, but good heavens! we can't esteem *them* so.

Of extreme laughter I know not in any annals a more satisfactory example than one that is to be found in Moore's *Life of Byron*. Both Byron and Moore were already in high spirits when, on an evening in the spring of 1813, they went "from some early assembly" to Mr. Rogers' house in St. James's Place and were regaled there with an impromptu meal. But not high spirits alone would have led the two young poets to such excess of laughter as made the evening so very memorable. Luckily they both venerated Rogers (strange as it may seem to us) as the greatest of living poets. Luckily, too, Mr. Rogers was ever the kind of man, the coldly and quietly suave kind of man, with whom you don't take liberties, if you can help it—with whom, if you can't help it, to take liberties is in itself a wildly exhilarating act. And he had just received a presentation copy of Lord Thurloe's latest book, *Poems on Several Occasions*. The two young poets found in this elder's Muse much that was so execrable as to be delightful. They were soon, as they turned the pages, held in throes of laughter, laughter that was but intensified by the endeavors of their correct and nettled host to point out the genuine merits of his friend's work. And then suddenly—oh joy!—"we lighted," Moore records, "on the discovery that our host, in addition to his sincere approbation of some of this book's contents, had also the motive of gratitude for standing by its author, as one of the poems was a warm, and I need not add, well-deserved panegyric on himself. We were, however"—the narrative has an added charm from Tom Moore's demure care not to offend or compromise the still-surviving Rogers —"too far gone in nonsense for even this eulogy, in which we both so heartily agreed, to stop us. The opening line of the poem was, as well as I can recollect, 'When Rogers o'er this labor bent'; and Lord Byron undertook to read it aloud;—but he found it impossible to get beyond the first two words. Our laughter had now increased to such a pitch that nothing could restrain it. Two or three times he began; but no sooner had the words 'When Rogers' passed his lips, than our fit burst out afresh,—till even Mr. Rogers himself, with all his feelings of our injustice, found it impossible not to join us; and we were, at last, all three in such a state of inextinguishable laughter, that, had the author himself been of our party, I question much whether he would have resisted the infection." The final fall and dissolution of Rogers, Rogers behaving as badly as either of them, is all that was needed to give perfection to this heart-warming scene. I like to think that on a certain night in spring, year after year, three ghosts revisit that old room and (without, I hope, inconvenience to Lord Northcliffe, who may happen to be there) sit rocking and writhing in the grip of that old shared rapture. Uncanny? Well, not more so than would have seemed to Byron and Moore and Rogers the notion that more than a hundred years away from them was someone joining in their laughter—as *I* do.

Alas, I cannot join in it more than gently. To imagine

a scene, however vividly, does not give us the sense of being, or even of having been, present at it. Indeed, the greater the glow of the scene reflected, the sharper is the pang of our realization that we were *not* there, and of our annoyance that we weren't. Such a pang comes to me with special force whenever my fancy posts itself outside the Temple's gate in Fleet Street, and there, at a late hour of the night of May 10th, 1773, observes a gigantic old man laughing wildly, but having no one with him to share and aggrandize his emotions. Not that he is alone; but the young man beside him laughs only in politeness and is inwardly puzzled, even shocked. Boswell has a keen, an exquisitely keen, scent for comedy, for the fun that is latent in fine shades of character; but imaginative burlesque, anything that borders on lovely nonsense, he was not formed to savor. All the more does one revel in his account of what led up to the moment when Johnson "to support himself, laid hold of one of the posts at the side of the foot pavement, and sent forth peals so loud that in the silence of the night his voice seemed to resound from Temple to Fleet Ditch."

No evening ever had an unlikelier ending. The omens were all for gloom. Johnson had gone to dine at General Paoli's but was so ill that he had to leave before the meal was over. Later he managed to go to Mr. Chambers' rooms in the Temple. He continued to be "very ill" there, but gradually felt better, and "talked with a noble enthusiasm of keeping up the representation of respectable families," and was great on "the dignity and propriety of male succession." Among his listeners, as it happened, was a gentleman for whom Mr. Chambers had that day drawn up a will devising his estate to his three sisters. The news of this might have been expected to make Johnson violent in wrath. But no, for some reason he grew violent only in laughter, and insisted thenceforth on calling that gentleman The Testator and chaffing him without mercy.

"I daresay he thinks he has done a mighty thing. He won't stay till he gets home to his seat in the country, to produce this wonderful deed; he'll call up the landlord of the first inn on the road; and after a suitable preface upon mortality and the uncertainty of life, will tell him that he should not delay in making his will; and Here, Sir, will he say, is *my* will, which I have just made, with the assistance of one of the ablest lawyers in the kingdom; and he will read it to him. He believes he has made this will; but he did not make it; you, Chambers, made it for him. I hope you have had more conscience than to make him say 'being of sound understanding!' ha, ha, ha! I hope he has left me a legacy. I'd have his will turned into verse, like a ballad."

These flights annoyed Mr. Chambers, and are recorded by Boswell with the apology that he wishes his readers to be "acquainted with the slightest occasional characteristics of so eminent a man." Certainly, there is nothing ridiculous in the fact of a man making a will. But this is the measure of Johnson's achievement. He had created gloriously much out of nothing at all. There he sat, old and ailing and unencouraged by the company, but soaring higher and higher in absurdity, more and more rejoicing, and still soaring and rejoicing after he had gone out into the night with Boswell, till at last in Fleet Street his paroxysms were too much for him and he could no more. Echoes of that huge laughter come ringing down the ages. But is there also perhaps a note of sadness for us in them? Johnson's endless sociability came of his inherent melancholy; he could not bear to be alone; and his mirth was but a mode of escape from the dark thoughts within him. Of these the thought of death was the most dreadful to him, and the most insistent. He was forever wondering how death would come to him, and how he would acquit himself in the extreme moment. A later but not less devoted Anglican, meditating on his own end, wrote in his diary that "to die in church appears to be a great euthanasia, but not," he quaintly and touchingly added, "at a time to disturb worshippers." Both the sentiment here expressed and the reservation drawn would have been as characteristic of Johnson as they were of Gladstone. But to die of laughter—this, too, seems to me a great euthanasia; and I think that for Johnson to have died thus, that night in Fleet Street, would have been a grand ending to "a life radically wretched." Well, he was destined to outlive another decade; and selfishly, who can wish such a life as his, or such a life as Boswell's, one jot shorter?

Strange, when you come to think of it, that of all the countless folk who have lived before our time on this planet not one is known in history or in legend as having died of laughter. Strange, too, that not to one of all the characters in romance has such an end been allotted. Has it ever struck you what a chance Shakespeare missed when he was finishing the Second Part of *King Henry the Fourth?* Falstaff was not the man to stand cowed and bowed while the new king lectured him and cast him off. Little by little, as Hal proceeded in that portentous allocution, the humor of the situation would have mastered old Sir John. His face, blank with surprise at first, would presently have glowed and widened, and his whole bulk have begun to quiver. Lest he should miss one word, he would have mastered himself. But the final words would have been the signal for release of all the roars pent up in him; the welkin would have rung; the roars, belike, would have gradually subsided in dreadful rumblings of more than utterable or conquerable mirth. Thus and thus only might his life have been rounded off with dramatic fitness, *secundum ipsius naturam.* He never should have been left to babble of green fields and die "an it had been any christom child."

Falstaff is a triumph of comedic creation because we are kept laughing equally at and with him. Nevertheless, if I had the choice of sitting with him at the Boar's Head or with Johnson at the Turk's, I shouldn't hesitate for an instant. The agility of Falstaff's mind gains much of its effect by contrast with the massiveness of his body; but in contrast with Johnson's equal agility is Johnson's moral as well as physical bulk. His sallies "tell" the more startlingly because of the noble weight of character behind them: they are the better because *he* makes them. In Falstaff there isn't this final incongruity and element of surprise. Falstaff is but a sublimated sample of "the funny man." We cannot, therefore, laugh so greatly with him as with Johnson. (Nor even *at* him; because we are not tickled so much by the weak points of a character whose points are all weak ones; also because we have no reverence trying to impose restraint on us.) Still, Falstaff has indubitably the power to convulse us. I don't mean we ever are convulsed in reading *Henry the Fourth.* No printed page, alas, can thrill us to extremities of laughter. These are ours only if the mirthmaker be a living man whose jests we hear as they come fresh from his own lips. All I claim for Falstaff is that he would be able to convulse us if he were alive and accessible. Few, as I have said, are the humorists who can induce this state. To master and dissolve us, to give us the joy of being worn down and tired out with laughter, is a success to be won by no man save in virtue of a rare staying power. Laughter becomes extreme only if it be consecutive. There must be no pauses for recovery. Touch-and-go humor, however happy, is not enough. The jester must be able to grapple his theme and hang on to it, twisting it this way and that, and making it yield magically all manner of strange and precious things, one after another, without pause. He must have invention keeping pace with utterance. He must be inexhaustible. Only so can he exhaust us.

I have a friend whom I would praise. There are many other of my friends to whom I am indebted for much laughter; but I do believe that if all of them sent in their bills tomorrow, and all of them overcharged me not a little, the total of all those totals would be less appalling than that which looms in my own vague estimate of what I owe to Comus. Comus I call him here in observance of the line drawn between public and private virtue, and in full knowledge that he would of all men be the least glad to be quite personally thanked and laurelled in the market-place for the hours he has made memorable among his cronies. No one is so diffident as he, no one as self-postponing. Many people have met him again and again without faintly suspecting "anything much" in him. Many of his acquaintances— friends, too—relatives, even—have lived and died in the belief that he was quite ordinary. Thus he is the more greatly valued by his cronies. Thus do we pride ourselves on having some curious right quality to which alone he is responsive. But it would seem that either this asset of ours or its effect on him is intermittent. He can be dull and null enough with us sometimes—a mere asker of questions or drawer of comparisons between this and that brand of cigarettes, or full expatiator on the merits of some new patent razor. A whole hour and more may be wasted in such humdrum and darkness. And then—something will have happened. There has come a spark in the murk; a flame now, presage of a radiance: Comus has begun. His face is a great part of his equipment. A cast of it might be somewhat akin to the comic mask of the ancients; but no cast could be worthy of it; nobility is the essence of it. It flickers and shifts in accord to the matter of his discourse, it contracts and it expands; is there anything its elastic can't express? Comus would be eloquent even were he dumb. And he is mellifluous. His voice, while he develops an idea or conjures up a scene, takes on a peculiar richness and unction. If he be describing an actual scene, voice and face are adaptable to those of the actual persons therein. But it is not in such mimicry that he excels. As a reporter he has rivals. For the most part, he moves on a higher plane than that of mere fact; he imagines, he creates, giving you not a person, but a type, a synthesis; and not what anywhere has been, but what anywhere might be—what, as one feels, for all the absurdity of it, just would be. He knows his world well, and nothing human is alien to him, but certain skeins of life have a special hold on him, and he on them. In his youth he wished to be a clergyman; and over the clergy of all grades and denominations his genius hovers and swoops and ranges with a special mastery. Lawyers he loves less; yet the legal mind seems to lie almost as wide-open to him as the sacerdotal; and the legal manner in all its phases he can unerringly burlesque. In the minds of journalists, diverse journalists, he is not less thoroughly at home, so that of the wild contingencies imagined by him there is none about which he cannot reel off an oral "leader" or "middle" in the likeliest style, and with as much ease as he can preach a High Church or a Low Church sermon on it. Nor are his improvisations limited by prose. If a theme calls for nobler treatment, he becomes an unflagging fountain of blank verse. Or again, he may deliver himself in rhyme. There is no form of utterance that comes amiss to him for interpreting the human comedy, or for broadening the farce into which that comedy is changed by him. Nothing can stop him when once he is in the vein. No appeals move him. He goes from strength to strength, while his audience is more and more piteously debilitated.

What a gift to have been endowed with! What a power to wield! And how often I have envied Comus! But this envy has never taken root. Incomparable laughtergiver, he is not much a laugher. He is vintner, not toper. I would not change places with him. I am well content to have been his beneficiary during thirty years, and to be for as many more as may be given us.

ON COMING TO AN END

BY HILAIRE BELLOC

OF ALL the simple actions in the world! Of all the simple actions in the world!

One would think it could be done with less effort than the heaving of a sigh. . . . Well—then, one would be wrong.

There is no case of Coming to an End but has about it something of an effort and a jerk, as though Nature abhorred it, and though it be true that some achieve a quiet and a perfect end to one thing or another (as, for instance, to Life), yet this achievement is not arrived at save through the utmost toil, and consequent upon the most persevering and exquisite art.

Now you can say that this may be true of sentient things but not of things inanimate. It is true even of things inanimate.

Look down some straight railway line for a vanishing point to the perspective: you will never find it. Or try to mark the moment when a small target becomes invisible. There is no gradation; a moment it was there, and you missed it—possibly because the Authorities were not going in for journalism that day, and had not chosen a dead calm with the light full on the canvas. A moment it was there and then, as you steamed on, it was gone. The same is true of a lark in the air. You see it and then you do not see it, you only hear its song. And the same is true of that song: you hear it and then suddenly you do not hear it. It is true of a human voice, which is familiar in your ear, living and inhabiting the

343

rooms of your house. There comes a day when it ceases altogether—and how positive, how definite and hard is that Coming to an End.

It does not leave an echo behind it, but a sharp edge of emptiness, and very often as one sits beside the fire the memory of that voice suddenly returning gives to the silence about one a personal force, as it were, of obsession and of control. So much happens when even one of all our million voices Comes to an End.

It is necessary, it is august and it is reasonable that the great story of our lives also should be accomplished and should reach a term: and yet there is something in that hidden duality of ours which makes the prospect of so natural a conclusion terrible, and it is the better judgment of mankind and the mature conclusion of civilizations in their age that there is not only a conclusion here but something of an adventure also. It may be so.

Those who solace mankind and are the principal benefactors of it, I mean the poets and the musicians, have attempted always to ease the prospect of Coming to an End, whether it were the Coming to an End of the things we love or of that daily habit and conversation which is our life and is the atmosphere wherein we loved them. Indeed this is a clear test whereby you may distinguish the great artists from the mean hucksters and charlatans, that they first approach and reveal what is dreadful with calm and, as it were, with a purpose to use it for a good, while the vulgar catch-penny fellows must liven up their bad dishes as with a cheap sauce of the horrible, caring nothing, so that their shrieks sell, whether we are the better for them or no.

The great poets, I say, bring us easily or grandly to the gate: as in that *Ode to a Nightingale* where it is thought good (in an immortal phrase) to pass painlessly at midnight, or, in the glorious line which Ronsard uses, like a salute with the sword, hailing *"la profitable mort."*

The noblest or the most perfect of English elegies leaves, as a sort of savour after the reading of it, no terror at all, nor even too much regret, but the landscape of England at evening, when the smoke of the cottages mixes with autumn vapours among the elms; and even that gloomy modern *Ode to the West Wind,* unfinished and touched with despair, though it will speak of—

> . . . *That outer place forlorn*
> *Which, like an infinite grey sea, surrounds*
> *With everlasting calm the land of human sounds;*

yet also returns to the sacramental earth of one's childhood where it says:

> *For now the Night completed tells her tale*
> *Of rest and dissolution: gathering round*
> *Her mist in such persuasion that the ground*
> *Of Home consents to falter and grow pale.*
> *And the stars are put out and the trees fail*
> *Nor anything remains but that which drones*
> *Enormous through the dark. . . .*

And again, in another place, where it prays that one may at last be fed with beauty—

> . . . *as the flowers are fed*
> *That fill their falling-time with generous breath:*
> *Let me attain a natural end of death,*
> *And on the mighty breast, as on a bed,*
> *Lay decently at last a drowsy head.*
> *Content to lapse in somnolence and fade*
> *In dreaming once again the dream of all things made.*

The most careful philosophy, the most heavenly music, the best choice of poetic or prosaic phrase prepare men properly for man's perpetual loss of this and of that, and introduce us proudly to the similar and greater business of departure from them all, from whatever of them all remains at the close.

To be introduced, to be prepared, to be armoured, all these are excellent things, but there is a question no foresight can answer nor any comprehension resolve. It is right to gather upon that question the varied affections or perceptions of varying men.

I knew a man once in the Tourdenoise, a gloomy man, but very rich, who cared little for the things he knew. This man took no pleasure in his fruitful orchards and his carefully ploughed fields and his harvests. He took pleasure in pine trees; he was a man of groves and of the dark. For him that things should come to an end was but part of an universal rhythm; a part pleasing to the general harmony, and making in the music of the world about him a solemn and, oh, a conclusive chord. This man would study the sky at night and take from it a larger and a larger draught of infinitude, finding in this exercise not a mere satisfaction, but an object and goal for the mind; when he had so wandered for a while under the night he seemed, for the moment, to have reached the object of his being.

And I knew another man in the Weald who worked with his hands, and was always kind, and knew his trade well; he smiled when he talked of scythes, and he could thatch. He could fish also, and he knew about grafting, and about the seasons of plants, and birds, and the way of seed. He had a face full of weather, he fatigued his body, he watched his land. He would not talk much of mysteries, he would rather hum songs. He loved new friends and old. He had lived with one wife for fifty years, and he had five children, who were a policeman, a schoolmistress, a son at home, and two who were sailors. This man said that what a man did and the life in which he did it was like the farm work upon a summer's day.

He said one works a little and rests, and works a little again, and one drinks, and there is a perpetual talk with those about one. Then (he would say) the shadows lengthen at evening, the wind falls, the birds get back home. And as for ourselves, we are sleepy before it is dark.

Then also I knew a third man who lived in a town and was clerical and did not work, for he had money of his own. This man said that all we do and the time in which we do it is rather a night than a day. He said that when we came to an end we vanished, we and our works, but that we vanished into a broadening light.

Which of these three knew best the nature of man and of his works, and which knew best of what nature was the end?

.   .   .   .   .   .

Why so glum, my Lad, or my Lass (as the case may be), why so heavy at heart? Did you not know that you also must Come to an End?

Why, that woman of Etaples who sold such Southern wine for the dissipation of the Picardian Mist, her time is over and gone and the wine has been drunk long ago and the singers in her house have departed, and the wind of the sea moans in and fills their hall. The Lords who died in Roncesvalles have been dead these thousand years and more, and the loud song about them grew very faint and dwindled and is silent now: there is nothing at all remains.

It is certain that the hills decay and that rivers as the dusty years proceed run feebly and lose themselves at last in desert sands; and in its æons the very firmament grows old. But evil also is perishable and bad men meet their judge. Be comforted.

Now of all endings, of all Comings to an End none is so hesitating as the ending of a book which the Publisher will have so long and the writer so short: and the Public (God Bless the Public) will have whatever it is given.

Books, however much their lingering, books also must Come to an End. It is abhorrent to their nature as to the life of man. They must be sharply cut off. Let it be done at once and fixed as by a spell and the power of a Word; the word

FINIS.

The Modern
Student's Library

NOVELS

AUSTEN: Pride and Prejudice
With an introduction by WILLIAM DEAN HOWELLS

BUNYAN: The Pilgrim's Progress
With an introduction by SAMUEL McCHORD CROTHERS

ELIOT: Adam Bede
With an introduction by LAURA JOHNSON WYLIE, formerly Professor of English, Vassar College

GALSWORTHY: The Patrician
With an introduction by BLISS PERRY, Professor of English Literature, Harvard University

HARDY: The Return of the Native
With an introduction by J. W. CUNLIFFE, Professor of English, Columbia University

HAWTHORNE: The Scarlet Letter
With an introduction by STUART P. SHERMAN, late Literary Editor of the New York *Herald Tribune*

MEREDITH: Evan Harrington
With an introduction by GEORGE F. REYNOLDS, Professor of English Literature, University of Colorado

MEREDITH: The Ordeal of Richard Feverel
With an introduction by FRANK W. CHANDLER, Professor of English and Comparative Literature, and Dean of the College of Liberal Arts, University of Cincinnati

SCOTT: The Heart of Midlothian
With an introduction by WILLIAM P. TRENT, Professor of English Literature, Columbia University

STEVENSON: The Master of Ballantrae
With an introduction by H. S. CANBY, Assistant Editor of the *Yale Review* and Editor of the *Saturday Review*

THACKERAY: The History of Pendennis
With an introduction by ROBERT MORSS LOVETT, Professor of English, University of Chicago
2 vols.; $1.50 *per set*

TROLLOPE: Barchester Towers
With an introduction by CLARENCE D. STEVENS, Professor of English, University of Cincinnati

WHARTON: Ethan Frome
With a special introduction by EDITH WHARTON

POETRY

BROWNING: Poems and Plays
Edited by HEWETTE E. JOYCE, Assistant Professor of English, Dartmouth College

BROWNING: The Ring and the Book
Edited by FREDERICK MORGAN PADELFORD, Professor of English, University of Washington

TENNYSON: Poems
Edited by J. F. A. PYRE, Professor of English, University of Wisconsin

WHITMAN: Leaves of Grass
Edited by STUART P. SHERMAN, late Literary Editor of the New York *Herald Tribune*

WORDSWORTH: Poems
Edited by GEORGE M. HARPER, Professor of English, Princeton University

AMERICAN SONGS AND BALLADS
Edited by LOUISE POUND, Professor of English, University of Nebraska

ENGLISH POETS OF THE EIGHTEENTH CENTURY
Edited by ERNEST BERNBAUM, Professor of English, University of Illinois

MINOR VICTORIAN POETS
Edited by JOHN D. COOKE, Professor of English, University of Southern California

ROMANTIC POETRY OF THE EARLY NINETEENTH CENTURY
Edited by ARTHUR BEATTY, Professor of English, University of Wisconsin

ESSAYS AND MISCELLANEOUS PROSE

ADDISON AND STEELE: Selections
Edited by WILL D. HOWE, formerly head of the Department of English, Indiana University

ARNOLD: Prose and Poetry
Edited by ARCHIBALD L. BOUTON, Professor of English and Dean of the Graduate School, New York University

BACON: Essays
Edited by MARY AUGUSTA SCOTT, late Professor of the English Language and Literature, Smith College

BROWNELL: American Prose Masters
Edited by STUART P. SHERMAN, late Literary Editor of the New York *Herald Tribune*

BURKE: Selections
Edited by LESLIE NATHAN BROUGHTON, Assistant Professor of English, Cornell University

CARLYLE: Past and Present
Edited by EDWIN MIMS, Professor of English, Vanderbilt University

CARLYLE: Sartor Resartus
Edited by ASHLEY H. THORNDIKE, Professor of English, Columbia University

EMERSON: Essays and Poems
Edited by ARTHUR HOBSON QUINN, Professor of English, University of Pennsylvania

FRANKLIN AND EDWARDS: Selections
Edited by CARL VAN DOREN, Associate Professor of English, Columbia University

HAZLITT: Essays
Edited by PERCY V. D. SHELLY, Professor of English, University of Pennsylvania

LINCOLN: Selections
Edited by NATHANIEL WRIGHT STEPHENSON, author of "Lincoln: His Personal Life "

MACAULAY: Historical Essays
Edited by CHARLES DOWNER HAZEN, Professor of History, Columbia University

3

MEREDITH: An Essay on Comedy
Edited by Lane Cooper, Professor of the English Language and Literature, Cornell University

PARKMAN: The Oregon Trail
Edited by James Cloyd Bowman, Professor of English, Northern State Normal College, Marquette, Mich.

POE: Tales
Edited by James Southall Wilson, Edgar Allan Poe Professor of English, University of Virginia

RUSKIN: Selections and Essays
Edited by Frederick William Roe, Professor of English, University of Wisconsin

STEVENSON: Essays
Edited by William Lyon Phelps, Lampson Professor of English Literature, Yale University

SWIFT: Selections
Edited by Hardin Craig, Professor of English, University of Iowa

THOREAU: A Week on the Concord and Merrimack Rivers
Edited by Odell Shepard, James J. Goodwin Professor of English, Trinity College

CONTEMPORARY ESSAYS
Edited by Odell Shepard, James J. Goodwin Professor of English, Trinity College

CRITICAL ESSAYS OF THE EARLY NINETEENTH CENTURY
Edited by Raymond M. Alden, late Professor of English, Leland Stanford University

NINETEENTH CENTURY LETTERS
Edited by Byron Johnson Rees, late Professor of English, Williams College

ROMANTIC PROSE OF THE EARLY NINETEENTH CENTURY
Edited by Carl H. Grabo, Professor of English, University of Chicago

SELECTIONS FROM THE FEDERALIST
Edited by John S. Bassett, late Professor of History, Smith College

SEVENTEENTH CENTURY ESSAYS
Edited by Jacob Zeitlin, Associate Professor of English, University of Illinois

4

BIOGRAPHY

BOSWELL: Life of Johnson
Abridged and Edited by CHARLES GROSVENOR OSGOOD, Professor of English, Princeton University

CROCKETT: Autobiography of David Crockett
Edited by HAMLIN GARLAND

VOLUMES IN PREPARATION

ELIOT: Middlemarch
With an introduction by ARTHUR BEATTY, Professor of English, University of Wisconsin

MELVILLE: Moby Dick
With an introduction by CARL VAN DOREN, Associate Professor of English, Columbia University

NEWMAN: Selections
Edited by HENRY A. LAPPIN, Professor of English, D'Youville College

PHILOSOPHY SERIES
Editor, Ralph Barton Perry
Professor of Philosophy, Harvard University

ARISTOTLE: Selections
Edited by W. D. ROSS, Professor of Philosophy, Oriel College, University of Oxford

BACON: Selections
Edited by MATTHEW THOMPSON MCCLURE, Professor of Philosophy, University of Illinois

DESCARTES: Selections
Edited by RALPH M. EATON, Assistant Professor of Philosophy, Harvard University

HEGEL: Selections
Edited by JACOB LOEWENBERG, Professor of Philosophy, University of California

HUME: Selections
Edited by CHARLES W. HENDEL, JR., Associate Professor of Philosophy, Princeton University

LOCKE: Selections
Edited by STERLING P. LAMPRECHT, Associate Professor of Philosophy, University of Illinois

PLATO: The Republic
With an introduction by C. M. BAKEWELL, Professor of Philosophy, Yale University

PLATO: Selections
Edited by RAPHAEL DEMOS, Assistant Professor of Philosophy, Harvard University

SCHOPENHAUER: Selections
Edited by DEWITT H. PARKER, Professor of Philosophy, University of Michigan

THE MODERN STUDENT'S LIBRARY

Volumes in Preparation

BERKELEY: Selections
Edited by MARY W. CALKINS, Professor of Philosophy, Wellesley College

KANT: Selections
Edited by THEODORE M. GREENE, Assistant Professor of Philosophy, Princeton University

MEDIÆVAL PHILOSOPHY
By RICHARD McKEON, Instructor in Philosophy, Columbia University

FRENCH SERIES
Editor, Horatio Smith
Professor of French Language and Literature, Brown University

BALZAC: Le Père Goriot
With an introduction by HORATIO SMITH, Professor of French Language and Literature, Brown University

FRENCH ROMANTIC PROSE
Edited by W. W. COMFORT, President, Haverford College

MOLIÈRE: Three Plays
Edited by WILLIAM A. NITZE, Professor of French Literature, University of Chicago